D1528787

Rousseau's Theory of Human Association

ROUSSEAU'S THEORY OF HUMAN ASSOCIATION
© Greg Hill, 2006.

First published in 2006 by
PALGRAVE MACMILLAN™
175 Fifth Avenue, New York, N.Y. 10010 and
Houndmills, Basingstoke, Hampshire, England RG21 6XS
Companies and representatives throughout the world.

PALGRAVE MACMILLAN is the global academic imprint of the Palgrave Macmillan division of St. Martin's Press, LLC and of Palgrave Macmillan Ltd. Macmillan® is a registered trademark in the United States, United Kingdom and other countries. Palgrave is a registered trademark in the European Union and other countries.

ISBN 1–4039–7259–1

Library of Congress Cataloging-in-Publication Data

Hill Greg, 1948–
    Rousseau's theory of human association : transparent and opaque communities / Greg Hill.
        p. cm.
    Includes bibliographical references and index.
    ISBN 1–4039–7259–1
        1. Rousseau, Jean-Jacques, 1712–1778. 2. Social contract. I. Title.

JC179. R9H55 2006
320.1′1—dc22   2005054650

A catalogue record for this book is available from the British Library.

Design by Newgen Imaging Systems (P) Ltd., Chennai, India.

First edition: May 2006

10 9 8 7 6 5 4 3 2 1

Printed in the United States of America.

Rousseau's Theory of Human Association

Transparent and Opaque Communities

Greg Hill

palgrave
macmillan

For Terry, Linda, and Shayna

CONTENTS

List of Tables   viii

List of Figures   ix

Previously Published Work   x

Acknowledgments   xii

Preface   xiii

One   Introduction   1

Two   Transparency and Opacity in Nature,
         Society, and State   11

Three   Association and Civil Society in Transparent
         and Opaque Communities   45

Four   Opaque Traders and the Invisible Hand   89

Five   The Ring of Gyges, the Perfect Shield,
         and the Veil of Ignorance   127

Six   Conclusion   154

Notes   161

Bibliography   188

Index   197

LIST OF TABLES

2.1	The *Amour de Soi* Game	13
2.2	The *Amour-Propre* Game	27
2.3	The Compassion Game	30
2.4	Cooperation under Different Motives	31
2.5	The Fraternity Game	33
2.6	A Rousseauean Typology of Social Interaction	41
3.1	Associations in Transparent and Opaque Societies	78
5.1	Symmetrical and Asymmetrical Modes of Interaction	133

LIST OF FIGURES

2.1 Expected Payoffs of Conditional Cooperation (CC) and
     Unconditional Defection (UD) with Different
     Probabilities of Recognition   16
2.2 Modes of Association and the Probability of Cooperation   44
3.1 The Unraveling of Association   72

PREVIOUSLY

PUBLISHED WORK

Publications in Philosophy and Political Theory

"Solidarity, Objectivity, and The Human Form of Life," *Critical Review* Vol. 11, No. 4 (1998): 555–580

"Justice and Natural Inequality," *The Journal of Social Philosophy* (Winter 1997): 16–30

"History, Necessity, and Rational Choice Theory," *Rationality & Society* (May 1997): 189–213

"The Moral Economy: Keynes's Critique of Capitalist Justice," *Critical Review* (Winter 1996): 33–61

"The Politics of Transparent and Opaque Communities," *Polity* (Fall 1996): 1–26

"Reason and Will in Contemporary Social Contract Theory," *Political Research Quarterly* (March 1995): 101–216

"Citizenship and Ontology in the Liberal State," *The Review of Politics* (Winter 1993): 67–84

"The Rational Justification of Moral Constraint," *The Southern Journal of Philosophy* Vol. XXI, No. 2 (1993): 179–191

Review of George Klosko, "The Principle of Fairness and Political Obligation" in *The Review of Politics* (Fall 1993): 727–728

Publications in Economic Theory

"From Hayek to Keynes," *Critical Review* (2004) Vol. 16, No. 1: 53–80

"Egalitarianism Old and New," *Briefing Notes in Economics* (March/April 2004): 1–12

"The Immiseration of the Landlords: Rent in a Kaldorian Theory of Income Distribution," *Cambridge Journal of Economics* Vol. 25, No. 4 (July 2001): 481–92

"The Investment Multiplier and the Aggregate Rate of Return: A Post-Keynesian View," *Economic Issues* Vol. 6, Part 2 (2001): 1–11

"Project Appraisal for the Keynesian Investment Planner," *Economics of Planning* (1999): 153–164

"Positional Goods and The Macroeconomy," *Briefing Notes in Economics* (May 1999): 1–6

"The Socialization of Investment: Comment on Meltzer," *Journal of Post Keynesian Economics* (1998): 309–313

"An Ultra-Keynesian Strikes Back: Reply to Horwitz," *Critical Review* (1998): 113–126

"Capitalism, Coordination, and Keynes: Rejoinder to Horwitz," *Critical Review* (Summer 1996): 373–387

"Massive Government Debt as an Economic Stabilizer," *Briefing Notes in Economics* (September 1996): 1–4

"Misreading Keynes: Reply to Garrison," *Critical Review* (Summer 1994): 441–446

"The Fair Allocation of Electricity Costs Over Time," *Electricity Journal* (November 1994): 74–78

Review of Robert J. Shiller, "Macro Markets" and John E. Roemer, "A Future for Socialism" in *Challenge* (May–June, 1995): 62–64

"From Recession to Recovery: A Prisoner's Dilemma and Its Solution," *Challenge* (January–February 1993): 61–62

ACKNOWLEDGMENTS

This book was made possible by the contributions of others. A long time ago, Michael Mosher introduced me to political theory in a way that only those who have attended his lectures can fully appreciate. He has also been kind enough to provide me stimulating comments on earlier drafts of my manuscript. I owe Bill Lund thanks for our long-distance conversations about Hobbes, Rousseau, and many other topics relevant to my work. I thank Jamie Mayerfeld for his penetrating comments, helpful suggestions, and kind encouragement. And, finally, I am grateful to my coworkers at the City of Seattle, who have taught me a great deal about how to search for the city's common good.

I thank Palgrave Macmillan for permission to reproduce parts of Greg Hill, "The Politics of Transparent and Opaque Communities," *Polity* (Fall 1996): 1–26.

PREFACE

Jean Starobinski's splendid book, *Jean-Jacques Rousseau: Transparency and Obstruction*, made vivid for its readers the significance of transparency and opacity in the way Rousseau came to understand his life and his relationship to others. "Rousseau desired communication and *transparency* of the heart," but, "meeting with disappointment," he "chose the opposite course, accepting—indeed provoking—*obstruction*, which enabled him to withdraw, certain of his innocence, into passive resignation."[1] I have appropriated Starobinski's wonderfully suggestive metaphor and put it to work with a different end in view: to explore some of the characteristic features of human interaction when the parties' intentions are easy to read, on the one hand, or difficult to discern, on the other. It is my contention that a substantial body of Rousseau's political thought—his conception of mankind's original condition, his critique of polite society, his understanding of how the market economy works, and his misgivings about intermediate associations, as well as his design of an ideal republican state—can be fruitfully explicated and critically appraised by focusing upon the essential aspects of transparent and opaque relations.

In speaking of "Rousseau's *theory* of human association," I do not mean to imply that the "citizen of Geneva" had a fully developed model of human interaction. Rather, I believe that we can find in Rousseau's work an inchoate theory of association, an assortment of provocative conjectures about the prospects for cooperation or conflict under conditions that vary according to the motives and transparency of the interacting parties. It is my task to weave these provocative conjectures together to produce a theory in terms of which we can elucidate, analyze, and assess Rousseau's understanding of human association. Put somewhat differently, I am interested in the logic of transparent and opaque communities and believe it is possible to derive interesting conclusions about human association by constructing simple models and thought experiments which embody alternative assumptions about the information that is available to the interacting parties. Although this kind of reasoning will, perhaps, seem alien to the spirit of Rousseau's thought, especially in the wake of the many excellent literary interpretations of his work that have appeared in recent years, Rousseau was, in fact, a bit of a modeler, himself, which is evident in his speculative and stylized history of the human species, in his account of the reasoning that leads men to embrace the social contract, and in his characterization of the "general will" as what remains after all the "pluses and minuses" of "particular wills" "cancel one another out."[2]

Rousseau describes the method he employs in his search for the origin of inequality as "conditional and hypothetical reasonings, rather calculated to explain the nature of things, than to ascertain their true origin."[3] In a similar fashion, he begins *The Social Contract* by acknowledging that he does not know how some men actually became masters of others. Rather, his aim is to develop a *rational reconstruction* of the state, which takes "men as they are and laws as they might be" and proceeds to show how a *legitimate* state could have arisen under these circumstances.[4] My "rational reconstructions" are not designed with the aim of justifying a particular set of political arrangements, but rather are intended to illuminate some of the essential characteristics of these arrangements. Of course many of these characteristics have important normative implications. Thus, I try to show that civic cooperation in Rousseau's model republic requires an extensive regime of mutual surveillance; that Hobbes's argument for a sovereign state requires as a necessary premise the natural opacity of human intention; that Adam Smith's argument for unfettered markets presupposes transparent intentions; and that freedom of association under transparent conditions draws a large portion of the citizenry into associations of unequal power, whereas free association under opaque conditions reduces the prevalence and power of such groups, but fosters the kind of "individualism" Tocqueville found latent in America's emerging democracy. Although my immediate objective is to describe the paradigmatic features of transparent and opaque relations, especially as they are exhibited in Rousseau's thought, this book is, for the most part, an exercise in political theory, which aims to disclose the implications of transparency and opacity for enduring controversies surrounding the nature of liberty, equality, civil society, and the democratic state.

CHAPTER ONE
_____

Introduction

Judging the quality of human life before "art had moulded our behavior," Rousseau concludes that "human nature was not at bottom better then than now; but men found their security in the ease with which they could see through one another, and this advantage, of which we no longer feel the value, prevented their having many vices."[1] In this passage and elsewhere, Rousseau invites us to imagine a form of life in which it was impossible to conceal one's real intentions from others, each person's outward demeanor being a true reflection of his immediate purpose. "What happiness would it be," Rousseau laments, "if our external appearance were always a true mirror of our hearts."[2] As long as human beings retained this quality, all those vices requiring duplicity were excluded from their social intercourse. With nothing to hide, men and women were content to live together in common huts and "to have the gods for witnesses to their actions."[3]

Once civilized, human intention lost its transparency. The guileless souls whose aims found spontaneous expression within the primitive societies of Rousseau's imagination gave way to a new kind of man whose demeanor was moulded in the service of new ambitions—to be admired, esteemed, envied. "Whoever sang or danced best, whoever was the handsomest, the strongest, the most dexterous, or the most eloquent, came to be of most consideration."[4] This drive for preeminence, which can only be satisfied at the expense of others, must be pursued under the cloak of anonymity or behind the mask of reputation. "It now became the interest of men to appear what they really were not."[5] Civil society, far from being the intricate web of cooperation depicted by Rousseau's contemporary, Adam Smith, is rather the site of rivalry and struggle, where the common good is pulverized into the dust of egotism.

If human beings are once more to live in harmony, then, Rousseau insists, we must again become transparent to each other. Yet our original lucidity, made possible by the lack of a *persona*—a being for others—lies too deeply buried in our past to be recovered. Rousseau's solution is, instead, to create close-knit communities in which citizens "will feel themselves always to be acting under the eyes of their fellow citizens,"[6] the ideal state being a small republic in which "neither the secret machinations of vice, nor the modesty of virtue [can] escape the notice and judgment of the public."[7] In this model republic, the citizen no longer lives in self-contradiction, but, in the words of one of Rousseau's most astute commentators, discovers "pure freedom, pure transparency, through intimate association with other free and transparent souls."[8]

These Rousseauean themes—the original lucidity of human intention, the loss of this transparency in the modern cities of Europe, and the possibility of its restoration within small republican communities—have been explored by writers seeking to disclose their meaning and significance within the context of Rousseau's emblematic life and the conflicting cultural forces that collided there.[9] My aim, by contrast, is to lay bare the practical logic that governs the interaction among the transparent and opaque selves of Rousseau's thought, and to explore the implications of this logic, not only for Rousseau's own views regarding interpersonal relations, social inequality, republican virtue, and kindred subjects, but more generally, for human association in some of its social, political, and economic dimensions.

Let me elaborate. Rousseau valued transparent interpersonal relations as an intrinsic good. And he regarded opaque relations as something intrinsically bad. But Rousseau also prized transparency as an instrumental good, being, among other things, the social condition necessary for civic cooperation. And he held a symmetrical view of opaque relations, which Rousseau regarded as the breeding ground for many vices, most importantly the pursuit of private advantage under the guise of virtue. I am primarily, though not exclusively, concerned with the latter two propositions, that is, with the practical consequences and theoretical implications of transparency and its negation.

To be more specific, I want to see whether the distinction between transparent and opaque relations can illuminate some questions in political theory. Can the differences between the social contract theories of Rousseau and Hobbes be explained by recourse to the practical consequences of transparent and opaque intentions? Do the political ramifications of Rousseau's trilogy of passions—*amour de soi, amour-propre,* and compassion—vary within the disparate media of transparent and opaque relations? How does the character of civil society differ when voluntary associations are formed by citizens who know a great deal about one another as opposed to when they know very little about each other? Does transparency necessarily strengthen the general will, and opacity necessarily weaken it? Can Rousseau's critique of "money and commerce" be elucidated and extended via a theory of opaque markets? And, finally, is it useful to construe civic republicanism as a model of a transparent political community and liberalism as a theory for people who are, in many respects, opaque to one another?

Rousseau, Rational Choice, and the Human Form of Life: A Note on Method

My approach to these questions is informed, in part, by rational choice theory, which traces out the consequences of choices undertaken with an end in view and in the face of one or more constraints, including, oftentimes, a lack of information about the plans and strategies of other agents. Because this kind of analysis, which includes the theory of games, is typically used to analyze the utility-maximizing behavior of rational egoists and the outcome of their interaction, some readers may have reservations regarding its application to Rousseau's thinking in light of his richer and more nuanced understanding of the human psyche. Although I am not unsympathetic to these concerns, I ask the skeptical reader to consider the following points. First, while Rousseau was, by no means, an early rational choice theorist in the way some now read Hobbes, he did have a practical, and not just an intrinsic, interest in transparency, as the opening citation of this chapter suggests. Second, in view of Rousseau's depiction of civilized society as *a field of maneuver* where sophisticated individuals compete for preeminence, there is reason to believe the theory of games can be illuminating for it allows a perspicuous presentation of each agent's alternatives and the social outcomes that result from their strategic interaction. Third, I try to incorporate within my simple models and thought experiments some of the subtleties of Rousseau's psychological observations, exploring the interplay between individuals moved by passions as well as by interests. Fourth, the emerging theory of information economics, which explores the systemic consequences of deception and defense against deception can, I believe, illuminate and extend some of Rousseau's ideas about the interaction among, and between, transparent and opaque agents. Finally, I contend that Rousseau has something important to teach the rational choice school, particularly some of its practitioners in the field of economics, and develop several Rousseauean criticisms of their most cherished institution—the market economy—criticisms which elaborate Rousseau's claim that exchange is seldom completely transparent.

Although there is much to learn by reading Rousseau's works with an eye fixed firmly on the social milieu in which they were written, my working premise is that Rousseau's reflections bear on the *human condition*, that is, on the possibilities and predicaments arising from our ability to conceal or communicate our intentions; from the fact that we are sometimes observed by others, but not always; from our capacity to control our facial expressions and countenance, but not completely; from the fact that we cannot always tell whether someone is trying to deceive us, and so on. Insofar as these circumstances belong to the human form of life, I am hopeful that the following discussion will bear upon those modes of human interaction that are shaped by the potentialities of transparency and concealment.[10]

Survey of My Themes

Opaque Cities and the Ring of Gyges

Rousseau was not the first, nor the last, to consider the problems originating in our capacity for deception. The greatest challenge ever posed to the life of virtue—Glaucon's demand that Socrates explain why someone who had the power to satisfy every desire with impunity should nevertheless act with self-restraint—gains much of its force from Glaucon's thought experiment in which a person, in possession of the magical Ring of Gyges, can become invisible at will.[11] Why act with restraint if you can take whatever you want without any risk of being punished? Having initially posed the question in this compelling, but supernatural form, Glaucon discards Gyges's Ring and envisions the next best alternative (which bears a close resemblance to Rousseau's worst nightmare), that is, maintaining a good reputation while surreptitiously engaging in self-aggrandizement. Why live a life of virtue when, by merely having a reputation for virtue, one gains all the advantages of being trusted without incurring any of the costs entailed in being trustworthy?

In the *Republic*, the fundamental question is what kind of life one should lead and, to eliminate extraneous considerations, the question is posed from the perspective of someone who has the power to deceive others. In Rousseau's critical discourses, by contrast, the focus shifts to the kind of life that is possible when *everyone* possesses considerable deceptive powers.[12] For, according to Rousseau, these are the circumstances that prevail in the dark cities of Europe, where "the war of all against all" is waged beneath the patina of polite society. If the "citizens" of Paris really were opaque to one another and if behind their masks of virtue they plotted assaults against each other, would they not welcome Hobbes's Leviathan?

A Transparent Republic

Rousseau's solution to the problems created by our capacity for dissimulation is presented to the king of Poland in the following words, "you must arrange things so that *every citizen will feel himself to be constantly under the public eye.*"[13] Although the opaque cities of Europe (and other continents) have grown much larger and more anonymous since Rousseau offered his advice to the Polish king, recent advances in information technology may retrieve the possibility of bringing every citizen's conduct "under the public eye." More than three centuries after Hobbes outlined the necessary conditions for political order among individuals whose declared intentions cannot be trusted, there can be found in England nearly 2 million miniature cameras which, mounted on lampposts, transmit continuous images of Britain's 60 million citizens to local constabularies, which report sharp reductions in public misconduct.[14]

Although anyone who values privacy has reason to worry about the deployment of these remote sensing technologies, some contemporary communitarians welcome the possibility that citizens may, once again, be able to *watch over one another.*[15] Consider the futuristic utopia described in a book appropriately entitled, *The Transparent Society*:

> Homes are sacrosanct, but out on the street any citizen, from the richest to the poorest, can both walk safely and use the godlike power [of ubiquitous cameras on lampposts] to zoom at will from vantage point to vantage point, viewing all the lively wonders of the vast but easily spanned village their metropolis has become, as if by some magic it had turned into a city not of people but of birds.[16]

There is exquisite irony in this populist celebration of advanced surveillance technology. It was, after all, "the progress of the arts and sciences" that, in Rousseau's account, made the city and its anonymity possible.

Now technology is eliminating the very shadows that abet what Rousseau regarded as "the worst of all abuses," citizens paying "apparent obedience to the laws, only in order to break them with security."[17] Unlike its dark predecessor, the postmodern metropolis might become an "easily spanned village" where neither vice nor virtue go unnoticed.[18]

Not everyone welcomes the possibility that the citizens of the contemporary democratic state will be able to watch over one another with the diligence Rousseau thought necessary for a successful republic. Such intrusiveness bears an uncomfortably close affinity to what Michel Foucault has called the "surveillance society," where an omnipresent gaze functions as a disciplinary mechanism, not to maintain the civic virtue essential to an egalitarian republic, but to establish and maintain the reign of "normalcy."[19] Transparency, we shall see, is a double-edged sword that can threaten our autonomy even when its scope is expanded with the aim of eliminating the hiding places which protect those who free ride on the sacrifices of virtuous citizens.

Opaque Markets and the Invisible Hand

Like Rousseau, Adam Smith also considered the anonymity of urban life and its pervasive interaction of strangers a defining feature of the modern world. But where Rousseau found in civil society a polite version of the Hobbesian struggle for supremacy, Smith discovered something quite different—a rational, harmonious order of exchange where self-centered traders, acting with the sole purpose of advancing their own interests, were led, "as if by an invisible hand," to increase the wealth of the entire community.[20] And where Rousseau complained that the division of labor brought with it an enslaving dependence on others, Smith countered with a conception of the market economy as an intricate network of *inter*dependence where individuals cooperate for mutual advantage.

The contemporary debate over globalization is, in many respects, a contest between Rousseau's vision of self-governing republics and Smith's vision of a global marketplace. For our modern-day communitarians, the trouble with expanding markets is that they restrict the scope of self-government.[21] The logic of competition, which compels firms to vie with one another for market share, also forces states to compete for investment capital and, to a lesser, but increasing, extent, for skilled labor. When firms can "exit" the nation-state, shifting their production to countries with less stringent regulations and lower tax rates, the people are no longer sovereign because the range of policy alternatives is constrained by the imperatives of global competition. For Smith's contemporary followers, on the other hand, the globalization of markets, like the increasingly popular Internet, promises a wider trading network within which people can cooperate for greater advantage.

At the present time, it is Smith's model of the market economy that is winning the day, extending its dominion over countries that, not so long ago, were devoted to its destruction. Nevertheless, some economists have come to appreciate the Rousseauean distinction between interactions among transparent agents, on the one hand, and interactions among opaque agents, on the other.[22] There is a contemporary school of economic thought which holds that markets are subject to "information asymmetries," that is, circumstances wherein one party to a transaction possesses information which, if it were available to the other party, would alter the terms of the exchange. Thus, merchants know more about the quality of their goods than their customers; workers know more about their propensity for shirking than their employers; borrowers typically know more about their prospects for repayment than their creditors; and people shopping for insurance usually know more about their risks than insurers. In these opaque conditions, even honest traders must think and act strategically. And when every market participant is either concealing information about her offer or taking measures to defend against such deception, the nature of "trade" begins to look less like Smith's depiction of honest barter, and more like Rousseau's characterization of commerce as an arena of calculated rivalry dominated by the clever and the powerful.

Intermediate Associations in Transparent and Opaque Societies

I have outlined a few of the problems that emerge when the character and intentions of human beings are not transparent. I want to conclude this overview of my themes by mentioning a couple of the difficulties that arise when the cooperative qualities of individuals *are* transparent. The central dilemma is that, while transparency is necessary for civic cooperation, it is also favorable to the formation of what Rousseau calls "partial societies," that is, secondary associations which advance the relatively narrow interests of their members. These intermediate associations divide the citizen's loyalties between the group that advances his or her particular interests and the wider political community that exists to serve the common good. In addition, the more people know about one another, about their capacity for self-discipline, for hard work, for intelligent decision making, and the like, the easier it is for those with valuable skills and assets to form exclusive associations amongst themselves, reinforcing social inequalities and fragmenting the community. Such outcomes need not be the intended result of one group of citizens seeking superiority over others, but may, for example, be the unintended consequence of affluent families looking for quality schools, safe neighborhoods, and well-kept yards.

In opaque societies, by contrast, citizens lack the information that is necessary to sort themselves into exclusive associations. Hence, the organizations formed by anonymous citizens tend to be more heterogeneous in composition and, given a plausible set of assumptions, more equal in power than the associations that emerge within transparent communities. In the limiting case, where association membership is a random draw from the population, the composition of associations will mirror that of the wider community, which renders them less threatening to the republic than the more homogenous associations that form within transparent communities. Although limiting cases can be theoretically interesting, it is more realistic to think about transparency and opacity as a continuum in which citizens can acquire more or less information about one another's character, resources, objectives, interests, and the like. Bearing these qualifications in mind, my aim is to show that freedom of association produces different kinds of organizations, with divergent political consequences, depending on the ease with which those joining together for mutual advantage can ascertain one another's assets and liabilities.

Plan of the Book

The book is organized in the following way. In chapter two, I outline several variations of the prisoner's dilemma game in order to illustrate the different kinds of interaction that take place in Rousseau's primitive communities, in the great European cities he despised, and in the ultra-transparent republic he urged upon his fellow citizens. These games vary in two dimensions: (1) the likelihood that players will recognize one another's real intentions; and (2) the interests and sentiments that motivate the players. I begin with "*amour de soi* games," which are played by simple souls whose intentions are immediately expressed in their outward bearing, giving them a transparency that makes cooperation possible even in encounters that take the form of a single-play prisoner's dilemma game. Next I explore the "*amour-propre* games" that are played in polite society, where individuals, desperately seeking to surpass one another, employ the arts of deception to conceal their real ambitions. Even

though these vainglorious men and women would prefer mutual
restraint to mutual aggression, their concern with relative position raises
the threshold level of transparency necessary for cooperation, while, at
the same time, they are becoming more opaque to one another. Finally,
I consider "compassion games" played by other-regarding individuals
whose cooperative disposition, like the character of Rousseau's citizens,
is well-publicized. This mode of transparency, where neither virtue nor
vice can "escape the notice and judgment of the public," provides the
mutual assurance necessary for civic cooperation, but only under
conditions of mutual surveillance.[23]

The subject of chapter three is Rousseau's critical view of intermediate
associations and the threat they pose to the unity of the republic. I analyze
the composition, character, and extent of association when citizens can
easily assess one another's character, abilities, and resources, and when
they cannot. My primary objective is to show that the transparency
which sustains civic virtue is also favorable to the formation of exclusive
and unequal associations that divide the citizen's loyalties between
the "partial societies" that advance his or her particular interests and the
republic that serves the common good. By contrast, associations in
opaque societies tend to be more diverse in composition, more equal in
power, and, ironically, more compatible with the demands of citizenship. Opacity can, however, engender the corrosive "individualism" and
unraveling of association that Tocqueville warned against in his study of
America's nascent democracy.[24] In order to illustrate Tocqueville's
point, I develop a simple model to explain why association membership
becomes less attractive when the cooperative quality of citizens becomes
less transparent and how the "exit" of productive association members
sets in motion a self-reinforcing process that can unravel the fabric of
civil society. In overly simple terms, freedom of association under
opaque conditions is favorable to equality, but also to dissociation.
Transparency corrects the problem of dissociation, of "individualism,"
but at the cost of greater inequality and a contraction of the common life
that is essential to republican democracy.

In chapter four I examine the scheme of social cooperation given
theoretical expression by Rousseau's contemporary, Adam Smith, who
discovered a hidden order beneath the turbulent surface of market
society. My principal aim is to show that Smith's argument in favor of
competitive markets requires as a necessary premise traders whose intentions are transparent. If, however, "we never know with whom we have
to deal," as Rousseau contends, then the impersonal rule of the price
system gives way to strategic interaction, which produces outcomes that

are less efficient and less fair than those advertised by contemporary advocates of laissez-faire, if not by Smith himself.[25] In addition to showing that opacity brings in train strategic decision making, which limits the feasible range of cooperation (even through contractual agreements), I explain how opaque labor and capital markets give rise to self-reinforcing inequalities of wealth and income, and then conclude by considering some of Rousseau's recommended institutional arrangements as ways of addressing the principal-agent problems that confront a republican form of government pursuing egalitarian policy objectives.

In chapter five, I employ the Rousseauean distinction between transparent and opaque societies to cast a different light upon some other thinkers both ancient and modern. I begin with a consideration of the attitudes toward promise-keeping exhibited by Glaucon's "wolf in sheep's clothing," Hobbes's "foole," and David Gauthier's "constrained maximizer," and explore the upshot of these divergent attitudes for social contract theory.[26] Next I examine Bruce Ackerman's conception of "perfect transactional flexibility" and its embodiment in an ideal communications device from the vantage point afforded by our own inquiry into the possibilities and hazards of free exchange under conditions transparent and otherwise.[27] Finally, I take up John Rawls's supreme instrument of opacity—the veil of ignorance—and try to show how a real-world surrogate for this veil can be put to use in defending Rawls's conception of a just society against communitarian critics who insist that its citizens would not willingly comply with the principles of justice that are chosen under the opaque conditions of Rawls's "original position."[28] In the concluding chapter, I bring to mind these fantastic technologies—Gyges's Ring, Ackerman's perfect transmitter-receiver-shield, and Rawls's veil of ignorance—to frame a few closing thoughts about transparency, opacity, and the human form of life.

CHAPTER TWO

Transparency and Opacity in Nature, Society, and State

In *The Spirit of the Laws*, Rousseau's great predecessor, Montesquieu, presents a typology of the forms of government which is based on the distinctive human passion that sets each type "in motion."[1] In Montesquieu's scheme, virtue is the mainspring of republics, honor the animating principle of monarchies, and fear the motive force in despotisms. In simplest terms, republics are sustained by the virtuous self-discipline of their citizens, monarchies by the fulfillment of the duties and responsibilities of rank, and despotisms by the fear of arbitrary coercion. Assessing Montesquieu's contribution to modern social theory, Raymond Aron singles out the mutual dependence between "the form of government on the one hand and the style of interpersonal relations on the other" as Montesquieu's "most important and valuable idea."[2] Rousseau, too, was a student and admirer of Montesquieu's work and had a keen interest in the political implications of different kinds of "interpersonal relations." Although Rousseau never developed a similar typology of his own, he did pay close attention to the political consequences of different passions, their expression and concealment, and, on the basis of these observations, we can construct a Rousseauean typology of the different forms of social interaction and their political ramifications.

The main body of the presentation that follows is divided into three parts each of which deals with a specific mode of human association. I begin with the transparent encounters of those guileless human beings who populate the primitive societies that have just emerged from Rousseau's state of nature. My aim is to explain why these simple souls act with mutual restraint even when their interaction assumes the form of a single-play prisoner's dilemma game in which self-restraint is generally thought to be a losing strategy. Next, I turn to the interaction between the opaque individuals who inhabit the European cities Rousseau despised and explore the dynamic relationship between the desire for superiority and the loss of transparency. This is a deadly combination that all but forecloses the possibility of cooperation even in repeated encounters that normally favor reciprocity. Finally, I take up the ideal republic of Rousseau's imagination, explaining why citizens who are both transparent and compassionate stand a good chance of solving their collective action problems. This achievement is not without its cost, however, as the crystalline lucidity of Rousseau's citizens can only be maintained by an intrusive discipline of mutual surveillance.

The Transparent Interaction of Simple Souls

In reasoning about the original condition of human kind, Rousseau urges us "not to conclude, with Hobbes, that because man has no idea of goodness, he must be naturally wicked."[3] Hobbes's mistake, according to Rousseau, was to improperly admit "as a part of savage man's care for self-preservation, the gratification of a multitude of passions which are the work of society."[4] Pride is the most destructive of these passions because, in its virulent form, as the drive for preeminence, it can *only* be gratified at the expense of others. Yet pride cannot have any bearing on man's *natural* condition because this passion is inconceivable outside an established social ecology. Before a person can be moved by pride, he must first have a conception of himself as the object of another person's judgment. In other words, he must have acquired the habit of "living in the opinion of others," an orientation which, according to Rousseau, was far removed from mankind's original state.[5]

Some contemporary Hobbesians, in method if not results, contend that pride is *not* a necessary condition of social strife, that the public good of social peace will not be supplied by rational agents even if they are unmoved by pride, envy, or malice.[6] This argument can be conveniently illustrated with the help of the prisoner's dilemma game in which two players must each choose between a cooperative move and a noncooperative move referred to as "defection." The combination of these choices yields four possible outcomes or "payoffs," which each player ranks in the following order (from best to worst): unilateral defection, mutual cooperation, mutual defection, unilateral cooperation. More specifically, Hobbes's reasoning can be depicted by locating rational

Table 2.1 The *Amour de Soi* Game

		Player B	
		Act with restraint (cooperate)	Act without restraint (defect)
Player A	Act with restraint (cooperate)	2, 2	0, 3
	Act without restraint (defect)	3, 0	1, 1

Note: The first number of each pair represents Player A's payoff and the second number Player B's payoff.

egoists in a single-play prisoner's dilemma game, which I call the *Amour de Soi* Game (see table 2.1) for reasons that will become clear shortly.

In this game, each player has a choice between two strategies—to act with self-restraint (cooperate) or not (defect). If one player acts with restraint and the other does not, then, according to Hobbes's account, the unrestrained agent enjoys the best outcome, temporary power over the other (a payoff of 3), while the self-restrained agent, now vulnerable to harm, suffers the worst (a payoff of 0). If both players act with restraint, the result is the second best outcome for each—peace (a payoff of 2 for both players). And if neither player acts with restraint, both must endure the third best outcome—war (a payoff of 1 for both).[7]

Trouble arises because while both players find mutual restraint more conducive to their self-preservation than mutual aggression, each finds it most advantageous to act without restraint no matter what the other player does. Suppose player A acts with restraint (cooperates). In this case, A's payoff is two if B also acts with restraint (cooperates) and is zero if B acts without restraint (defects). Now suppose player A acts without restraint (defects). In this case A's payoff is three if B acts with restraint (cooperates) and is one if B acts without restraint (defects). Thus, A does best for herself by acting without restraint (defecting) regardless of what B does. And, of course, the same logic applies to B, who also does best by acting without restraint (defecting). Assuming A and B aim to maximize their own payoffs and, therefore, both act without restraint (defect), the result is war (mutual defection). It is this logic, which does not require the introduction of "a multitude of passions," but rather proceeds simply from man's *amour de soi* to the condition of collective insecurity, that harbors the potential for conflict even among those who bear no enmity toward one another. As one of Hobbes's contemporary interpreters puts it, "Even moderate people, who have no desire for power or glory for its own sake and who may have no specific quarrels with one, may, for defensive purposes, engage in *anticipatory* violence against one."[8]

Hobbes was convinced that the destructive consequences of human interaction in the state of nature could only be avoided by creating a sovereign authority with the power to punish those who failed to restrain themselves.[9] Mutual promises of self-restraint are not sufficient because "he that performeth first has no assurance that the other will performe after."[10] Rousseau envisioned a different possibility, where "men found their security in the ease with which they could see through one another."[11] To see how such innocent souls could live in peace, let us return to the encounter depicted in the *Amour de Soi* Game, where each player can act with or without restraint. One strategy for playing this game is to act with restraint (cooperate) only if you expect the other player to do the same, otherwise you act without restraint (defect) so as not to be exploited. This strategy is called "conditional cooperation" for obvious reasons. Alternatively, a player may choose a strategy of "unconditional defection" in which the player always acts without restraint (defects) no matter what she expects the other player to do.[12] In a population composed of these two types of players, conditional cooperators will enjoy the greatest gains from social interaction. Unconditional defectors *can do no better than* the low-valued defect/defect payoff [1,1 in the *Amour de Soi* Game] because conditional cooperators will defect in interactions with unconditional defectors. Conditional cooperators *can do no worse than* the defect/defect payoff, and, in addition, they enjoy the benefits of mutual restraint in interactions with each other, that is, the cooperate/cooperate payoff of [2,2].[13]

The Hobbesian will, of course, deny that the strategy of conditional cooperation is superior to unconditional defection, which, she contends, is the best strategy no matter what the other player does.[14] But this rejoinder fails to take seriously Rousseau's premise of transparency. If each player's true intention were plainly visible to the other, then each would know with certainty what move the other planned to make. In this respect, *transparent intentions are a perfect substitute for binding commitments of self-restraint.*[15] Still, the Hobbesian may insist, as soon as one player successfully convinces the other of her cooperative intentions, she will *then* find it advantageous to defect.[16] Granted, deception is a promising strategy for sophisticated players capable of disguising their real intentions. It is, however, inconceivable for naïve souls whose behavior proclaims "at first glance" their true disposition. A strategy requiring duplicity is simply not possible for people whose "external appearance" is "always a true mirror" of what is in their hearts.[17]

It must be acknowledged that transparent intentions alone cannot sustain forms of cooperation that require long-term commitments. For, it would be possible for someone to make a promise with the transparent (and sincere) intention of keeping it, yet sometime later act with the transparent intention of breaking it. *Naïve transparency rules out deception, not weakness of will.* Hence, the innocent lucidity of Rousseau's simple souls does not solve the Hobbesian problem of assurance, which arises when one party must comply with a promise before the other is called upon to do so. Rather, Rousseauean transparence comes into play when people are face-to-face and act with self-restraint rather than pressing for an uncertain advantage. Mutual security is possible in such encounters because Rousseau's artless innocents can "see through one another," taking their cues from the facial expression, posture, and demeanor of the other person.

Rousseau's conjecture about the harmonious relations that were possible for human beings before "art had moulded our behavior" gains some measure of plausibility when we take account of the fact that, even *after* art has molded much of our behavior, we still cannot control many of our facial muscles or the pitch of our voices when we lie.[18] It is as if we had been designed by nature so that some of our emotions are expressed involuntarily, which is perhaps why, in many experiments, mutual cooperation in the prisoner's dilemma game occurs with greater frequency when the players can see one another, even though they cannot communicate.[19]

The Calculus of Recognition and the Dynamics of Cooperation

Let us be a little more precise. If the advantages of conditional cooperation are to exceed those of unconditional defection, the following conditions must be satisfied: (1) conditional cooperators must be able to identify one another in order to successfully cooperate; and (2) conditional cooperators must be able to accurately recognize unconditional defectors in order to avoid being exploited. Once these requirements are met, conditional cooperators will enjoy the benefits of mutual cooperation, while unconditional defectors will suffer the costs of mutual defection.

Although conditional cooperation will flourish whenever people can easily read one another's intentions, its success does not require perfect transparency. It is easy to imagine that the naïve creatures who inhabit Rousseau's first societies would occasionally make mistakes about one another's real intentions, even if they were still too innocent to engage in calculated deception. Conditional cooperators are subject to two kinds of error. They can mistake unconditional defectors for conditional cooperators, thereby exposing themselves to exploitation (the cooperate/defect outcome). Or, they can mistake one another for unconditional defectors, thereby missing an opportunity to cooperate for mutual advantage.[20]

Although mistakes about another person's intentions are costly to conditional cooperators and beneficial to unconditional defectors, conditional cooperation continues to be the superior disposition as long as the likelihood of accurate recognition remains relatively high. In general, the higher the probability of recognition, the greater are the expected benefits of conditional cooperation and the smaller are the expected benefits of unconditional defection.[21] Figure 2.1 displays the expected payoffs of the two strategies under varying probabilities of accurate recognition, assuming the population is evenly divided between conditional cooperators and unconditional defectors, and taking the payoffs from the *Amour de Soi* Game explained earlier.

Given these premises, the expected payoff of conditional cooperation will be greater than the expected payoff of unconditional defection provided the probability of accurate recognition exceeds 75 percent, that

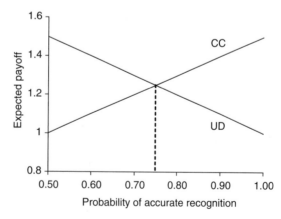

Figure 2.1   Expected payoffs of conditional cooperation (CC) and unconditional defection (UD) with different probabilities of recognition.

is, provided conditional cooperators recognize both one another and unconditional defectors in more than three-quarters of their encounters.

As long as the probability of recognition exceeds the threshold level at which conditional cooperation becomes the superior strategy, then, by the process of natural selection, or through the emulation of successful behavior, the proportion of conditional cooperators in the population will rise.[22] And this increase, in turn, will be self-reinforcing because conditional cooperators enjoy larger gains relative to unconditional defectors as the proportion of conditional cooperators in the population rises.[23] Once they comprise more than half of the population, the expected payoff of conditional cooperation will exceed the expected payoff of unconditional defection, so that if there are no other changes, the percentage of conditional cooperators in the population will increase. If the degree of transparency, that is, the probability of accurate recognition, remains unchanged, the population will gravitate toward one composed entirely of conditional cooperators.[24]

Transparent Intentions and the Logic of Leviathan

Life among Rousseau's simple souls is more harmonious than life in Hobbes's state of nature because human beings who can "see through one another" find self-restraint more advantageous than self-assertion.[25] Yet the original transparency of human intention is not sufficient to explain the differences between the two accounts of mankind's natural condition, nor is it entirely fair to Hobbes, who regarded the consequences, and not the probability, of misjudging another person's character as the crucial fact of life without a sovereign authority. If "violent death" is the outcome awaiting anyone who misconstrues another person's intentions, then conditional cooperation will only be attractive if people are, indeed, perfectly transparent, so that the possibility of misperception is ruled out altogether.[26] It seems unlikely that even the uncorrupted inhabitants of Rousseau's early communities could be this transparent. But then they do not have to be, for the cost of misjudgment among these artless creatures is something well short of violent death. And if the risk of acting with self-restraint is relatively small, then, as we have already seen, conditional cooperation will yield advantages even if human intentions are not fully transparent, and unconditional defectors are occasionally mistaken for those who would conditionally cooperate.

By the same token, if human beings were so opaque that their attempts to ascertain one another's intentions were hardly more successful than random guesses, then the prospects for cooperation would be slim even when the costs of miscalculation were relatively small. The grave risk incurred in unilaterally choosing self-restraint, which is central to Hobbes's account of life without Leviathan, is not, then, a necessary condition of cooperative failure. If people cannot read one another's intentions with any consistency, conditional cooperation will not prove advantageous even if the cost incurred in choosing self-restraint when the other player chooses self-assertion is relatively small.[27] Thus the logic, if not the full psychological force, of Hobbes's *Leviathan* applies not just to individuals who fear violent death, but to any agents who are opaque to one another, for this condition, even in the absence of grave risk, is sufficient to foreclose the possibility of cooperation without a mechanism of enforcement.[28]

Are Rousseau's Primitives Human?

In Rousseau's speculative anthropology, the probability of misconstruing another person's intentions rises in proportion to the degree of human refinement. But before we explore the nature and consequences of human opacity in polite society, we should pause to consider *why* Rousseau's primitives are so transparent and whether his explanation of this trait is at least plausible, if not compelling. Given the superior payoff that accrues to the unconditional defector who appears ready to cooperate, why do Rousseau's early humans fail to exploit this opportunity? We have already drawn attention to the difficulty facing would-be deceivers whose intentions find immediate, involuntary expression in their outward demeanor. We may now add that, in order to reap the benefits of such deception, individuals must be able to self-consciously fashion a public identity that will win the confidence of others. This task was beyond the comprehension of the unrefined souls who populated Rousseau's primitive societies because they did not yet have a conception of how they appeared to others.[29] Rather, "each man regarded himself as the only observer of his actions."[30] Such beings would be transparent to one another, not only because of their irrepressible emotions, but also because they lack an understanding of what it is to present oneself to others, that is, to have a social identity, a *persona*.

Is the notion of a human being without a social identity a coherent conception? Before we address this question, let us note that the absence of a conception of oneself as the object of another's judgment is not a necessary condition of deception. There are many animal species whose behavioral repertoire includes some form of deception. Elephants make "bluff attacks" to thwart the aggression of other elephants. Foxes, coyotes, and weasels have been observed feigning injury, and monkeys engage in a variety of complex behaviors to divert the attention of dominant males.[31]

These are not, of course, the kinds of deception Rousseau had in mind in his critique of polite society. Animals do not calculate, and the point of their deception is survival, not self-aggrandizement. Nonetheless, these examples from the animal kingdom show that the absence of a social identity does not preclude several varieties of deception in the ordinary sense of the word.

There is, however, a more serious objection to be raised against Rousseau's understanding of primitive transparency. This objection turns on the question of whether it is possible to learn a language without developing a conception of oneself as the object of another person's judgment, that is to say, without acquiring the idea of "me" to go along with "I."[32] Learning a language involves, in addition to many other things, learning to make judgments. When a child is taught the meaning of words like "smaller" and "larger," she is also taught how to make judgments using these words, for example, "this tree is larger than that one, but smaller than the one over there."[33] And these judgments, in turn, are corrected on countless occasions, for example, when the child's parent says, "no, that tree is taller, but not really bigger, than the other one." There are, in addition, many words and phrases, such as "making a promise," which involve learning how to do things in accordance with the rules governing a social practice. In learning how to use these words, the child may be criticized for failing to conform to the rules of the practice: "you promised to do such and such, but you have not done as you promised." Given the pervasive nature of this kind of training, it is hard to imagine how someone who has been subjected to so many judgments could *avoid* acquiring a conception of herself as a person who is judged by others.[34]

In fact, many common language games presuppose this self-understanding. The practice of praising and blaming is inconceivable without the companion notion that one's behavior may be the object of another person's judgment. If we think of Rousseau's references to primitive society, to people living together in "common huts," rather than his references to isolated savages, then, to make Rousseau's view self-consistent, we must imagine that praising and blaming are foreign to the life that is carried on within these common quarters, that somehow their inhabitants learn to speak without acquiring a conception of themselves as objects of one another's appraisal, or we must imagine that these primitives could acquire such practices, and conceive of themselves as objects of judgments made by others, without, at the same time, learning how to manage their public identity.[35]

Although I have argued that learning a language is part of a process in which one's speech and conduct are judged by others, and that many language games and their interwoven social practices entail the idea of an agent whose actions are appraised by others, I do not want to rule out what might be called naïve spontaneity. Language does not abolish natural inclination, but gives it a new form. In Wittgenstein's instructive example, the instinctive cry of pain is replaced by "pain behavior."[36] With this example in mind, it seems plausible to suppose that there comes a point in a child's development when a few verbal expressions have become second nature, as spontaneous as the natural cry of pain, even though the child has yet to learn the more complex patterns of behavior necessary for the sophisticated deceit Rousseau found so pervasive among adults.[37] Perhaps there are even cultures that remain closer to nature in this sense than, say, cultures with elaborate forms of politesse. It may be recalled that Tocqueville found the manners of egalitarian America more "natural" than those of aristocratic France.[38] Nevertheless, I want to reiterate the point that there is little prospect of establishing transparent social relations by creating communities in which no one regards himself as the object of anyone else's judgment, at least not if the members of these communities are to speak a language. And, in fact, Rousseau did not pursue this elusive notion, but rather envisioned its opposite, a republican form of life in which citizens would become the *continuous objects of one another's judgment.*

The Opaque Cities of Hobbesian Men

Given the prerequisites for strategic deception, we can mark the end of mankind's innocent lucidity as the moment human beings began to consider how they appeared to others and record as a second turning point the moment they gained control of their outward bearing. Once a person's demeanor no longer "proclaimed at first glance" his true disposition, mutual restraint based on the immediate transparence of human intention vanished forever. In this section, we explore the damaging consequences of our capacity to conceal our real motives, which is fully realized in "civilized" society where each person, desperately seeking the admiration and esteem of those around him, derives his self-worth entirely from the opinion of others. But first let us note that Rousseau's conjectural history of human development chronicles other changes which are favorable to social cooperation, albeit of a different kind. In particular, Rousseau describes how specialization and a growing dependence on others brought individuals into repeated interactions, which, on the standard game-theoretic view, creates the possibility of conditional cooperation in an iterated prisoner's dilemma game.

Deep Duplicity and the Premises of Tit-for-Tat

It has been demonstrated by deductive reasoning, by experiment, and by historical example that, under the right conditions, cooperation will emerge even among rational egoists.[39] Players in an iterated prisoner's dilemma game will find it advantageous to adopt a strategy of conditional cooperation provided they expect to interact with one another an indefinite number of times and do not discount the costs and benefits of future outcomes too sharply.[40] Under these conditions, the best individual strategy is to play "tit-for-tat," that is, to cooperate if the other player has been cooperative and to defect if she has not. Once other players realize that this is the invariable rule guiding one's conduct, they will find it beneficial to cooperate for mutual advantage rather than play strategies that elicit retaliation and therefore result in mutual defection.

This kind of cooperation was not possible among Rousseau's early humans both because their interaction was too sporadic and because they had no idea of the future.[41] But, according to Rousseau's conjecture, human beings ultimately developed their imaginative capacities and began to value future states of affairs.[42] In addition, Rousseau reports, albeit regretfully, that individuals became dependent on one another and so found themselves engaged in a continuing process of social interaction.[43] In short, the two conditions necessary for the success of a "tit-for-tat" strategy were eventually satisfied, and, thus, from the vantage point of the contemporary game theorist, there would be reason for optimism about the prospects for cooperation as human beings gradually abandoned their original condition for civilized life. Yet, as their interactions increase in number and importance—the very set of circumstances *most* conducive to cooperation in the standard game-theoretic view—Rousseau finds not harmony, but "rivalry and competition."[44] Our first task, then, is to explain why, when the social conditions necessary for cooperation based on reciprocity appear to have been met, the outcome is not harmony, but discord.

Let us begin with the transitional moment that separates the existence of the isolated savage from that of the civilized man, that is, the period during which human life was carried on within the "common huts" of

Rousseau's imagination.[45] In these communal living quarters, Rousseau conjectures that men and women had nothing to hide and lived together in harmony. Contemporary anthropological accounts of primitive societies paint a similar picture, though, in these accounts, it is the great difficulty involved in concealing misbehavior, a constraint imposed by the absence of doors and separate rooms, which is responsible for the relative lack of intense conflict in simple societies.[46] Even without the complete Hobbesian machinery necessary to investigate transgressions and to punish their perpetrators, crime is seldom widespread in primitive societies because the entire community is effectively enlisted as informants, and privacy, whether in the form of separate living quarters or other hiding places, provides no shield against the group's surveillance. In these circumstances, "everyone knows everything about everyone else," and deception is therefore exceedingly difficult.[47]

Once human beings abandoned their "common huts" in favor of private living quarters; once they relinquished their independence in favor of specialization and the division of labor; once they ceased living "within themselves" and began to live only in the "opinion of others"; it then "became the interest of men to appear what they really were not."[48] And with this development, the immediate transparency of thought and feeling, wherein a man's demeanor "proclaimed at first glance his true disposition," was lost forever. Henceforth, men would know one another only by their reputation.

Acquaintance by reputation is by no means fatal to cooperation. Quite the contrary, people interested in cooperating for mutual advantage will naturally seek out individuals who are known to follow through on their commitments. Thus it becomes profitable to have a reputation for trustworthiness, which can be achieved either by actually being trustworthy, or, if one can pull it off, by appearing to be trustworthy. Of course, the latter strategy will not work in interactions where it is obvious whether one has kept a commitment or not. For example, if a farmer who received help during last year's harvest refuses to return the favor, his defection will be manifest, and he will receive no help during next year's harvest.[49]

Yet the difference between cooperation and defection is not always so straightforward, particularly once people have learned the art of duplicity. To begin with, the two strategies often admit of subtle variation. Thus the farmer who decides not to follow through on a commitment at harvest time may nevertheless pretend to help while actually shirking her responsibilities, harvesting the minimum amount she believes is necessary to induce the cooperation of other farmers during next year's harvest.

Similarly, the farmer who is being cheated may not find it worthwhile to carefully monitor his neighbor's effort, but may, when it is his turn to help others, instead employ the same strategy of pretending to fully cooperate. In this case, both of the shirking farmers might be better off than they would have been had neither helped at all, but still not as well off as they could have been had each devoted a full effort to harvesting one another's crops.[50]

When we turn to the interaction among sophisticated men and women who wished to impress one another in the salons of Paris, we might imagine, as Rousseau did, that the opportunities for deception are much greater.[51] In polite society, treating others with respect sustains a public good: the social conditions favorable to self-esteem. But while people have a common interest in mutual admiration, Rousseau finds that in stratified societies, where status is important, each person most prefers to be admired by others without deferring to them in turn.[52] Each one will therefore seek to appear as though he is expressing regard for others, when, in fact, he may be doing just the opposite. In some interactions, the person who is the object of ridicule may even become an accomplice in the charade, for once people derive their self-worth from the judgments of others, they have a stake in believing they are being treated with respect when, in reality, they are the object of derision. In this fashion, our propensity for self-deception joins forces with our powers of deceit to create a house of mirrors in which no "virtue" is what it seems to be.

Yet neither the subtleties of politesse, nor the human propensity for self-denial, will always be sufficient to conceal the fact that one person's self-restraint has been repaid with acts of self-assertion. If the social good of mutual respect is to be maintained, then defections intended to improve one person's status at the expense of another's dignity must become well-publicized so the offending party can be punished or excluded from future interactions.[53] Yet the alternatives open to those who believe they have been slighted are often uninviting. If the victim shares her experience with others who believe her story, she may be regarded as a fool. This damages one's self-esteem and may invite further acts of denigration. On the other hand, if others do not give credence to the complaint, perhaps because of the subtle and ambiguous quality of polite behavior, then the victim is apt to become known as a whiner and maybe as a conniver as well. For "social man," who "only knows how to live in the opinion of others," the costs of such disclosure must oftentimes outweigh the benefits.[54] As a consequence, the character of individuals will remain opaque, and the prospects for mutual respect will be correspondingly diminished.

Those who, despite these pitfalls, are nevertheless disposed to cooperate must be careful. On the one hand, they must be crystal clear in communicating their intentions, a task made difficult by the nuances of politesse, by the multitude of impostors, and by the need to distinguish themselves not only from predatory defectors, but also from *un*conditional cooperators who always cooperate and, hence, are especially vulnerable to exploitation.[55] On the other hand, they must be equally assiduous in assessing the character of those around them, many of whom are skilled in the art of deception. And, of course, unconditional defectors will not find it advantageous to stand by idly while their prospective prey improve their ability to discern the character of those with whom they interact, but will redouble their efforts to find more effective means of concealment and disguise.

Thus there emerges a kind of arms race in which some make increasing investments in the techniques of deception, while others, for a time at least, invest in the skills and information necessary to uncover deceit.[56] The outcome of this contest depends on (1) the costs incurred by unconditional defectors in their efforts to reduce the likelihood that their true intentions will be recognized versus (2) the costs incurred by conditional cooperators in trying to increase their chances of recognizing the character of others. These costs will depend, in turn, on such factors as the social milieu in which people interact, the frequency of interaction between the same individuals, the extent to which people talk about their interaction, and so on. In the next section I describe how Rousseau hoped to alter this cost calculus in favor of conditional cooperation. But in the absence of such special measures, Rousseau was convinced that the field of play was tipped in favor of the deceitful, that improvements in the means of masquerade eventually outrun our ability to penetrate the veil of false appearance, with the consequence that "we never know with whom we have to deal."[57]

If we now return to the question of why Rousseau finds conflict where the contemporary game theorist would expect cooperation, part of the answer is that Rousseau attributes to human beings a capacity for deception that is rarely found in the works of contemporary game theory. The deceit Rousseau depicts is more thoroughgoing because it includes the ability, not only to give the impression that one is going to cooperate when, in fact, one plans to defect, but also the ability to act in such a way that it is not always clear to others, *after the fact*, whether one has cooperated or not.[58] Although this kind of deception is apt to be most effective in sporadic interactions between people who do not know one another very well, Rousseau believed it to be pervasive even among people who considered themselves friends.[59]

For the most part, the rational choice school has restricted its attention to forms of interaction that resemble board games where the players have a clear and comprehensive view of one another's strategic options and are in complete command of their own moves. In Rousseau's portrayal of the contest for preeminence, by contrast, the individuals contending for superiority have neither a dispassionate, synoptic view of their strategic possibilities, nor full control over their own resources. Men and women whose self-esteem is tethered to the "opinion of others" cannot perceive the world as it is, nor can they carry through strategies requiring great self-discipline. Instead, deception and self-deception reinforce each other, as men and women, vulnerable to every snub and slight, conceal from themselves the mistreatment they receive at the hands of their "friends." Unable to look at their interaction with open eyes, civilized people cannot play the simple, but effective, strategy of tit-for-tat because its modus operandi demands a true accounting of the players' deeds.[60]

Cooperation and Amour-Propre

As individuals become more opaque to one another and the probability of accurate recognition diminishes, the expected benefits of conditional cooperation will decrease in comparison to the expected benefits of unconditional defection. If the probability of accurate recognition falls below the threshold level at which conditional cooperation becomes the superior strategy, 75 percent in our original example, then the ratio of unconditional defectors to conditional cooperators will rise, which, in turn, will further increase the relative advantage of unconditional defection over conditional cooperation.[61] In this case, the cumulative process described earlier, in which a rising proportion of conditional cooperators was self-reinforcing, works in reverse, as a falling proportion of conditional cooperators is also self-reinforcing.[62] If there are no intervening changes, the population will gravitate toward one composed entirely of unconditional defectors.

Unlike the contemporary game theorist, who regards an increase in the frequency of social interaction as an expanded opportunity for rational egoists to cooperate for mutual advantage, Rousseau sees in this same thickening web of social interdependence a transformation of rational egoists themselves.[63] As individuals interact more frequently with one another, they not only come to have a conception of how they appear to others, which is necessary in order to conduct a campaign of deception, they also acquire a new motive, *amour-propre*, which leads them to judge social outcomes, not by how well they themselves fare but by how well they do in comparison to others. "Thus it is that we find our advantage in the misfortunes of our fellow-creatures, and that the loss of one man almost always constitutes the prosperity of another."[64] Those who profit at the expense of others do not openly proclaim their triumph, for such a declaration would reveal their true ambitions and alert their potential prey. Instead, this "vile propensity to injure one another . . . puts on the mask of benevolence, to carry its point with greater security."[65] These two traits, the desire to surpass others and the capacity to deceive them, thus emerge as the "inseparable attendants of growing inequality."[66]

Within the scheme we have been developing, duplicity and *amour-propre* combine in such a manner that as human beings are becoming less transparent to one another, their growing preoccupation with relative position is raising the threshold level of transparency at which conditional cooperation becomes the favored strategy. Because successful exploitation in a prisoner's dilemma game produces a superior payoff for one player and an inferior payoff for the other (the defect/cooperate outcome), players motivated by *amour-propre* will assign an added value to their own reward when they succeed in taking advantage of the other player. Thus, for any given set of objective payoffs, "the temptation to defect," that is, the difference between the subjectively valued payoff to the defector in the defect/cooperate outcome and his subjectively valued payoff in the cooperate/cooperate outcome, will be greater when players are moved by *amour-propre* than when they are moved solely by *amour de soi*.[67]

Individuals driven by *amour-propre* are not only more tempted to defect by the prospect of relative gains, they also find cooperation more risky because of the prospect of relative losses. Whatever the objective payoff awaiting the player who is exploited in the cooperate/defect outcome, the subjective assessment of this payoff will be lower for those preoccupied with relative position than for those who care only about their own payoffs.[68] *Amour-propre* thus works in two ways to complicate the problem of cooperation, first by increasing the temptation to defect, and second by increasing the risk in not defecting.

These attitudes are illustrated in the *Amour-Propre* Game, where each player may express regard for the other (cooperate) or not (defect). In this game, each player most prefers the outcome in which he is deferred to, a result that occurs when one player withholds regard for the other, who, in turn, expresses regard for him. The second best result for both players is the outcome in which each expresses regard for the other

Table 2.2   The *Amour-Propre* Game

		Player B	
		Show respect (cooperate)	Don't show respect (defect)
Player A	Show respect (cooperate)	2, 2	−1, 4
	Don't show respect (defect)	4, −1	1, 1

(mutual respect), while the third best outcome results when neither expresses regard for the other (mutual derision). The worst outcome, an inferior social status, results when one person expresses regard for the other without receiving the same measure of respect in return. To illustrate the consequences of this preoccupation with relative position, I have replaced the cooperate/defect payoffs of the *Amour de Soi* Game, zero and three, respectively, with the payoffs of negative one and four, respectively, for players moved by *amour-propre*. See table 2.2 for a clear understanding.

If we assume, as before, that the population is equally divided between conditional cooperators, that is, those who show respect if they believe it will be reciprocated, and unconditional defectors, that is, those who always disrespect others, then the probability of accurate recognition in the *Amour-Propre* Game described earlier must exceed 83 percent, versus 75 percent in the *Amour de Soi* Game, if players are to choose the strategy of conditional cooperation and thereby enjoy the mutual respect that it entails.[69] Although the payoffs in the *Amour-Propre* Game, and the 83 percent threshold probability of recognition derived therefrom, are merely illustrative, the threshold probability of recognition must *always* be higher when the players are moved by *amour-propre* than when they are moved by *amour de soi*, that is, when the players are exclusively concerned with their own payoffs.

From Rousseau to Hobbes to Montesquieu

The effect of *amour-propre* in diminishing the prospects for mutual restraint leads us back to Hobbes, who hoped to persuade England's vainglorious aristocrats to become mere egoists—self-interested, prudent, but no longer driven by a desire for preeminence. In Oakeshott's words, "proud men must become tame men in order to remain alive."[70] Yet, while a diminished concern for relative position does indeed enhance the prospects for cooperation, it is not a necessary condition of mutual restraint. If people care about their absolute gains and losses as well as their relative position, that is, if they are moved by *amour de soi* as well as by *amour-propre*, then they may still have something to gain from cooperation. For example, suppose the members of a social class compete for status through conspicuous consumption. Because individuals can offset one another's drive for superior status by making costly purchases themselves, this kind of competition can be collectively self-defeating insofar as each round of expenditure leaves everyone poorer without improving anyone's relative position.[71] In these circumstances, individuals can improve their lot by refraining from actions that, if undertaken by everyone, cannot achieve their aim, provided they are assured others will act with similar restraint.[72] Of course the requisite assurance may not be easy to achieve, especially among people like Rousseau's sophisticates. Nonetheless, the theoretical possibility remains; the adverse consequences of *amour-propre* can be mitigated without eliminating the passion, itself, *provided those moved by it are sufficiently transparent.*

This possibility leads from Hobbes to Montesquieu, who depicted honor, the characteristic sentiment of monarchy, not as a vainglorious drive for preeminence, but as the forthright pursuit of greatness. In Montesquieu's account, frankness "is a mark of breeding and boldness."[73] Here transparency becomes a vehicle, indeed a requirement, of honor. Moreover, for Montesquieu, such noble candor is an ally of liberty because it is the willingness of the nobility to confront the king *forthrightly* that distinguishes monarchy from tyranny.[74]

But if greatness sometimes demands open defiance, what happens when great men confront one another? Within our scheme, the answer depends on two considerations: (1) the value they attach to the possible outcomes of a confrontation; and (2) the transparency of their motives, or what we have been calling the probability of accurate recognition. If the potential gain from acting without restraint is not too great and the risk incurred in acting with restraint is not too grave, and if these rivals are confident in their assessment of one another's intentions, then they will find it advantageous to draw back from a contest of wills neither can be assured of winning. In this fashion, a chastened quest for glory, when coupled with sufficient transparency of character, can produce mutual restraint, an outcome noble adversaries might rationalize as what great men owe each other.

Although even Hobbes's vainglorious aristocrats would find it advantageous to act with self-restraint provided their motives were sufficiently transparent, Rousseau gives us reason to doubt the psychological plausibility of vainglorious men whose character and intentions are ultra-transparent.[75] It is hard to imagine that individuals driven by a desire for distinction could remain as transparent as their naïve ancestors. In Rousseau's speculative anthropology, human vanity and the capacity for deception—a combination fatal to cooperation—develop hand-in-hand and reinforce each other. This particular "style of interpersonal relations," which is pervaded by "jealousy, suspicion, fear, coldness, reserve, hate, and fraud," must, by its own logic, give rise to "a horrible state of war" the violence, if not the origin, of which was well described by Hobbes. In fact, the Leviathan state is the only regime possible for opaque subjects bent on dominating one another.[76]

Once human beings have acquired a conception of, and an interest in, how they appear to others, there can be no return to the innocent transparence that prevailed among creatures who had no reputation. If people who have acquired a public identity are to enjoy the advantages of cooperation, then not only must their desire for superiority be held in check, but a new means of making their true character known to one another must be introduced.

Rousseau's Transparent Republic

In interactions between opaque agents, unconditional defection is the individually rational strategy to choose, and mutual aggression is the collective outcome that follows. In Hobbes's account, this "war of all against all" can only be circumvented by the creation of a coercive state that enforces our promises of mutual restraint. By contrast, Rousseau finds, even in the opaque cities of Europe, a force that moderates the destructive consequences of our propensity for self-aggrandizement. Compassion, though enfeebled in civilized people, is a sentiment so deeply rooted in human nature that it has survived "the greatest depravity of morals."[77]

Compassion and Cooperation

Although the human capacity for sympathy cannot be extinguished, even by the progress of civilization, its range can be circumscribed by the barriers of class and status. Thus Rousseau' rhetorically asks:

> Why are kings without pity for their subjects? Because they count on never being mere men. Why are the rich so hard toward the

poor? It is because they have no fear of becoming poor. Why does the nobility have so great a contempt for the people? It is because a noble will never be a commoner.[78]

If men are going to become citizens, then each one must come to realize that all alike are vulnerable to misfortune and can be thrown into dire straits by events beyond their control. With this realization, each person naturally identifies with his neighbor's distress and is ready to undertake the responsibilities of citizenship in a spirit of fellowship.[79]

To see the effect compassion has on the kind of interaction we have been considering, that is, variations of the prisoner's dilemma game, let us suppose that a player in the Compassion Game may choose between helping the other player (cooperate) or not (defect). Since we are trying to model the "enfeebled" compassion of civilized men and women, let us also suppose that each player most prefers the outcome in which she declines to help (defects), while the other player lends a helping hand (cooperates), and least prefers the opposite outcome. Mutual assistance (both cooperate) is the second best outcome, and mutual non-assistance (both defect) is the third best outcome. This preference ordering, like the orderings incorporated in the *Amour de Soi* and *Amour- Propre* games, is consistent with the prisoner's dilemma preference ordering. To bring the essential characteristic of compassion into our scheme, we may assume that while compassionate players still prefer the defect/cooperate outcome, a compassionate player's "innate repugnance at seeing a fellow-creature suffer" leads him to discount his own payoff when it is won at the expense of the other player.[80] In order to embody this sentiment within our familiar game matrix, we may reduce the defector's payoff in the defect/cooperate outcome from 3 in the *Amour de Soi* Game to 2.5 in the Compassion Game (see table 2.3), leaving all other payoffs unchanged.[81]

Table 2.3   The Compassion Game

		Player B	
		Help A (cooperate)	Don't help A (defect)
Player A	Help B (cooperate)	2, 2	0, 2.5
	Don't help B (defect)	2.5, 0	1, 1

Since players moved by compassion discount their own payoffs when these are gained at the expense of others, it follows that, for any given set of objective payoffs, the subjectively valued gain, or utility, from defecting when the other player cooperates will always be less for the compassionate player than for the player motivated exclusively by *amour de soi*, whose utility from defecting will, in turn, always be less than that of the player moved by *amour-propre*.[82] This reduction in the temptation to defect reduces, in turn, the threshold probability of accurate recognition at which conditional cooperation becomes the rational strategy for compassionate players. Thus, if we return to our original assumption of a population equally divided between unconditional defectors and conditional cooperators, then the threshold probability of recognition in the Compassion Game above is only 71 percent, less than the 75 percent and 83 percent thresholds of the *Amour de Soi* and *Amour-Propre* games, respectively.[83]

Although these percentages are based on the particular payoffs we have chosen to illustrate the social consequences of different motives, it is nevertheless true, and necessarily so, that the more compassionate individuals are, that is, the more they discount their prospective payoffs when these are won at the expense of others, the weaker is their temptation to defect. Consequently, compassionate players do not need to be as transparent as players moved exclusively by *amour de soi* or *amour-propre* in order to cooperate for mutual advantage.[84] Table 2.4 summarizes the prospects for cooperation under each of Rousseau's paradigmatic motives.

Although compassion is naturally engaged at the sight of a fellow creature in pain, its range can be extended by the power of imagination. In fact, if compassion is to restrain a person "before the fact," then it must be awakened by the *prospect* of another person's suffering. Thus, in

Table 2.4 Cooperation under different motives

Motive	Temptation to Defect [a]	Degree of Transparency Necessary for Cooperation [b]
Amour de soi	Moderate	Moderate
Amour-propre	High	High
Compassion	Low	Low

Notes: [a] The "temptation to defect" is equal to the difference between the subjectively valued payoff to the defector in the (D/C) outcome and the subjectively valued payoff to the same player in the (C/C) outcome.

[b] The "degree of transparency necessary for cooperation" is the probability of accurate recognition necessary for the expected utility of conditional cooperation to exceed the expected utility of unconditional defection.

the Compassion Game, imagination is important because it is only *after* the players have chosen not to lend a helping hand that each may experience the hurt which comes when assistance is denied. While this kind of imaginative identification with another is no doubt less demanding when the person of concern is a friend or neighbor, Rousseau believed that, in the absence of class distinctions, its range could extend much more broadly. Hence, we might suppose, as Tocqueville did, that in egalitarian societies, interpersonal relations are "gentle" because the scope of human sympathy is not circumscribed by the barriers of rank and status that divide aristocratic societies into nobles and commoners.[85]

Hannah Arendt directed a much less flattering light upon Rousseau's tenderhearted sentiment, arguing that by the time of the French Revolution, "compassion" had become synonymous with the "misfortune and unhappiness" of the downtrodden, forming an integral part of the skein of ideas invoked by Robbespierre to justify the violence of the Reign of Terror.[86] I do not wish to challenge the merits of Arendt's interpretation of compassion *as an ideology*. I do, however, want to stress, as a countervailing point, that the *feeling* of compassion, in as much as it tempers human selfishness, performs a useful service, facilitating cooperation that would be less likely to emerge from the interaction of individuals who are indifferent to the interests of those who are harmed by their self-centered choices. Of course, people who keep their commitments, in part, because they care about the welfare of others may not fulfill the heroic requirements of Arendtian citizenship. But there is no reason to think citizens moved by this kind of compassion would find Robbespiere's politics appealing either.

Compassion as we have characterized it, that is, as the discounting of the compassionate player's prospective payoff when she defects and the other player cooperates, does not open the compassionate player to exploitation by players who are unmoved by this sentiment.[87] A compassionate player who has adopted a strategy of conditional cooperation has just as strong a reason to defect if she expects the other player to defect as a conditional cooperator moved only by *amour de soi*. The fact that the compassionate player in our example gets a subjectively valued payoff of 2.5, rather than three, when she defects and the other player cooperates, does not increase the player's vulnerability to exploitation by unconditional defectors, provided the remaining payoffs, the composition of the population, and the probability of accurate recognition remain unchanged. Compassion only invites exploitation if it distorts a player's judgment about the intentions of other players, in particular if compassion leads one to persistently mistake unconditional defectors for

Table 2.5 The Fraternity Game

		Player B	
		Cooperate	Defect
Player A	Cooperate	2.4, 2.4	0.6, 3
	Defect	3, 0.6	1.2, 1.2

conditional cooperators. If, on the other hand, compassion improves a player's ability to judge the character of other players, then the expected benefits of conditional cooperation will rise still further.[88]

In addition to drawing on our natural feeling of compassion, Rousseau hoped to enlist fraternity, "the love of one's countrymen," in sustaining civic cooperation. We can illustrate the effect of fraternity on the prospects for cooperation by assuming that each player derives some benefit, or utility, not only from his own payoff, but also from the other player's payoff. Thus, if we let "i" stand for a player's own payoff, "y" for the other player's payoff, and "w" for the weight a player attaches to the other player's payoff, then the total payoff to each player moved by the sentiment of fraternity will be "i + wy." To illustrate, we can simply take the payoffs from the *Amour de Soi* Game and let "w" equal 0.2 for both players. The resulting payoffs are displayed in the Fraternity Game (see table 2.5).

Given these payoffs, and assuming the community is evenly divided between conditional cooperators and unconditional defectors, the threshold probability of accurate recognition at which conditional cooperation becomes the dominant strategy is only 67 percent, compared with the 75 percent threshold probability of recognition in the *Amour de Soi* Game. More generally, the greater the weight each player assigns to the other player's payoff, the more likely it is the players will cooperate.

We began with Rousseau's belief that equality extends the effective range of compassion and have shown that, all else being the same, compassionate citizens are more likely to cooperate with one another than are citizens moved by *amour de soi*, not to mention those driven by *amour-propre*. I now want to suggest that cooperation, itself, tends to preserve the egalitarian conditions in which compassion achieves its broadest reach. To begin with, we may take note of the fact that, in a prisoner's dilemma game, the payoffs in the cooperate/cooperate outcome are more equal than the payoffs in the defect/cooperate outcome in which one player gains at the expense of the other. To return to an earlier example, we may compare a community of farmers, who all help one another at harvest time, with a group of farmers in which some help others when the harvest comes, but do not receive the same amount of help in return. All else being the same, the "payoffs" enjoyed by the farmers who all cooperate will tend to be more equal than the "payoffs" in the group in which some farmers take advantage of others.

Of course, we cannot proceed directly from the "micro equality" of mutual cooperation in a prisoner's dilemma game to the conclusion that incomes in a community where everyone cooperates will be more equal than incomes in a community where some people successfully exploit others. For example, if those who are favored by nature tend to cooperate more often with each other than with those less favored, then the cumulative outcome of many such interactions could be significant inequalities of wealth and income (a possibility I explore in chapter three). From Rousseau's vantage point, however, social and economic inequality is much more deeply rooted in the knave's exploitation of the naïve (the defect/cooperate scenario) than in cooperative arrangements among the naturally advantaged. Moreover, Rousseau was not inclined to leave the egalitarian foundations of his republic to chance, recommending tax policies and regulations designed to forestall the "great inequality of fortunes" that "inflames vanity and stifles compassion."[89] When we combine these effects together, we get a mutually reinforcing network that can be summarized as follows: (1) reciprocal cooperation produces more equal gains than exploitation; (2) in a community where income is more equally distributed, the range of compassionate identification extends more broadly; and (3) the greater the scope of compassion, the more likely it is that people will cooperate for mutual advantage, which completes what might be called "a virtuous cycle."

Civic Virtue and the Discipline of Mutual Surveillance

One may object that I have portrayed Rousseau's transparent republic as nothing more than a collection of social and psychological mechanisms designed to induce self-interested individuals to cooperate for mutual advantage when, in fact, Rousseau is interested in the formation of citizens who will advance the common good for its own sake. I grant that he *is* mainly concerned with the creation of citizens whose love of virtue and of their countrymen inclines them to willingly meet their public responsibilities. But Rousseau, who vows to "take men as they are," was also alert to the many temptations that distract citizens from performing their duties.[90] Hence, many of his institutional proposals are intended to strengthen the citizen's resolve in resisting the temptations of narrow self-interest. Indeed Rousseau believed that even the most patriotic citizen is sometimes tempted to regard "what he owes to the common cause as a gratuitous contribution," reasoning that the withdrawal of his cooperative effort "will do less harm to others than the payment of it is burdensome to himself." Thus there is a constant danger that citizens will "wish to enjoy the rights of citizenship without being ready to fulfill the duties of a subject."[91]

Those who choose to free ride on the cooperative efforts of their fellow citizens do not announce their intentions, for if they did, they would either be denied the benefits of citizenship or compelled to make a contribution to the common good. Instead, they adopt a strategy of duplicity, pretending to cooperate, which is more difficult to counteract and, hence, more threatening to the republic. "The worst of all abuses," according to Rousseau, "is to pay apparent obedience to the laws, only in order to break them with security."[92] This risk is especially great in large states where citizens can easily conceal their conduct "from the public eye." Because "vice is a friend of the shadows," danger lurks in communities that afford a life of privacy and anonymity.[93] In such places, citizens often adopt a hybrid strategy, choosing to cooperate for mutual advantage in private interactions where betrayal is more easily exposed, while defecting in more impersonal settings where one's conduct is less visible to others.

Individual citizens can reduce the risk of being duped by gathering information about the character of their neighbors. Of course this information is costly to obtain. In addition to the time and effort involved, the citizen may acquire a reputation for being meddlesome. In deciding whether to investigate the character of others, the citizen must weigh the cost of this investment against the likelihood of interacting with untrustworthy individuals and the consequences of being exploited. Given this decision calculus, we can envision an equilibrium that is sustained by two opposing forces. On the one hand, the number of unconditional defectors cannot rise above a certain threshold because conditional cooperators will find it rational to carefully monitor the conduct of their neighbors whenever the probability of interacting with an unconditional defector is relatively high, which will reduce, in turn, the expected payoffs to unconditional defection. On the other hand, the number of unconditional defectors cannot fall below this threshold because conditional cooperators will not incur monitoring costs when the probability of interacting with unconditional defectors is relatively low.[94]

Rousseau's characterization of the special risks inherent in large states, where anonymity veils the contradiction between one's outward demeanor and one's true character, leads naturally to his proposed solution: the citizens of an ideal community remain transparent to one another because so much of their lives is conducted in public view. Before I consider Rousseau's own words, let me be clear about the nature of his remedy. The problem to be solved is that, in a republic where most citizens meet their commitments, no one has an incentive to monitor the performance of others, which creates a niche for those who only pretend to cooperate. Rousseau's solution to this problem is to minimize the cost of surveillance, and to maximize the cost of deception, by arranging the affairs of his republic so that its citizens must often act under the watchful eyes of one another.[95]

"To know men," Rousseau affirms, "one must see them act."[96] In the opaque cities of Europe, it is impossible to know one's fellow citizens in this way "because each, easily hiding his conduct from the public eye, shows himself only by his reputation."[97] Here people feign virtue while pursuing selfish ends. But in small communities, "where individuals, always in the public eye, are born censors of one another and where the police can easily watch everyone, contrary maxims must be followed."[98] This is not just a casual observation, but a description of the conditions necessary for civic cooperation. Thus, in his *Considerations on the Government of Poland*, Rousseau advances the proposition that "almost all small states, republics or monarchies, prosper for the sole reason that they are small, that all their citizens know each other and observe one another."[99] And when he concentrates his mind on "the strongest, most powerful" means of bringing "patriotism to the highest pitch," Rousseau recommends a method "which is infallible in its effects if properly executed; this is to arrange things so that every citizen will feel himself to be constantly under the public eye."[100]

When the public life of the community is so expansive that citizens must perpetually act under one another's penetrating gaze, they will find no advantage in shirking their responsibilities, for under these conditions the probability of accurate recognition must be very high, and the expected benefit of unconditional defection, however much disguised, must be very low. When "neither the secret machinations of vice, nor the modesty of virtue [can] escape the notice and judgment of the public," every citizen's character becomes public knowledge and, their real motives being transparent to one another, citizens will find it prudent to renounce deception, choosing instead to comply with the commitments that advance their common good.[101]

Rousseau proposed to supplement this scheme of mutual surveillance by granting "purely honorific rewards" that would be distributed by a committee assigned the responsibility of drawing up "a roster of those peasants who were distinguished for good conduct."[102] For a Polish noble who aspired to public service, Rousseau urged an even more exacting discipline, viz. "that a faithful account [be kept] of all his good and evil deeds, and that this account influence the whole subsequent course of his life."[103] By making rewards contingent upon good deeds, "patriotism alone" becomes the means to all public offices, and "the whole state is knit together."[104]

Even Rousseau's defense of the right of property, which he characterizes as "the true foundation of civil society, and the true guarantee for the engagement of the citizens," is based, in part, on the fact that it makes the citizen's activities more public, "for if the goods were not responded for [i.e., possessed] by anybody, nothing would be as easy as to elude one's duties and mock the laws."[105] Unlike money, which constantly changes hands, providing all its temporary owners anonymity, property is fixed, its ownership, if not immediately transparent, can be at least ascertained.

In contemplating those aspects of republican life that induce citizens to discharge their public duties, Rousseau seems to have had in mind something in addition to the constraining influence that is exerted by the physical presence of others, or even by their overt expression of approval or disapproval. Rousseau's citizens, whose training is intended to accustom them to "living under the eyes of their fellow-citizens" and "to desiring public approbation," continue to conduct themselves as if they were being watched even when their actions are hidden from view.[106] Thus, while Rousseau is usually explicit in urging the actual presence of others as a force capable of restraining the behavior of citizens, he sometimes suggests that the same results can be achieved if citizens "feel" themselves to be in public view.[107]

From a game-theoretic vantage point, citizens who comply with mutually advantageous commitments because they believe they are being watched are no different than citizens who behave this way because they are actually being observed. Moreover, the inculcation of a belief that one's conduct is being monitored is all the more effective because it follows individuals into those places where their behavior is not visible to others. One way of interpreting this self-monitoring is to imagine that citizens will, to borrow a phrase from psychoanalytic theory, "internalize the viewpoint of the other."[108] According to this understanding, those who experience the psychic pain caused by the disapprobation of other people will, by degrees, incorporate the other's judgmental gaze within their own psyche. To the extent that the citizen's particular will remains untamed, the experience of being observed, even if it is by "the public eye" internalized, will still be one of constraint. Although this feeling is unpleasant, it is a necessary condition of social cooperation among people who are not yet inclined to spontaneously discharge their public responsibilities. If, however, citizens come to identify with their countrymen, then their conduct, whether or not in public view, will be undertaken without the feeling of restraint and inner conflict that plagues those who are still tempted to defect from commitments which advance the common good.

The General Will, Transparency, and the "unhappiness of having equals as masters"

Although I have been considering the practical advantages Rousseau attributes to transparent intentions, I have now reached the point where my inquiry dovetails with Starobinski's classic account of Rousseau's intrinsic interest in human transparency. Individuals who have made the common good their own no longer have any reason to conceal their true aims from one another, and this transparency not only enhances their prospects for cooperation, it also makes possible relations in which " each person sees and loves himself in the others. "[109] Whereas double dealers dread the watchful eyes of their neighbors, true citizens delight in their gaze. Rousseau's cherished communal festivals, with their "rapture of public joy," are, for Starobinski, the psychological expression of the social contract itself. In these public gatherings, "every man is both *actor* and *spectator*," just as he is at once " member of the sovereign and member of the state. "[110] When Rousseau writes, "each person, in giving himself to all the others, gives himself to no one," Starobinski adds, "each person is 'alienated' in the gaze of others, and each is restored to himself by universal 'recognition.' " In the perfect republic of Rousseau's imagination, human beings no longer live in contradiction with themselves. Rather, in Starobinski's words, the self discovers its "pure freedom, pure transparency, through its intimate association with other free and transparent souls."[111] But let us add that until such time as the citizen's heart is pure, Rousseau insists that "all his conduct must be seen and judged by his fellow citizens; he must know that his every step is being watched."[112]

Rousseau lamented the loss of our natural transparence, but found another basis on which citizens could cooperate for mutual advantage.

His conception of the "general will" is one of a limited number of solutions to the problem of collective action: citizens who evaluate alternatives from the vantage point of their common interests and are prepared to act upon this judgment can avoid the unwanted outcomes awaiting rational egoists whose wills are fixed upon a narrower object.[113] From a game-theoretic standpoint, Rousseau has every right to proclaim, "create citizens, and you have everything you need."[114]

The difficulty lies in getting people to abide by mutually advantageous constraints. Rousseau acknowledged, as had Hobbes before him, that every individual will insist, "Either give me guarantees against all unjust undertakings or do not expect me to refrain from them in turn."[115] Such guarantees are hard to come by once the desire for superiority has increased the temptation to defect, and mastery of the art of deception has made the task of uncovering deceit more difficult. The original transparency of human intention having been lost behind the civilized person's carefully contrived public identity, Rousseau hoped to provide mutual assurance—a necessary condition of public virtue—within a civic life designed to open each citizen's character to public view.[116]

There is an extra dimension to the mutual assurance citizens require in order to *confidently* cooperate for mutual advantage: each citizen must know that every other citizen knows that all alike are obeying the laws.[117] In the game-theoretic literature, this is known as "common knowledge," and, according to one contemporary theorist, it is sometimes most effectively established, not sequentially, from person-to-person by word-of-mouth, but through public meetings, rituals, and celebrations where many people are brought together in one place.[118] Although Rousseau would not have put it this way, his cherished community festivals may be construed as a mechanism through which citizens acquire common knowledge about the quality of their citizenship. And if citizens of the republic rejoice in the contemplation of their collective virtue, their jubilation will owe something to the republic's regime of mutual surveillance, which is also most effective when each citizen knows that all alike are being watched.

The social arrangements that make republican citizenship possible will no doubt be repellent to those who believe that every person should enjoy an extended sphere of privacy within which to conduct life without having to constantly look over one's shoulder.[119] It is noteworthy that Michel Foucault, one of the sharpest critics of contemporary "democracy," insists that we live "in the panoptic machine" where, like the inmates in Bentham's Panopticon, we are under constant observation.[120] Although Foucault's choice of the Panopticon as the quintessential model of modern "discipline" is not surprising, his neglect of Rousseau's republican discipline of mutual surveillance does seem curious.[121] For there is a very short distance between what Foucault calls "disciplinary power," which takes the form of "permanent, exhaustive, omnipresent surveillance," and Rousseau's favored means of maintaining the citizen's self-discipline, that is, by arranging the social order "so that every citizen will feel himself to be constantly under the public eye."[122] Although Foucault may exaggerate the scope of "disciplinary power," his characterization of a "discipline" that "homogenizes, excludes . . . *normalizes*" bears a family resemblance to Rousseau's small, unified republic.[123] And when Foucault, like Tocqueville before him, points out that equality brings with it a homogeneity that calls immediate attention to *difference*, we must see in Rousseau's little republic the danger of "a normalizing gaze, a surveillance [that] establishes over individuals a visibility through which one differentiates and judges them."[124]

After Geneva burned his books, Rousseau, himself, worried that "in so small a state where no one can hide in a crowd, who will not live in eternal terror, and not feel at each moment the unhappiness of having his equals for masters."[125] And yet, if Rousseau is right in thinking that the freedom to avoid the notice and judgment of the public poses an insurmountable obstacle to social cooperation, then there is more at stake in choosing between transparent and opaque communities than the values of privacy and autonomy. By arranging our public life so as to conceal the quality of our citizenship from one another, we not only protect nonconformists, but also create niches for free riders.[126] Cooperation depends on our ability to recognize one another's real intentions, and insofar as we reject the social conditions necessary for such transparence, choosing instead to live in opaque communities, we must either leave ourselves vulnerable to exploitation or rely upon the state to enforce many of the commitments we make to one another.

Modes of Association: A Rousseauean Typology

Our consideration of Rousseau's thought has revolved around three paradigmatic modes of social interaction: (1) the peaceful encounters of naïve souls moved by *amour de soi*; (2) the mutually destructive interplay between opaque sophisticates driven by *amour-propre*; and (3) the civic cooperation of compassionate citizens whose character is public knowledge. These forms of association vary in two dimensions: the motives of the interacting parties and the transparence or opacity of their intentions.

Table 2.6 A Rousseauean typology of social interaction

	Amour de soi	Motive *Amour-propre*	*Compassion*
Transparent intentions	1. Interaction among Rousseau's primitives	3. Montesquieu's monarchy with its principle of honor	5. Rousseau's republic
Opaque intentions	2. Some game-theoretic interpretations of Hobbes's state of nature	4. Rousseau's depiction of civilized society	6. Liberal democracy?

Although I have focused upon the three types of interaction just mentioned, Rousseau's trilogy of motives, when combined with the transparent/opaque dichotomy, yield six permutations. These combinations are displayed in table 2.6 along with illustrative examples.

We have examined in some detail Rousseau's romantic depiction of primitive social interaction, his disparaging account of social relations in polite society, and his portrait of a communitarian life among virtuous citizens in a transparent republic, types one, four, and five, respectively. We have also briefly considered the interaction of opaque egoists, which forms the basis of several contemporary game-theoretic interpretations of Hobbes's state of nature.[127] Montesquieu's conception of despotism also fits within this category insofar as the dissociation produced by fear is, roughly speaking, the social condition that may be expected to prevail among self-centered individuals whose character is opaque. It is worth reiterating that the difference between the unappealing outcomes of this second type of interaction and the mutually advantageous outcomes of the first type is due entirely to the greater transparency of the agents in the first type. Among straightforward egoists, clear intentions produce mutual restraint, whereas opaque intentions produce, in the limiting case, "the war of all against all," an outcome which, in Hobbes's chain of reasoning, can only be avoided by the creation of a sovereign authority.

I also mentioned, though just briefly, Montesquieu's monarchical regime, which is included in the table as an example of type three, interaction among transparent agents moved by honor. This is a bit of a Procrustean fit because what Montesquieu means by "honor" is somewhat different than what Rousseau means by "*amour-propre*." We might contrast the two by saying that while Rousseau insists that men moved by *amour-propre* cannot be trusted, Montesquieu contemplates the possibility of forthright (ultra-transparent) men of honor who act with mutual restraint. Without taking sides, let me simply reiterate my point that men and women who judge the outcome of their interaction in terms of relative payoffs must be more transparent than self-regarding individuals if they are going to reap the benefits of cooperation.

I have characterized Rousseau's republican citizens as transparent and compassionate, exemplars of type five in the table. With respect to cooperation, these citizens are doubly blessed, for both transparency and compassion improve the prospects for successful collaboration. Of course it should not be forgotten that republican transparency is the hard-earned achievement of diligent surveillance, which is not without its cost.

What about type six, which envisions people who are compassionate but opaque, people who care about the welfare of others, but whose character is hard to read? To begin with, let us recall that while Rousseau seems to rule out the possibility of men and women who are both deeply compassionate and deceitful, there are other causes of opacity besides deception, and these impediments to transparency, such as anonymity, are not necessarily incompatible with sympathy.[128] Many barriers to transparent interaction emerge when small, undifferentiated communities give way to larger, more heterogeneous societies that sustain disparate "life worlds."[129] Because communication across this diversity of experience can be difficult, the inhabitants of modern societies are, for this reason alone, sometimes opaque to one another.

It is reasonable to suppose that "modernization" and, more specifically, "social differentiation," limit the scope of compassion, if only because human beings identify more easily with people like themselves than with those different from themselves. For Rousseau, of course, the greatest *difference* in civilized society is the gulf separating rich and poor. The poor resent the wealthy, and the wealthy regard the poor as another species; hence, there is no community of feeling between them. But compassion *can* flow between citizens when inequalities are small enough that the more advantaged can imagine the loss of their advantages and the less advantaged believe they are equal, or superior to the advantaged, in character or contentment if not in possessions or influence.[130] Reasoning along these Rousseauean lines, Tocqueville argued that "when ranks are almost equal among a people . . . each instantaneously can judge the feelings of all the others . . . so there is no misery that he cannot readily understand."[131] And, we may add, the modern idea of *mankind*, which Rousseau himself helped to create, provides the conceptual channel through which compassion can flow without running into barriers of class or status.

A great deal more would have to be said in order to sketch in the details of a compassionate, but opaque, mode of association. The foregoing remarks are only intended to suggest that modern democratic states, which are too large to sustain the immediate transparency that is possible in small, close-knit communities, but which are not permanently divided into classes, may afford a site for such interaction. If so, we could, for the reasons noted earlier, expect social interaction within these polities to be more cooperative than social relations in Hobbes's state of nature or in the polite society depicted by Rousseau, but not as harmonious as life in Rousseau's republic.

I have presented this Rousseauean typology as a two-by-three matrix composed of the transparent/opaque dichotomy and the three paradigmatic motives of *amour de soi*, *amour-propre*, and compassion. Yet the transparent/opaque dichotomy may also be regarded as a continuum in the probability of recognition, that is, in the likelihood that two players in a prisoner's dilemma game will recognize one another's intention or disposition. And Rousseau's trilogy of passions can also be expressed as a continuum, in this case in the temptation to defect, which is weakest in the case of compassionate players, stronger for players moved by *amour de soi*, and strongest for players driven by *amour-propre*.[132] Using these two variables, we can represent the prospects for cooperation in a single diagram.

In figure 2.2, the probability of accurate recognition decreases as we move upward along the vertical axis, and the temptation to defect increases as we move rightward along the horizontal axis. The prospects for cooperation are, therefore, greatest close to the origin and diminish with increasing distance from the origin. In this presentation, the likelihood of cooperation depends, not on a particular motive, nor on the absolute transparency or opacity of the players, but rather on the combination of the two factors together. For purposes of illustration, I have indicated where each of the six types might be located within this scheme.

By way of illustrative explanation, I have located Rousseau's primitive societies and his ideal republic, types one and five, respectively, an equal distance up the vertical axis, which assumes that the probability of accurate recognition is the same in the two cases. The prospects of cooperation are somewhat greater in Rousseau's republic because I have assumed that compassion is more fully developed among Rousseau's ideal citizens than among his isolated savages, hence type five is closer to the origin than type one. I have located Montesquieu's monarchy (type three) and liberal democracy (type six) about the same distance from the origin, assuming that while Montesquieu's candid aristocrats are more transparent to one another than are the citizens of large, socially differentiated, liberal states, the latter, at least in Tocqueville's view, are

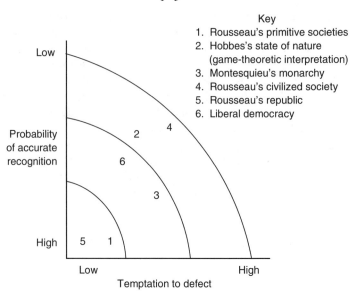

Figure 2.2   Modes of association and the probability of cooperation.

more compassionate, and, therefore, are less tempted to defect. I have placed the game-theoretic interpretation of Hobbes's state of nature (type two), whose inhabitants are straightforward egoists rather than vainglorious aristocrats, closer to the origin than Rousseau's civilized society (type four) because while both are opaque, Rousseau's sophisticates, moved by *amour-propre*, are more tempted to defect in prisoner's dilemma-type interactions.

One advantage of this way of presenting the interrelation between motives and transparency, that is, between differences in the temptation to defect and in the probability of accurate recognition, is that it highlights their combined effect on the prospects for cooperation. Thus, cooperation may occur even if people's dispositions are only partially transparent, provided their sense of compassion is sufficiently well-developed. This may be optimistically construed as a promising possibility for the liberal who wishes to encourage civic cooperation, but rejects the intrusive surveillance that sustains transparency and virtue in Rousseau's republic.

CHAPTER THREE

Association and Civil Society in Transparent and Opaque Communities

Civil society has enjoyed a remarkable resurgence in recent years. I am referring not only to the revival of associational life within the countries of the former communist bloc, but also to the renewed appreciation of civil society by political thinkers of varied persuasion.[1] Intermediate associations are now commonly praised as a counterbalance to the power of the state, as schools of citizenship and social responsibility, and as the natural expression of pluralism in a free society. One contemporary civil society theorist speculates that "if the twentieth century was about the steady erosion of civil society through neglect or conscious abandonment, the twenty-first century may represent the era of its restoration."[2]

There is, however, a different and less favorable view of associations that also belongs to the political culture of the West. This alternative understanding finds expression in criticisms of *special* interests, which divide the community and distort the democratic process through which the *public* interest is articulated. According to this understanding, a republic must be on guard against groups of ambitious citizens seeking to advance their own interests at the expense of the common good, a line of reasoning most forcefully argued by Rousseau, who regarded such associations as "partial societies" that threaten the unity of the people and imperil the general will.[3]

In this chapter I examine the logic of association among citizens whose "cooperative quality," and other assets and attributes, are either transparent, on the one hand, or opaque, on the other. To give some idea of where we are headed, let me summarize some of my conclusions without argument or qualification:

1. The condition Rousseau finds necessary to civic virtue—transparency of character—is also favorable to the formation of "partial societies," which divide the citizen's loyalties between the association that advances his or her particular interests and the republic that serves the common good;
2. Given Rousseau's premises, he can have *either* equality within associations *or* equality among associations, but he cannot have both;
3. The free association of transparent citizens reinforces social inequality insofar as the well-endowed find it more advantageous to interact with one another than with the less well-endowed *and* can differentiate between the two;
4. In transparent communities, the most self-disciplined and productive members of associations will find the duties of citizenship more onerous than the less disciplined and least productive association members;
5. Uncertainty about the character of one's fellow citizens reduces the prevalence and power of "partial societies," but can engender the kind of atomistic individualism Tocqueville found latent in America's emerging democracy;
6. In opaque societies, large associations tend to reflect the composition of the wider population and are therefore less threatening to the general will than the more homogenous associations that form within transparent communities; and
7. Association members in transparent communities are likely to find "exit" a more attractive response to dissatisfaction than "voice," whereas opacity tends to reverse this order.

In developing these themes, I begin by outlining Rousseau's misgivings about "partial societies" and the conditions that must be satisfied if the general will is to prevail in its contest with particular wills. In the next section, I undertake a thought experiment in which citizens form associations with full knowledge of the skills and resources of their fellows, and examine both the character of these associations and their ramifications for Rousseau's republic. Part three develops a second thought experiment in which each citizen's cooperative disposition and other attributes are opaque to others. I analyze the nature of the associations that form within this milieu and consider their somewhat surprising import for a republican state. Part four explains how associations can unravel in opaque societies, as individuals "withdraw into a small circle of family and friends," to invoke Tocqueville's characterization of "individualism."[4] In section five, I explore the implications of Albert O. Hirschman's suggestive trilogy of "exit, voice, and loyalty" for our scheme of transparent and opaque relations.[5] In section six, I summarize the results of these investigations and draw some general conclusions about transparency, opacity, and their consequences for the associational life of democratic societies. And in the final section, I bring some of my Rousseauean arguments to bear upon the contemporary debate about the character of civil society and its uneasy coexistence with republican democracy.

"Partial Societies" and the Republican State

Rousseau thought he discovered a necessary connection between the transparency of individual character and the prospects for republican liberty. If, for the sake of this liberty, each citizen is required to forego the pursuit of private advantage in favor of the common good, then each citizen must be assured that other citizens are making the same sacrifice. "The worst of all abuses," according to Rousseau, "is to pay apparent obedience to the laws only to break them with security."[6] Ideally, citizens will come to regard the community as an extension of themselves and willingly discharge their duties in the spirit of patriotism. But Rousseau, who vows to take men "as they are and laws as they might be," is not content to assume such devotion.[7] Rather, he insists that free people must live in small communities where citizens "know each other and observe one another," where "neither the secret machinations of vice, nor the modesty of virtue [can] escape the notice and judgment of the public," and where, once accustomed to acting under the eyes of others, each person's demeanor will "proclaim at first glance his true disposition."[8] (This kind of mutual surveillance can, of course, be oppressive, but that is not my concern in this chapter.)

Although transparency prevents citizens from free riding on the cooperative efforts of their fellows, it also poses a threat to the unity of republican communities because clear intentions are favorable to social cooperation among individuals who comprise only a part of the republic, that is, to the formation of "partial societies." If the quality of each person's character is public knowledge, and if there are benefits to be gained by cooperating with others, then trustworthy individuals moved only by their private interests—by *amour de soi* in Rousseau's words—will seek out other reliable individuals in order to collaborate for mutual advantage. Such combinations do not depend in any way upon a desire for preeminence—upon *amour-propre*—nor do they even require a taste for luxury.[9] What could be more practical than an association of farmers who have agreed to share their tools and to help one another at harvest time?

Herein lies an ironic, but formidable obstacle to the success of the republican state. On the one hand, the civic virtue that sustains the republic is only possible if citizens are able to resist the temptation to free ride on the cooperative efforts of their fellows. On the other hand, citizens capable of such self-discipline will, quite naturally, form smaller associations within the republic in order to further their common interests. Rousseau does not criticize the ends of these "partial societies," which, he acknowledges, are "general" in relation to their members. Rather, the threat to a republican state arises from the fact that while "the will of these particular societies" is a general will "for the members of the association," it is a particular will "for the great society; and it is often right with regard to the first object, and wrong as to the second."[10] The reason for this incongruity is straightforward; the common interests of a particular association will not, except by accident, be coextensive with the common interests of the community as a whole. For example, a policy that is most advantageous for one region of a country will not necessarily be most advantageous for the country as a whole. Thus, if the members of an association devoted to advancing a particular region's common interests vote with this objective in mind, their votes will not, except in rare cases, be "right" with regard to the republic's common good.

The foregoing argument is largely a matter of definition: the general will is directed toward the good of the republic as a whole, and any will that is directed toward the good of a less inclusive body is necessarily a "particular will" in relation to the larger body. But there is also a psychological dimension to the problem. For, while "particular societies" are "subordinate to the general society," and while "the duty of a citizen always takes precedence to that of a senator," Rousseau argues that "personal interest is always found in inverse ratio to duty, and increases as the association grows narrower and the engagement less sacred."[11] In simple terms, an individual has a greater "personal interest" as a member of a small association than as a member of a larger body because one's share of the association's costs and benefits will be greater in a small association than in a large one.[12] "Partial societies" pose a problem, therefore, because the common interests of the republic and the corresponding duties of a citizen often conflict with the personal stake individuals have in the secondary associations that serve their more parochial interests.

These complications are exacerbated when "partial societies" become participants in the legislative process. "Carefully determine what happens in every public deliberation," Rousseau advises, "and it will be seen that the general will is always for the common good, but very often there is a secret division, a tacit confederacy, which, for particular ends, causes the natural disposition of the assembly to be set at naught."[13] Rousseau is here registering two familiar complaints. First, he draws attention to the role of special interests that seek advantages for themselves at the expense of the common good. And second, he complains that such "factions" do not pursue their objectives in the open, but rather "pay some sort of homage to the public faith" so as to conceal their real ambitions and thereby increase their chances of molding the public will in their favor. When "the people is [thus] seduced by private interests," Rousseau concludes, "the general will will be one thing, and the result of the public deliberation another."[14]

"If the general will is to express itself," then, Rousseau insists, "there should be no partial society within the State." Besides being parochial and sometimes duplicitous, "partial societies" impede one of the mechanisms through which the general will is disclosed. Rousseau gives a brief description of this mechanism in his somewhat obscure suggestion that if one takes away from all the divergent particular wills "the pluses and minuses that cancel one another," then "the general will remains as the sum of the differences."[15] One provocative explication of this notion draws upon Condorcet's voting theorem, which, roughly speaking, holds that if each voter has a better than even chance of arriving at the correct decision in a particular case, then the probability of a majority vote being correct rises as the number of voters increases.[16] It is important to add that this proposition only holds true if each voter makes an *independent* decision, which, it may be noted, squares with Rousseau's insistence that, when voting, citizens must have "no communication one with another."[17] The trouble with "partial societies," in this regard, is that instead of there being "as many votes as there are men," there are "only as many as there are associations," so that "the differences become less numerous and give a less general result."[18] In other words, the presence of "partial societies" reduces the probability that a majority vote will give the correct result, that is, will be in agreement with the general will, because when association members vote as a herd, the number of *independent* votes is sharply diminished, and the likelihood of a majority vote being correct is correspondingly reduced.[19]

Having made his case against the presence of "partial societies" within the state, Rousseau then considers the second-best solution to the problem posed by secondary associations. "If there are partial societies," then Rousseau recommends that "it is best to have as many as possible and to prevent them from being unequal."[20] In part, this advice flows from the previous argument about the necessity of having many independent votes so that particular interests will "cancel out." But, in addition, Rousseau is concerned about the possibility that a large and powerful association may eventually overcome its rivals or combine with some of them to defeat the remainder, in which case "there is no longer a general will, and the opinion which prevails is purely particular."[21] If, by contrast, there are many "partial societies," which are roughly equal in power, then they will tend to counterbalance one another, thereby preventing any one association, or coalition of associations, from gaining ascendancy over the rest. Although civic virtue is the ideal foundation for the republic, the imperatives of human partiality may require not only mutual surveillance in small communities, but also recourse to the logic of countervailing power in order to secure the republic against "factions" that would otherwise divide the people.[22]

With these concerns in mind, let us now consider the kinds of associations, or "partial societies," that would be formed by individuals whose cooperative disposition and other attributes are transparent, and then examine the nature of the "partial societies" that would be formed by individuals whose disposition and other endowments are opaque, in each case paying close attention to the implications these different kinds of association hold for Rousseau's model republic.

Transparency and Association: A Thought Experiment

To begin, suppose that citizens can be divided into two categories, C_1 citizens, who make large contributions to the associations they join, and C_2 citizens, who make small contributions to the associations they join. Let us also stipulate, at least initially, that this difference is entirely due to the fact that C_1 citizens never free ride on the cooperative efforts of their fellows whereas C_2 citizens do occasionally free ride. In making this assumption, I depart (for present purposes) from the usual approach to collective action where the choice facing the rational agent is whether to defect to one's individually best strategy, that is, to free ride in this case, or to cooperate for mutual advantage. In this chapter, I wish to conceive of each citizen as having acquired a disposition through education and experience that fixes the level of effort the citizen devotes to whatever association he or she joins. Specifically, I wish to characterize C_1 citizens as having acquired a disposition to always "do their part" in the collective undertakings of the associations they join, and C_2 citizens as having acquired a disposition to let others "do the heavy lifting." The choice facing these citizens is not, then, whether to cooperate or free ride, but *with whom* to join in association.

The distinction between citizens who never free ride on the cooperative efforts of their fellow association members and citizens who do occasionally free ride becomes important when a member's share of association benefits is independent of his or her particular contribution to the group. This will of course be the case for any collective goods provided by an association because such goods, by definition, cannot be divided up and allocated to individual association members on the basis of contribution (or any other principle of distribution).[23] But even where the goods generated by an association *can* be divided among the members according to contribution, an association may forego this option because extensive monitoring would be required in order to measure each person's contribution. Let us provisionally assume, then, that the benefits generated by associations are distributed equally among their membership regardless of contribution. Each member receives an equal share of any non-collective goods provided by the association, has equal access to the association's common resources, is entitled to assistance from the group with the same frequency, benefits in roughly the same degree from the association's influence with public officials, and so forth.

To give a concrete form to Rousseau's ideal of transparency, we assume that citizens can readily discern the cooperative quality of the individuals with whom they might associate. In other words, they can easily differentiate between C_1 and C_2 citizens. There are several ways in which citizens might acquire this information. In rustic communities, where people have not yet learned the art of politesse, Rousseau believed a person's demeanor still reflected his true character. A willingness to look others in the eye, a firm handshake, unpretentious speech and clothing are, even in contemporary societies, sometimes taken as signs of a trustworthy neighbor. Where a person's countenance is not immediately revealing, her reputation may convey the required information, particularly in small communities where "word gets around."[24] In any case, I shall initially suppose that, on the basis of a person's bearing or reputation, citizens are able to form reliable judgments about the cooperative quality of those with whom they might join in association.

These assumptions can be summarized in the following three points: (1) there are citizens who make relatively large or relatively small contributions to the associations they join, that is, C_1 and C_2 citizens respectively; (2) association benefits are distributed equally among the membership; and (3) the cooperative quality of each citizen is transparent to others. Later I shall explore the consequences of modifying each of these conditions, but let us now develop the results of our first thought experiment.

If people are interested in getting the most out of the associations they join (which is a plausible reading of Rousseau's commitment to "take men as they are"), then they will seek membership in associations with a high proportion of C_1 citizens because the benefits enjoyed by the members of these associations will be greater than the benefits enjoyed by members of associations in which, all else being the same, the ratio of C_1 to C_2 citizens is smaller.[25] However, since the cooperative quality of each citizen is known or easily discerned, individual C_1 citizens will maximize their benefits by associating exclusively with other C_1 citizens, leaving C_2 citizens to associate among themselves.[26] *When benefits are equally distributed within associations and the cooperative quality of individual citizens is fully transparent, associations will be homogenous; they will either be composed entirely of highly disciplined C_1 citizens or entirely of less disciplined C_2 citizens.*

Before we consider the ramifications of this result, it is worth briefly mentioning a recent experimental study that investigated the composition of associations formed to provide public goods.[27] In this experiment, the subjects combined into four-person teams that played a finite sequence of prisoner's dilemma games in which each player could either make a contribution to the group, that is, contribute to the provision of a public good, or free ride on the contributions of the other team members. The experiment was unique in that the players were afforded a periodic opportunity to choose new associates and regroup. Moreover, they could form new associations with complete information about each of the other subject's past contributions. Under these transparent conditions, the subjects sorted themselves with fine precision into homogenous teams of "higher and lower contributors," just as the C_1 and C_2 citizens in our thought experiment did.

A society divided into homogenous associations of C_1 and C_2 citizens will not satisfy Rousseau's requirement that, if there are "partial societies" within the republic, they should be equal in power. Other things being the same, groups of self-disciplined C_1 citizens, who resist the temptation to free ride on one another's efforts, will be more effective in achieving their objectives than will groups of less disciplined C_2 citizens. To illustrate, consider two associations whose members are equal with respect to their talents, resources, and the like. Next, suppose that the members of the first association honor mutually advantageous commitments, while the members of the second association often fail to honor such commitments. Thus, in one association, farmers help each other at harvest time, while in the other some do not. In one credit union, the members promptly repay their debts, while in the other they are less reliable. In one association, everyone attends a meeting with elected officials, while in the other many do not. As these examples and the words, "*mutually advantageous* commitments," suggest, an association of trustworthy individuals will secure greater benefits for its members than an association of unreliable individuals will achieve for its members.

At first thought, one naturally takes pleasure in this outcome: it is good that combinations of the most reliable citizens are more effective, more powerful, than combinations of the less reliable. Yet the triumph of self-discipline over selfish impulse creates, or at least exacerbates, a serious problem for the republican polity—the conflict between the general interest of the community as a whole and the particular interests of the "partial societies" within it. For the more steadfast the members of these secondary associations are in pursuit of their mutual, but *special*, interests, the more intense will be the conflict between the particular will and the general will.

The opposition between the interests of "partial societies," on the one hand, and the public good, on the other, cannot be finessed away by redefining the common good as the totality of group interests, at least not within the terms of Rousseau's political theory. The general interest only comes into view, in Rousseau's account, when citizens ask themselves what serves the common good; it cannot be discerned from the collage of answers given by association members to the question—what serves the association's interest?—even if the association is composed exclusively of C_1 citizens who never free ride on the efforts of their fellow members.[28]

I have been implicitly assuming that C_1 citizens always meet their responsibilities as members of *local* associations. Of course we could redefine C_1 citizens as those who always set aside narrower interests in favor of broader ones—individual interests in favor of association interests, and association interests in favor of the public or national interest. But such a "resolution" of the conflict between the particular will and the general will would not be faithful to Rousseau's moral psychology, which holds that the strength of personal interest "increases in proportion as the association grows narrower, and the engagement less sacred" (quoted earlier).[29] Had Rousseau believed that citizens could be moved to act according to the precept that less inclusive interests should always be set aside in favor of more inclusive interests, he would not have inveighed so forcefully against the formation of secondary associations, nor would he have had any reason to prefer many equal associations to a few unequal ones.[30]

There is another troublesome aspect to the superior organizational power of exclusive associations formed by C_1 citizens. Since the members of these associations enjoy greater benefits than the members of associations composed entirely of C_2 citizens, C_1 citizens will face greater costs than C_2 citizens when pressed to set aside the particular interests of their respective "partial societies" in favor of the general interest. There are at least two considerations supporting this conclusion. First, since C_1 citizens enjoy greater gains from their homogenous associations than C_2 citizens enjoy from theirs, C_1 citizens will have more to lose if the state enacts laws weakening or constraining associations in general, for example, laws limiting the political activities of "interest groups." And second, since republican life is founded on the principle of equality, the members of homogenous associations of C_1 citizens, who, others things being same, possess greater resources as a result of their organizational superiority, will also face greater potential losses than C_2 citizens whenever the state aims to bring about a more equal distribution of resources.[31]

It would be a mistake to dismiss this problem by assuming that every reliable member of a secondary association must also be a good citizen. There are many forms of praiseworthy conduct, and while some of them are loosely connected, the possession of a single virtue does not guarantee possession of all the rest.[32] In Rousseau's own words, "an individual may be a devout priest, a brave soldier, or a zealous senator, and yet a bad citizen."[33] Nancy Rosenblum, a contemporary student of "membership and morals," reaches a similar conclusion, pointing out that "cooperation enables the worst as well as the best social actions—'force and fraud are most effectively pursued by teams.' "[34] I am not insisting that those who never free ride on the cooperative efforts of their fellow association members, C_1 citizens in our lexicon, are less virtuous than association members who do occasionally free ride. Rather, my point is that the civic virtue of the C_1 citizen must be greater than that of the C_2 citizen because the C_1 citizen must make a greater sacrifice in renouncing the particular interest of her association than the sacrifice required of the C_2 citizen in renouncing his.

The formation of associations whose memberships differ in cooperative quality becomes much more threatening to Rousseau's republican objectives if this division reinforces other inequalities. For example, if the self-discipline characteristic of C_1 citizens is correlated with such virtues and talents as good judgment and superior planning skills, then the greater power exercised by groups of self-disciplined C_1 citizens will be magnified by their disproportionate share of other valuable resources. Should the trustworthy and the talented turn out to be the same people, in other words, their combination in exclusive associations will further corrode the egalitarian foundations of the republic.[35]

For example, consider the case of elite universities, which are among the most prominent members of civil society. These universities, like other colleges, screen applicants for academic performance, paying close attention to a student's grades and test scores. Before the introduction of means-tested scholarships and affirmative action programs, the applicants who gained admission to elite universities tended to be rich and well-connected. Although "cooperative quality" per se has never been a criterion for admission to an elite university, the self-discipline that is required for high academic performance is not unlike the self-discipline that is necessary if one is to be a good cooperation partner. In both cases, short-term benefits must be foregone in order to enjoy long-term advantages.[36] Those who graduate from elite universities will typically have a combination of highly valued assets: intelligence, a capacity for sustained effort, a first-rate education, helpful social connections, and a diploma that signals the likely possession of many other sought-after qualities as well. The expansion of opportunities for admission to elite universities through scholarships, subsidized loans, and affirmative action programs has increased the diversity of these universities in important respects, but the use of merit-based admission and graduation criteria, which is a necessary condition for the existence of elite universities, assures that their graduates will remain alike, though not, of course, perfectly homogenous, in their possession of skills and assets that are highly valued in contemporary societies.

Citizens with such valuable abilities and endowments are more likely to associate with one another than with less fortunate citizens. The favored and not-so-favored live in different neighborhoods, send their children to different schools, run in different social circles, and separate themselves in a dozen other ways. Such sorting need not arise from *amour-propre* or other malevolent motives. Affluent families may prefer to live in affluent neighborhoods for purely self-regarding reasons, such as quality schools, low crime rates, well-kept yards, and the like.

Nevertheless, this kind of sorting can have unwanted consequences. For example, when middle- and upper-income city residents leave the city, either literally by moving to the suburbs, or functionally by moving to a fortified condominium in a gentrified downtown neighborhood, their secession reduces the city's resources, while exacerbating its social problems. In the United States, this exodus of relatively well-off citizens has been facilitated by the formation of more than 150,000 condominium and single-family detached homeowner associations, which encompass more than 32 million Americans, who, having withdrawn to private enclaves, are likely to have "a decreasing sense of loyalty and commitment to the national community and the local communities in which their RCAs [Residential Community Associations] are located."[37]

In addition to diminishing the scope of common concerns and attachments, sorting reinforces social stratification because "associational spillovers" in affluent neighborhoods are more favorable than "spillovers" in poor neighborhoods.[38] For example, studies have found that high school dropout rates and teenage pregnancy rates are negatively correlated with the percentage of professional and managerial workers among adults in a community; and that a high percentage of families receiving public assistance in a neighborhood reduces the expected adult wage of children in the neighborhood.[39] As one contemporary student of "social dynamics" concludes, stratification emerges "in contexts ranging from neighborhoods to firms, despite adverse [social consequences], because individual agents seek associational configurations that maximize their own payoffs."[40] *Inequality may originate in* amour-propre, *the division of labor, and the institution of private property, but it will be amplified by free association as long as the well-endowed find it more advantageous to interact with one another than with those less well-endowed and can differentiate between the two.*

The citizen who lacks the credentials necessary to gain admission to a high-quality association is not only deprived of the important benefits these associations provide to their members. There is a further loss. Since association members often develop strong attachments to one another and, as a consequence, make more pressing claims on one another's time and energy, they will have less time and energy to devote to the interests of those citizens who do not belong to their association. In a community that values friendship, the close personal ties that develop within an association furnish its members with what Samuel Scheffler characterizes as "the moral equivalent of a tax shelter," that is, "a moral justification for channeling their time, energy, and other resources into rewarding relations and associations and away from people who are needier."[41]

Although it may seem that these "agent-relative" rights and responsibilities simply provide a rationalization for being self-centered, it is important to remember that "agent-relative" claims are rooted in the close interpersonal relationships that comprise the fabric of much of our lives, relationships which Rousseau, himself, valued deeply (though they often remained beyond his grasp). The conflict between the claims of citizenship and those prerogatives that emanate from our own personal standpoint is nicely summed up in the title of Thomas Nagel's book, *Equality and Partiality*.[42] The notion that we are sometimes torn between our duties to the community and the moral claims originating in our personal relationships captures something that is missing from Rousseau's more starkly drawn opposition between narrow self-interest—our particular will—and equality—the essence of the general will. Although we may be able to focus all of our attention upon the common good in the voting booth and in a limited range of other communal activities, we cannot, as Nagel writes, "sustain an impersonal indifference to the things in [our] life which matter to [us] personally."[43] When Rousseau celebrates the triumph of virtue over personal ties by recounting the story of a mother who was more interested in the outcome of a battle than in the fate of her sons who fought in it, we are given a vivid impression of what Rousseau's republic demands of us, not just as self-regarding individuals, but as parents, neighbors, and friends.[44]

Let us summarize our results to this point. If the cooperative quality of citizens is transparent and association benefits are equally distributed, then the most self-disciplined citizens will form exclusive associations among themselves, leaving less disciplined citizens to form their own associations. Other things being the same, associations of C_1 citizens will be more powerful than associations of C_2 citizens, while, at the same time, the C_1 citizens who belong to the most powerful associations will face greater costs than the C_2 citizens who belong to the least powerful associations when asked to set aside the interests of their respective "partial societies" for the sake of the common good. In addition to forming exclusive organizations, citizens with valuable assets tend to associate with one another in less formal networks, which enhances their advantages over time, widening the gap between the more and less advantaged. When everyone's cooperative quality is public knowledge, the social unity essential to the republican way of life will be threatened both by the formation of exclusive associations of unequal power, and by the social stratification that results from the free association of individuals who, largely in pursuit of private ends, sort themselves into social classes.

I began by differentiating between citizens who readily meet their obligations as association members, on the one hand, and citizens who are less reliable, on the other, in order to show that the cooperative virtues, which Rousseau believed were essential to a republic, become problematic when they are unequally distributed among its citizens, transparent for all to see, and put to work in pursuit of less encompassing objectives. However, even if we ignore the distinction between more and less reliable cooperation partners and assume, instead, that other valued qualities are unequally distributed across the citizenry, *and that these qualities are transparent to others*, then the general results we derived initially will still hold, results which, it may be added, are consistent with those derived from more rigorous models, as well as with the findings of several experimental and empirical studies.[45] As long as citizens who possess valuable qualities find it advantageous to form exclusive associations among themselves and are able to identify one another, the community will remain divided into associations of unequal power.

Needless to say, this conclusion will be jarring if you are thinking of a book club or the church around the corner. There are, of course, many associations that do not screen membership applicants for "cooperative quality" or other attributes that might be converted into social or political advantage. Nevertheless, one would be hard-pressed to argue that the many groups which populate contemporary pluralist democracies are symmetrically organized so as to produce a more or less equal distribution of power and influence in civil society. On the contrary, it is the *unequal* opportunities afforded by associations that *do* screen membership applicants, formally or informally, on the basis of race, gender, class, and so on, which have prompted some governments to limit freedom of association, in particular an association's right to admit or reject membership applicants on whatever grounds it pleases.[46] The problem is exacerbated by the fact that the more powerful an association becomes, the more attractive it is to citizens with valuable resources, which increases the association's power still further. As Michael Walzer, a prominent defender of both pluralism and equality, observes, "it is a general rule of civil society that its strongest members get stronger," a propensity which, Walzer goes on to say, has "found little recognition" in "the recent literature on civil society."[47]

It may be fruitful to introduce a concrete illustration of how divergent cooperative dispositions have shaped the social and political life of a contemporary democratic state. In *Making Democracy Work: Civic Traditions in Modern Italy*, Robert Putnam describes the political practices, governmental performance, and pace of economic development in various regions of southern and northern Italy.[48] The culture of the southern regions has been characterized as one of "amoral familism," an ethos that is captured in the following rule: "maximize the material, short-run advantage of the nuclear family; assume that all others will do likewise."[49] People who act in this fashion resemble our C_2 citizens insofar as their orientation prevents them from effectively cooperating for mutual advantage. Putnam argues that because of this ethos, southern Italy remains backward both politically and economically, a relatively poor region where citizens, like the rational egoists depicted in Hobbes's *Leviathan*, "are forced to rely on what Italians call 'the forces of order,' that is, the police."[50] In the north, by contrast, citizens conform to "norms of reciprocity" and, like our C_1 citizens, have formed a multitude of secondary associations, including "guilds, mutual aid societies, cooperatives, unions, and even soccer clubs and literary societies."[51] In this region, Putnam argues, government is effective and the people have prospered, so much so that it is as if Italy comprised two countries instead of one.

Putnam draws several lessons from the disparate circumstances of Italy's two political cultures, one of which is that strong intermediate associations, effective government, and economic prosperity are mutually reinforcing. I consider this claim in more detail later on, but for now I simply wish to point out that Putnam's description of Italy's contrasting civic traditions provides an instructive illustration of how different cooperative dispositions can give rise to self-reinforcing inequalities and a sharp divergence of social, political, and economic conditions within the same nation-state. Of course it is tempting to embrace Putnam's implicit judgment that the impoverished citizens of southern Italy, with their "amoral familism," have the authoritarian politics and stagnant economy they deserve. But according to Edward Banfield's original study of this region, the ethos of "amoral familism" was, itself, a rational response to the difficult circumstances prevailing in southern Italy, where life expectancy was much shorter than in the north, and where there was a high probability that one's children would become orphans.[52] Whether the C_1 citizens of northern Italy and the C_2 citizens of southern Italy deserve their disparate life prospects is not my principal concern. The essential point is that, whether it is just or not, citizens who are capable of forming effective associations will enjoy greater prosperity and have more influence in law-making than their less disciplined neighbors, advantages which are incompatible with the egalitarian and communal requirements of the republican state.

Unequal Association Benefits

The rise of homogenous and unequal associations within our model flows, ironically, from the premise that association benefits are equally distributed. If, instead, associations offered benefits proportionate to each member's contribution to the group, which requires that associations generate some non-collective goods (leadership positions would qualify), C_1 citizens would no longer find it advantageous to form exclusive associations among themselves. On the contrary, C_1 citizens could enjoy greater benefits by offering C_2 citizens membership in otherwise homogenous associations of C_1 citizens, provided that the marginal contributions of C_2 citizens to the association's total benefits exceeded the rewards offered to them in return.[53] C_2 citizens would find it advantageous to join these heterogeneous associations provided that they received greater benefits than the benefits offered by homogenous associations of C_2 citizens.[54] Although the division of benefits *within* these heterogeneous associations will be unequal (C_1 citizens will still enjoy greater membership benefits than C_2 citizens), there will be less inequality *across* these associations than across the homogenous associations of C_1 and C_2 citizens that form when association benefits are equally divided.

Since we have been assuming that every citizen's cooperative disposition, or level of effort, is fixed, the introduction of unequal rewards will not increase the total benefits supplied by associations in the aggregate, at least not as a result of incentive effects. If, however, we assume that C_1 and C_2 citizens *can* each vary their level of effort within some range, then the introduction of unequal rewards creates an incentive structure that will call forth greater exertion, thereby increasing the average benefit generated by all associations. While such an arrangement will be good for association members, it may be harmful to the republic, or at least to the kind of republic Rousseau envisioned. For the greater the membership benefits conferred by "partial societies," the greater will be the sacrifice required when the association's particular interest comes into conflict with the common good. Thus, while unequal rewards give rise to heterogeneous associations of roughly equal power, they can also intensify the conflict between a citizen's particular will and the general will.

The logic of association among citizens whose cooperative character is transparent poses the following dilemma for Rousseau's republican politics. Insofar as associations generate benefits that are equally distributed among their membership, the most productive association members (either by virtue of their reliability alone or in combination with other talents) will find it advantageous to form exclusive groups amongst themselves, leaving less disciplined individuals to combine with one another for smaller gains. In this case, equality will prevail *within* associations but not *among* them. If, on the other hand, associations generate benefits that are divided up and distributed to the membership on the basis of each member's contribution to the group, there will be inequalities within each association, but associations, in their external relations, will tend to be more equal in power, as the most disciplined and productive individuals will be dispersed across many associations instead of being concentrated within a few groups.

The latter arrangement, in which an aristocracy of talented and self-disciplined citizens is scattered across many secondary associations, may coexist with republican government *if* the leaders of these "partial societies" can either be persuaded to pledge their first allegiance to the community as a whole, or, acting in the interests of their particular group, they counterbalance one another's political influence.[55] The first outcome, though not ideal from Rousseau's vantage point, resembles some aspects of the Roman republic he admired.[56] The second pattern, with its stress on countervailing interests, comes closer to Rousseau's second-best requirement that, if there must be "partial societies," they should be "equal in power."

Association in Opaque Societies

We began by working out the "pure" logic of association among citizens who differ in cooperative quality and whose unequal endowments are immediately apparent. In this section, I want to start by setting out the "pure" logic of association under opaque conditions in which citizens cannot ascertain differences in cooperative quality at a cost that justifies the effort. Once we have a clear conception of the perfectly opaque scenario, we can explore more realistic variations of this theme.

If the cooperative quality of citizens cannot be discerned, then, by definition, associations cannot differentiate between C_1 and C_2 citizens and, therefore, cannot directly control the composition of their membership. To consider the limiting case, let us stipulate that it is impractical to measure individual contributions to the group even after new applicants have become members of an association. Lacking the information necessary to distribute benefits in proportion to each member's contribution, I assume that the goods supplied by associations are equally available to all members.

How can associations make rational decisions about their membership if they do not know the cooperative quality of membership applicants? One approach is to rely on trial and error. For example, an association might admit new members and assess from time to time, and in a rough-and-ready way, whether the quality of the association and the benefits it supplies were rising, falling, or remaining unchanged. Operating under this rule, an association would continue admitting new members as long as the benefits provided by the association were increasing. Assuming, for simplicity, that there are no economies of scale, nor any complementarities of skill, accepting new members will increase association benefits as long as the average cooperative quality of the existing membership remains below the average cooperative quality of the population as a whole. When membership benefits begin to level off, or fall, an association will close its doors to new applicants.[57]

Even though associations cannot ascertain the cooperative virtues of membership applicants, we can nevertheless draw some inferences about the composition of these associations by bringing the "law of large numbers" to bear upon the problem. Most importantly, if we assume association members are drawn randomly from the population, then, applying the law of large numbers, we may infer that the more members an association has, the closer its composition will correspond to that of the wider society. Thus, if C_1 citizens comprise half of the population, then the percentage of C_1 citizens in an association will approach fifty percent as the association grows in size. By the same reasoning, if there were any homogenous associations of C_1 citizens in opaque societies, they would be small for the same reason that, when a coin is tossed repeatedly, it is unlikely that there will be a run of, say, ten "heads" in a row.[58]

The upshot of this brief exercise is that, unlike association under transparent conditions, where the community sorts itself into homogenous associations of C_1 and C_2 citizens, the associations formed under opaque conditions will tend to be heterogeneous groups that include both C_1 and C_2 citizens. The political significance of this exceedingly sparse scenario is that citizens who are especially skilled in cooperating for mutual advantage will, for the most part, be dispersed across a number of heterogeneous associations in which the ratio of C_1 to C_2 citizens within each association will be similar to the ratio of C_1 to C_2 citizens in the population as a whole. Thus, the condition Rousseau finds at the root of so many evils—opacity—actually precludes the disconcerting outcome of our first thought experiment in which citizens with transparent cooperative abilities separated themselves into homogenous associations of unequal power. *Whereas transparency facilitates sorting, opacity impedes it by substituting a random draw (in the limiting case) for the information-rich process through which citizens with unequal abilities separate themselves into exclusive groups.*

Rousseau emphasizes that organized interest groups are not the only "partial societies" that influence the affairs of the republic. In addition, there are the informal relationships that develop among people with common backgrounds and circumstances, and these loose-knit associations can also influence the public will.[59] As I mentioned earlier, the more and less advantaged tend to live in different neighborhoods, send their children to different schools, often seek out different entertainments, and separate themselves in many other ways. If people's cooperative abilities and other assets could *not* be so readily discerned, however, social stratification would be less pronounced because citizens with valuable assets would find it more difficult to capitalize on the positive "associational spillovers" that are generated by their combination in informal social networks. Citizens with valuable qualities would still enjoy advantages, but these would not be multiplied further by the concentration of the more fortunate in self-selected groups. Moreover, under completely opaque conditions, the most advantaged citizens would have no bargaining power in negotiating the terms of cooperation with less advantaged citizens. A "veil of ignorance" that prevents *others* from knowing the value of one's talents has much the same effect as John Rawls's veil of ignorance, which prevents one from knowing the value of *one's own* assets.[60] *In these respects, opacity is the ally of equality.*

Let us pause for a moment to recall Rousseau's speculations about the different social milieu in which transparent and opaque relations predominate. In small communities, where "individuals know and watch over one another," citizens will have, or can easily acquire, information about the interests, skills, resources, and character of their neighbors. Moreover, insofar as the members of such communities share a common set of circumstances—live in the same locality, earn a living in similar occupations, especially farming, and confront the same problems, for example, drought, floods, competition from nonlocal producers, and the like—they are apt to share many values and beliefs in common as well. In close-knit rustic villages, where communication among citizens is facilitated by the social uniformity of the inhabitants and by the dense social networks that interconnect them, the community and its standards will remain constantly "before their eyes," and "differences," when they do arise, will be difficult to conceal.[61] In other words, transparency and homogeneity are mutually reinforcing.

By contrast, the locus of opaque relations is, for Rousseau, the city, which was made possible by the division of labor and the exploitation of the countryside, and which bears the scars of social differentiation and the struggle for advantage. In addition to social fragmentation, which makes it difficult for urban dwellers to confidently assess one another's real aims and objectives, the anonymity afforded by the city, the constant mobility within and across its boundaries, the ceaseless jostling for relative position, and many other aspects of urban life, also contribute to the opaque character of the city. It is no wonder, then, that in Rousseau's account, the inhabitants of the city are strangers to one another, that each person, hiding "his conduct from the public eye, shows himself only by his reputation." Whereas transparency and *Gemeinschaft* (community) are mutually reinforcing in the countryside of Rousseau's imagination, so, too, are opacity and *Gesellschaft* (civil society) in the cities of his mind.[62]

It is easy to understand why Rousseau was so pessimistic about the prospects of forming a general will in societies that are divided into many separate, and often conflicting, interests. Would these prospects be improved if every citizen's character, social attributes, interests, and aims could be easily, even costlessly, ascertained? It is a difficult question to answer with much confidence, but some of the emerging social and political ramifications of the Internet may shed a little light on the question. Given our concerns, the essential feature of the Internet lies in its "search" function, which allows a person to seek out others who share his interests, outlook, or identity. As David Bohnett, founder of geocities.com, enthusiastically observes, "The Internet gives you the opportunity to meet other people who are interested in the same things you are, no matter how specialized, no matter how weird, no matter how big or how small."[63] Although this is a welcome new power for many citizens, the vastly enhanced ability to find others with the same interests or a shared identity may produce a horizontal version of the sorting that occurred in our first thought experiment, where citizens with unequal cooperative abilities separated themselves into exclusive groups. While it is not yet clear whether the "partial societies" formed in cyberspace will increase social inequality, some worry that these associations may reduce the scope of common experience that is essential to republican government. In *Republic.com*, Cass Sunstein argues that the Internet fosters "group polarization" because, in addition to affording citizens increased opportunities to find others with a similar outlook, interest, or identity, the Internet also gives people the ability to wall themselves off from others with different viewpoints, interests, and identities.[64] For example, partisan sites on the Internet typically offer many links to similar viewpoints, but very few, if any, links to opposing perspectives. Indeed, one study of "democratic discourse on the Web" concluded that "far from fostering deliberative political discourse, most of the surveyed Websites sought to consolidate speech power and served to balkanize the public forum."[65]

It is not surprising that people use the Internet to seek out others who are similar to themselves in some respect. Human beings are subject to the "homophily principle," which is simply to say that we tend to interact with, and form associations with, people who resemble us.[66] This tendency, which is partly the result of the constraining effects of social structure, typically situates individuals within personal networks that are relatively homogenous with regard to important social and demographic characteristics. This homogeneity, in turn, has a constraining effect on the information we receive and the attitudes we form, which will tend to resemble the information received, and the attitudes formed, by others who are similarly situated. If we are thinking of Rousseau's rustic village, then the homophily principle will reinforce the common life that sustains his model republic. But if we are thinking of a socially differentiated polity, then the homophily principle becomes a problem, for, among other things, it creates an obstacle to any public dialogue that seeks to find common interests across diverse social groups. To the extent the Internet facilitates the operation of this principle, making it easier for people to associate with others like themselves, it works against the realization of republican objectives within a modern state.

Rousseau's ideal republic, with its absence of "partial societies," is not a plausible alternative for a socially differentiated polity that recognizes freedom of association. On the other hand, the results Rousseau hoped to achieve in his "second-best" republic, with many small associations, may, in fact, be better served (in a modern society at least) by the presence of large *heterogeneous* associations. To begin with, citizens in more heterogeneous societies tend to be less engaged in intermediate associations than their counterparts in more homogeneous societies.[67] Although this lower rate of association membership will be troubling to the champions of civil society, it would not be disquieting for Rousseau, who was less favorably disposed toward the "partial societies" that populate civil society. When heterogeneous associations do form in diverse societies, they face difficulties in reaching agreement, in coordinating their actions, and in discouraging free riders because they typically lack the shared identity and common norms that facilitate decision making and organizational discipline in more homogeneous associations.[68]

On the other hand, studies have shown that while the presence of homogenous associations in heterogeneous societies tends to increase trust *within* these homogenous groups, they tend to weaken trust *between* them, whereas heterogeneous associations strengthen trust both within and between such groups.[69] Thus, while Rousseau envisioned a second-best scenario in which many small, and implicitly, homogeneous "partial societies" counterbalance one another in their efforts to shape the public will in favor of one or another "special interest," we are contemplating a scenario in which this counterbalancing of "special interests" takes place within large heterogeneous associations which face unique obstacles in trying to advance narrow objectives, and which, unwittingly, strengthen trust throughout the society.

Rousseau's contention that large associations effectively reduce the number of independent votes, thereby impairing the mechanism through which the "pluses and minuses" of "particular wills" cancel out, is also less compelling under quasi-opaque conditions. We may grant that Rousseau's argument carries considerable weight in the case of *homogenous* associations formed by *transparent* citizens who are able to combine resources in pursuit of relatively narrow interests. But his argument is much weaker in the case of "partial societies" formed under more opaque conditions because these associations tend to be more heterogeneous and, in the limit, resemble the larger society of which they are a microcosm. In this case, the "canceling out" of opposing interests is accomplished *within* associations rather than through "bloc voting," where idiosyncratic interests cancel out through offsetting ballots.

We have considered the formation and composition of associations under two limiting conditions, complete transparency and complete opacity. Real societies lie along a continuum between these two limiting cases. Typically, people choose their associates on the basis of incomplete information and the inferences they can draw therefrom. For example, we may attend to a person's speech or demeanor in order to predict whether he or she will be a reliable cooperation partner. Alternatively, we may consider a person's achievements, such as the possession of a college diploma or professional license, as an indicator of self-discipline, reliability, or other valued qualities. In addition to observable signs of achievement, people may also take account of ascriptive characteristics, such as family background, if these attributes are believed to be correlated with dependability, trustworthiness, or other cooperative virtues.

Although this kind of "statistical discrimination" is unfair to individuals, it can be a rational approach to membership decision making when the cooperative attributes of individual applicants cannot be ascertained at low cost. If, for example, there are social groups that are known for their "work ethic," then, all else being the same, associations looking for hard-working members can increase their chances of finding such people by focusing their recruiting efforts among these groups.[70] In a similar fashion, associations composed largely of people who belong to a particular ethnic group may believe, and be justified in believing, that they can make better predictions about the behavior of people with the same ethnic background than about people with different backgrounds. If so, they will incur less risk by restricting the membership of their organization accordingly. However, while such practices may be a rational response to a lack of low-cost information, statistical discrimination nevertheless favors self-enclosed associations, which, like the exclusive associations that form within transparent communities, tend to reinforce social divisions within the republic.

There is another drawback to statistical discrimination. Suppose you belong to an ethnic group or social class that has a reputation for free riding, which, in turn, makes you an unattractive candidate for association membership. Yet, suppose you could undertake certain activities which require considerable sacrifice in the short run, but which would be rightly regarded as a good predictor of your high value to an association. The hitch is that, unless information concerning your undertakings were available at a low cost, associations would continue to assess your membership application on the basis of group stereotypes, and you would not enjoy the anticipated return on your disciplined undertakings. In other words, your request for membership would be rejected. Of course, if you know that this is the way things would turn out, then you would not undertake these disciplined activities in the first place. And if other members of your group reason in a similar fashion, then the stereotypical view of your group will be reinforced, and its members will continue to be excluded from the best organizations.[71]

In summary, the composition of "partial societies" will vary depending on the extent and kind of information that is available. If associations have no knowledge about the character of prospective members and cannot make accurate inferences on the basis of observable characteristics, then such associations will tend to be heterogeneous. The larger these associations are, the more the composition of their membership will resemble that of the wider society, and the less intense will be the conflict between the group's interest and the public interest.[72] If, however, associations rely on easily observed characteristics to draw inferences about (unobservable) cooperative qualities, then associations will be less heterogeneous and may be formed around class, status, ethnicity, or other attributes that are readily distinguished. In this case, the citizen's identity, as well as her loyalty, may be divided between the republic that advances the community's common interests, and the "partial society" that advances her particular interests.

The Unraveling of Association:
A Digression on Tocqueville

In exploring the character of associations that form under transparent and opaque conditions, I have implicitly assumed that individual citizens find it advantageous to combine forces rather than pursuing their interests independently of one another. Alexis de Tocqueville, writing nearly a hundred years after Rousseau, perceived a new threat to democracy—"individualism"—which Tocqueville characterized as the tendency of citizens "to withdraw into the circle of family and friends," content to leave "the greater society to look after itself."[73] It is this "isolation of men" which Tocqueville, following Montesquieu, regarded as the social condition most favorable to despotism.

In America, Tocqueville found an antidote to individualism. "Americans of all ages, all stations in life, and all types of dispositions are," he observed, "forever forming associations."[74] And within these associations, which have "carried to the highest perfection the art of pursuing in common the objects of common desires," individuals are required, in some measure, "to know and adapt themselves to one another."[75] People are drawn into associations by their particular interests, but once assembled, they are drawn out of themselves and "learn to submit their own will to that of all the rest and to make their own exertions subordinate to the common action."[76] Needless to say, the moral psychology at work in Tocqueville's portrait of American democracy differs from Rousseau's understanding of the conditions necessary for civic virtue. For Tocqueville, the individual's participation in "partial societies" is a preparation for, not a distraction from, the tasks and responsibilities of citizenship.[77]

To consider Tocqueville's admonitions about "individualism" within our model, let us expand the citizen's range of options to include the alternative of withdrawing from public life in favor of purely private pursuits. With this additional option, each citizen now has two decisions to make: (1) whether or not to join an association; and (2) with whom to associate in the event the citizen chooses to combine his or her efforts with others. These decisions are not, of course, independent of one another. Whether a citizen chooses to join an association will depend on the quality of the association to which he or she can gain admission.

There are many things that affect the relative advantages of private life versus the common pursuit of mutual interests. These include such variables as family size and structure, levels of income and education, the scope of government and the quality of the public goods it supplies, as well as the prevalence of norms sustaining trust and civic participation. These and other factors shape the environment in which citizens allocate their time and energy between civic life and more intimate relationships.[78] Since we are interested in the bearing of transparency and opacity on the propensity toward individualism versus civic engagement, we must again invoke the "all else being equal" clause, abstracting from other considerations. Our aim is to analyze the comparative appeal of attending solely to one's private interests versus the collective pursuit of common interests under circumstances in which the cooperative abilities and other assets of citizens are easily discerned or not.

We begin with the transparent scenario in which C_1 and C_2 citizens can easily identify one another. Let us also suppose that association benefits are equally distributed among the members and that at least some C_1 citizens form homogenous associations to further their interests. For easy reference, I shall call these "A_1 associations," which provide the same "B_1 benefits" to all their members. Similarly, we assume at least some C_2 citizens form homogenous associations called "A_2 associations," which provide "B_2 benefits" to all their members. Given these assumptions, a C_1 citizen will join an A_1 association if the B_1 benefit it offers exceeds the citizen's opportunity cost, that is, the marginal benefit he or she derives from private activity. And a C_2 citizen will join an A_2 association if the B_2 benefit it provides exceeds the citizen's opportunity cost, that is, the marginal benefit he or she derives from private activity.

Since, under these transparent conditions, citizens have complete information about the benefits offered by associations, and associations have, or can easily acquire, complete information about the cooperative quality of membership applicants, we may infer that every citizen who wishes to belong to an association can join one, bearing in mind that less favored C_2 citizens must settle for membership in A_2 associations offering B_2 benefits. The only citizens who will not belong to associations in this scenario are those who, at the margin, derive greater benefits from their "circle of family and friends" than they would gain from association membership. No citizen is precluded from civic life because she cannot find equally gifted cooperation partners, or because these potential collaborators cannot readily discern her cooperative attributes.

Transparency thus tends to counteract "individualism" by facilitating the matching of citizens who seek to cooperate for mutual advantage. In this respect, transparent societies resemble the perfectly transparent markets of the economist's general equilibrium model in which traders are assumed to have complete information about the costs and benefits of all potential trades.[79] Under these idealized circumstances, trading proceeds until all gains from trade have been exploited. Similarly, under the transparent scenario we have described, which, needless to say, is also an idealized construction, individuals will exploit all gains from cooperation by combining into associational groupings that maximize their rewards.

Even under these transparent conditions, however, there will be some C_2 citizens who would join a high-quality, A_1 association, if they could gain admission to one, but who, only being eligible for membership in a lower quality, A_2 association, forego this opportunity in favor of private pursuits. This outcome will be troubling for egalitarians because some citizens will have fewer opportunities than others, especially if membership in a high-quality association brings with it other advantages and benefits.[80] It will also be troubling for Tocquevillians because it means that a segment of the public, perhaps a large segment, will be isolated from society, ignorant of "the art of pursuing in common the objects of common desires." Given our present concerns, I simply wish to take note of the fact that both of these disquieting results depend on the transparent circumstances that allow more advantaged citizens to form exclusive associations among themselves, leaving less advantaged citizens with diminished opportunities in civil society and, hence, a greater likelihood of being cut off from the rest of the community.[81]

How do opaque conditions affect the citizen's allocation of time and resources between civic life and private pursuits? We may approach this question by assuming that, not only do associations lack the information necessary to ascertain the cooperative quality of membership applicants, but that citizens, themselves, cannot precisely discern the level of benefits offered by particular associations. Rather, we assume that associations include a mix of C_1 and C_2 citizens, and that these heterogeneous groups provide "B_{ave} benefits," which are less than the B_1 benefits provided by A_1 associations in our transparent scenario, but greater than the B_2 benefits provided by A_2 associations in the transparent scenario, in other words, $B_1 > B_{ave} > B_2$. All else remaining the same, association under opaque conditions will differ from association under transparent conditions in two respects. First, a greater number of less advantaged, C_2 citizens, will join associations under opaque conditions than under transparent conditions because $B_{ave} > B_2$; and second, a smaller number of more advantaged, C_1 citizens, will join associations under opaque conditions than under transparent conditions because $B_{ave} < B_1$. In this case, opacity is again an ally of equality because, as we have seen before, opaque conditions prevent well-endowed, C_1 citizens, from joining together in exclusive associations, while affording less favored, C_2 citizens, greater benefits as members of heterogeneous associations.

If we adopt the notation that follows, we can say something about total association membership under transparent and opaque conditions.

C_1^{trans} = number of C_1 citizens in associations under transparent
         conditions
C_1^{opaque} = number of C_1 citizens in associations under opaque
         conditions
C_2^{trans} = number of C_2 citizens in associations under transparent
         conditions
C_2^{opaque} = number of C_2 citizens in associations under opaque
         conditions

In the simple scenario we have just described, there are fewer C_1 citizens in association under opaque conditions than under transparent conditions, that is, $C_1^{trans} > C_1^{opaque}$. But there are more C_2 citizens in association under opaque conditions than under transparent conditions, that is, $C_2^{opaque} > C_2^{trans}$. Hence, it follows that the total number of citizens in associations will be greater under transparent conditions if $(C_1^{trans} - C_1^{opaque}) > (C_2^{opaque} - C_2^{trans})$. Contrariwise, the total number of citizens in associations will be greater under opaque conditions if $(C_2^{opaque} - C_2^{trans}) > (C_1^{trans} - C_1^{opaque})$. In other words, total association membership will be greater under transparent conditions if the number of C_1 citizens joining associations (because they can reap the benefits of exclusivity) is greater than the number of C_2 citizens leaving associations (because they no longer enjoy the benefits of collaborating with more productive citizens).[82] On the other hand, total association membership will be greater under opaque conditions if the number of C_2 citizens joining associations (because they can reap the benefits of collaborating with C_1 citizens) exceeds the number of C_1 citizens leaving associations (because they no longer enjoy the benefits of exclusivity).

These results are, however, short-lived because we have not yet taken account of the dynamic relationship between the composition of associations and the level of benefits they provide. To understand the dynamics involved, let us assume that in our transparent society there are equal numbers of C_1 and C_2 citizens who belong to homogenous A_1 and A_2

associations, which provide benefits of ten and five, respectively. Next, suppose this transparent society is instantly transformed into an opaque society that is populated by heterogeneous associations which include a mixture of C_1 and C_2 citizens, and which provide a B_{ave} benefit of 7.5 to all association members. Following this instantaneous transition, we may reasonably expect that some C_1 citizens, who found association membership attractive when (under transparent conditions) they enjoyed a membership benefit of ten, will now exit a heterogeneous association providing a benefit of only 7.5. On the other hand, we can also expect that some C_2 citizens, who were not interested in joining an association providing a benefit of five (under transparent conditions), will eagerly join an association offering a benefit of 7.5. As soon as the decisions of these C_1 and C_2 citizens are taken, however, the initial level of benefits provided by heterogeneous associations, that is, $B_{ave} = 7.5$, will decline. For, as the ratio of C_1 to C_2 citizens within associations decreases, B_{ave} will decrease. Moreover, this is just the beginning of a cumulative process, because a reduction in B_{ave} will bring forth another round of adjustments in which some additional C_1 citizens, and even some C_2 citizens, will withdraw from associations because the benefits of association membership are lower following the initial exit of C_1 citizens.

This self-reinforcing process, which engenders an "unraveling of association," is illustrated in figure 3.1. The benefits of association

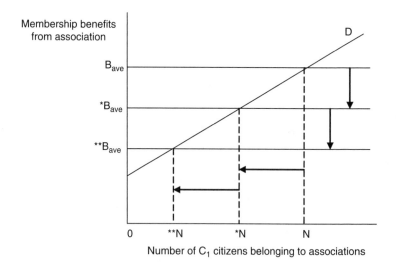

Figure 3.1   The unraveling of association.

membership are represented on the vertical axis, while the number of C_1 citizens belonging to associations is measured along the horizontal axis. The horizontal lines, B_{ave}, $^*B_{ave}$, and $^{**}B_{ave}$, represent the membership benefits of association, which depend on the ratio of C_1 to C_2 citizens within associations. The upward sloping line, D, represents the total demand for association membership among C_1 citizens, which rises with increasing membership benefits.

Figure 3.1 may be interpreted in the following way. As the number of C_1 citizens belonging to associations decreases from N to $^*N$, the benefits provided by associations decrease from B_{ave} to $^*B_{ave}$. When association benefits decline from B_{ave} to $^*B_{ave}$, additional C_1 citizens will exit associations, driving benefits down from $^*B_{ave}$ to $^{**}B_{ave}$, as the number of C_1 citizens belonging to associations falls from $^*N$ to $^{**}N$.

Although figure 3.1 only depicts the circumstances of C_1 citizens, it is easy to infer that as C_1 citizens exit associations, and B_{ave} falls, the number of C_2 citizens in associations will also decline. This exodus of C_1 and C_2 citizens will continue until the ratio of C_1 to C_2 citizens in associations, and, hence, B_{ave}, stabilizes. An equilibrium will be reached either when B_{ave} equals B_2, if all C_1 citizens retire to private life, or at a point when B_{ave} is greater than B_2, if there are some C_1 citizens willing to remain in associations offering fewer benefits. It is also worth pointing out that, in this model, there is an upper limit on association membership which depends, not only on the willingness of C_1 citizens to participate in associations when B_{ave} is less than B_1, but also on the choices of C_2 citizens regarding civic engagement. In particular, any large influx of C_2 citizens into associations will be self-limiting because such an inrush will reduce B_{ave}, thereby diminishing the appeal of association membership to both C_1 and C_2 citizens alike.

We can draw a few tentative conclusions from this exercise. To begin with, the number of citizens who find it worthwhile to join an association will likely be larger in transparent societies than in opaque societies because information about the character of individual citizens, and the benefits offered by specific associations, is readily available. In simplest terms, a transparent society is one in which "search costs" are low, making it easier for citizens to "match up," thereby increasing the appeal of civic engagement. We have seen that transparency allows C_1 citizens to combine in exclusive associations, but low search costs also facilitate the combination of citizens with similar backgrounds, beliefs, or interests, a point well-illustrated by the "virtual communities" that have sprung up with the expansion of the Internet, which has sharply reduced search costs for many citizens.[83] (This is, as we have already seen, a potentially problematic development. I shall have more to say about associations formed in cyberspace and their implications for republican democracy in chapter five.)

By contrast, when the cooperative attributes of individual citizens and the benefits offered by associations are difficult to ascertain, fewer citizens will choose to combine their efforts because they cannot easily identify other citizens who possess comparable abilities or similar interests. Those citizens who derive great enjoyment from their "circle of family and friends" and, hence, would only join high-quality associations, will turn away from civic life under opaque conditions because the information necessary to maintain "quality control" is lacking. If a disproportionate share of the citizens who fall into this category have a lot to offer any association they would otherwise join—C_1 citizens in our scheme—their absence from associations under opaque conditions will reduce the average benefits offered by associations, which, in turn, will reduce the appeal of civic engagement to other citizens.

In terms of association dynamics, an increase or decrease in transparency will set in motion self-reinforcing changes in the composition of associations. Although I concentrated on the case where a transparent society becomes opaque, it is important to add that the self-reinforcing process described in this case can also work in reverse. If a society is becoming more transparent, perhaps because of improvements in information and communications technology, then more resourceful citizens may be drawn into associations, which, in turn, will increase the benefits provided by these associations. This self-reinforcing influx of C_1 citizens into associations will continue if associations with an increasing proportion of C_1 citizens can screen new applicants for cooperative quality. If they cannot, then the influx of C_1 citizens will also attract more C_2 citizens into associations, thereby putting downward pressure on association benefits. As in the converse of this case, an equilibrium will be reached when the ratio of C_1 to C_2 citizens in associations stabilizes.

Finally, it is worth pointing out that an increase in transparency does not necessarily work to the advantage of everyone who belongs to, or might want to belong to, an association. In opaque societies, some highly productive citizens may belong to associations that include less productive citizens who benefit from the efforts of their more resourceful comrades. But as each citizen's cooperative quality comes into focus under more transparent conditions, some C_1 citizens who belong to associations offering a B_{ave} benefit under opaque conditions will now leave these heterogeneous associations to join homogenous A_1 associations providing B_1 benefits (where $B_1 > B_{ave}$). This will leave the C_2 citizens who have been "abandoned" by their more productive associates with the choice of either joining an A_2 association offering a B_2 benefit (where $B_{ave} > B_2$) or withdrawing, perhaps resentfully, to private life.

The logic at work in the case of increasing transparency is similar to the dynamic process that is set in motion when careers become "open to talents," a transformation which, itself, requires a certain threshold level of transparency. As candidates for positions in organizations are increasingly judged on their merits, some of the most talented members of the disadvantaged classes will leave their original associations in favor of the higher quality organizations to which they can now gain entry. As a consequence, those less talented will find themselves bereft of the benefits they enjoyed as members of associations that once included their more resourceful neighbors.[84] Thus, while equality of opportunity breaks the hold of social privileges based on ascriptive criteria, it can also give rise to new kinds of inequality, which may be reinforced by new patterns of association.[85]

Exit, Voice, and Loyalty

Tocqueville's concern with individualism and association, withdrawal and engagement, finds contemporary expression in Albert O. Hirschman's fertile typology of "exit, voice, and loyalty."[86] These concepts name alternative responses to dissatisfaction of one kind or another. A discontented individual can either withdraw (exit) from an organization or other kind of unsatisfactory relationship, or take steps to improve matters, such as complaining to management (voice). Loyalty, the third leg of Hirschman's triad, is manifest in the Rousseauean disposition toward participation, toward voice rather than exit.

Exit and voice are, of course, the characteristic responses to dissatisfaction within the market economy and the democratic state, respectively. Dissatisfied consumers can "vote with their feet," abandoning one seller for another, whereas disgruntled citizens may try to solve problems by persuading elected officials to address them, or, failing this, by organizing themselves to take action. In Hirschman's account, voluntary associations occupy an interesting niche between the market and the democratic state because they are subject to the pressures exerted by both voice and exit, as association members may either "speak up" or quit the association (in favor of joining another one or retreating to private life).

How does our dichotomy of transparent and opaque societies bear on Hirschman's typology and vice versa? In the first place, and most importantly, transparency tends to favor "exit" over "voice." If there are many associations and their quality is transparent, then the dissatisfied member of an association need not incur any search costs in finding an alternative association.[87] In effect, the decision to quit an association of declining quality in favor of a superior alternative is risk-free; the disappointed member of an association simply joins another organization the higher quality of which is known with certainty. By contrast, if the quality of associations is opaque, then a disaffected member will incur a risk in changing associations. Other things being the same, voice becomes a more attractive option than exit under conditions of opacity.[88]

In the limiting case of complete transparency, "partial societies" will proliferate, but "exit" rather than "voice" will be the primary response to dissatisfaction.[89] Of course, everyone cannot be "exiting" all of the time. Some members of associations must remain behind to patch things up or there will be no associations for migrating members to join. Nevertheless, the proportion of association loyalists who exercise the "voice" option will be relatively small compared to the analogous ratio in opaque societies, and therefore associations will not function as the schools of citizenship Tocqueville and his contemporary followers envision for them, because it is voice—the activity of participation—that is essential to the citizen's civic education. From Rousseau's vantage point, however, the absence of voice within intermediate associations is not such a bad thing.[90] In fact, the more often individuals shift between organizations, the weaker will be their attachments and loyalties to any one association, and, hence, the less intense will be the conflict between their particular will and the general will.

There is another aspect of Hirschman's analysis that bears on our theme and this is the fact that associations are not spread with equal density across the quality range.[91] Typically, the number and variety of associational alternatives are smaller at the top of the quality scale than at the bottom, that is, there are fewer A_1 associations than A_2 associations in our jargon. As a consequence, the members of A_1 associations will usually have fewer associational alternatives to choose from than will the members of A_2 associations. Thus, the relative appeal of "voice" over "exit" will be greater for members of A_1 associations than for members of A_2 associations. Moreover, insofar as A_1 associations have fewer members, each one can have a greater influence on the group's decisions, hence the members of A_1 associations have a greater incentive to participate than do the members of A_2 associations. Further, if the members of A_1 associations are more inclined to take action to maintain or improve the quality of their associations, then these associations are likely to continue generating greater benefits than those generated by A_2 associations, whose members are prone to "exit" rather than "voice."

Hirschman summarizes the foregoing logic in the following way, "since voice will be forthcoming more readily at the upper than at the lower quality ranges, the cleavages between the quality of life at the top and at the middle or lower levels will tend to be more marked."[92] If we add to this observation our own conclusion that transparency tends to favor the "exit" alternative, we then have a state of affairs in which the most advantaged citizens become loyal members of their own high-quality "partial societies," while those citizens with less to offer move among the larger number of lower quality associations, forming relatively weak attachments to their temporary groups. For the contemporary Tocquevillian, it is the latter consequence that will be most troubling because many citizens will fail to develop the participatory skills and broad outlook that are necessary for effective citizenship. But from the Rousseauean vantage point we have been constructing, it is the former condition—the loyalty of advantaged individuals to their high-quality associations—that is most disconcerting, first because powerful associations of well-endowed individuals will exacerbate social and economic inequalities, and second because the strong group loyalties formed by members of these organizations will conflict with their duties to the wider community.[93]

This view contrasts sharply with the perspective of contemporary Tocquevillians who worry that, in a society where citizens exit associations rather than complaining about their shortcomings ("voice" in Hirschman's lexicon), the quality of democracy will suffer for lack of an active public. It is difficult to dismiss such concerns. How are citizens to learn the skills and habits essential to democracy if not in the intermediate associations that encompass so much of our lives? But if Tocqueville correctly seized upon the crucial role of associations in a democratic polity, did he not, perhaps, pass too quickly over Rousseau's point that the more effective "partial societies" are, the more difficult it will be for citizens to see beyond the immediate horizons of the associations that advance their particular interests?

Transparent and Opaque Associations:
The Two Models Summarized

We have now investigated several characteristics of associations formed by individuals whose cooperative dispositions and other assets are either transparent or opaque, as well as some of the implications these different kinds of "partial society" hold for Rousseau's republic. The main premises and results of our thought experiments are summarized in table 3.1.

In constructing the first model displayed in the table, I stressed some of the unexpected consequences of transparency. To summarize, the condition most auspicious for the development of civic virtue— transparency of character—is also favorable to the formation of "partial societies" because citizens who can confidently read one another's intentions will find it advantageous to combine within intermediate associations to advance their mutual interests. Moreover, if association benefits are equally distributed among the membership, then the most productive citizens will do best for themselves by joining together in exclusive associations. This propensity to combine within homogeneous groups will divide each citizen's loyalties between the association that advances his or her particular interests and the republic that serves the common good, while, at the same time, dividing the community into self-enclosed associations of the more and less advantaged.

The threat posed to the republican state by these "partial societies" is somewhat mitigated by the fact that "exit" takes precedence over

Table 3.1   Associations in transparent and opaque societies[a]

	Model I Transparent Societies	Model II Opaque Societies
Composition of associations	Homogeneous	Heterogeneous
Distribution of power across associations	Less equal	More equal
Proportion of citizenry in associations	Relatively high	Relatively low
Conflict between the general will and the particular will	More intense	Less intense
Primary response to dissatisfaction	"Exit"	"Voice"

Note: [a]Assuming association benefits are equally distributed among the members.

"voice" in transparent societies, and the relative ease of leaving one's current association in favor of a more promising alternative weakens the power of all associations over their members.[94] If individuals are in the habit of "voting with their feet," gravitating to whichever association offers the most advantages at any given moment, then their loyalty to these "partial societies" cannot run too deep. Thus, if the primary threat to republican government arises from special interest groups, from "factions" rather than from "individualism," then the "easy exit" option fostered by transparency will mitigate to some degree its effects in facilitating the formation of "partial societies." The formation of exclusive associations of the more and less advantaged will also be tempered to some extent if benefits are distributed according to contribution, which draws citizens with greater and lesser cooperative skills into heterogeneous associations of roughly equal power, but only through the mechanism of unequal rewards.

Some of the features of transparent societies that reinforce social inequality arise from the premise, retained throughout all but one of the thought experiments of this chapter, that a person's cooperative disposition, once formed, cannot be altered. Given this constraint, individuals are limited in their decision making to the choice of cooperation partners. If, however, citizens *are* able to alter their character, then, under conditions of transparency, every citizen ready to renounce free riding would be able to gain entry into associations that accepted only reliable applicants. And if reliability, in turn, were the *only* trait on which a person's cooperative contribution depended, equality would then prevail both within *and* across associations.

There are, however, two reasons for skepticism regarding this possibility. In the first place, a person's contribution to an association usually depends on more than his or her reliability. Judgment, foresight, creativity, conviviality, the capacity for sustained, physically demanding work—all of these virtues, and many others, are valued by associations. If these attributes are not spread evenly across the population, but instead are concentrated within certain segments of it, and if individuals, moved solely by *amour de soi*, choose their cooperation partners with the aim of advancing their interests, then one undesirable feature of associations formed by transparent citizens will reassert itself, viz. the emergence of self-reinforcing inequalities across both individuals and groups.

The second reason for skepticism concerning this rosy scenario is that the moral psychology presupposed in the case of universally alterable dispositions does not give sufficient weight to Rousseau's pessimism about our capacity for sustained self-mastery.[95] The problem is not just the sanguine assumption that *everyone* can mold himself into a cooperative partner who never free rides on the efforts of the group. Even if this premise were granted, the resulting multitude of highly effective associations would pose a further problem. For every citizen who is called upon to set aside the particular interest of her partial society in favor of the public good must overcome two powerful forces—self-interest, which is all the more well-served by a successful association, and loyalty, which must be especially strong within associations whose members never free ride on the cooperative efforts of the group.[96]

Association in opaque societies proceeds according to a different logic and produces organizations whose composition and character diverge from the typical groups that form within transparent societies. Lacking information about the cooperative quality and resourcefulness of their neighbors, the citizens of opaque societies will not form associations as readily as their counterparts in transparent societies, hence, associations in opaque societies will encompass a smaller proportion of the citizenry. The associations that do emerge within opaque societies will be more heterogeneous in composition and more equal in power than the "partial societies" that flourish in transparent societies. Without the information that is necessary in order to sort themselves into exclusive groups, the most productive citizens in opaque societies will either withdraw to private life or be dispersed across an array of associations.

To the extent that associations in opaque societies are a random draw from the community at large, their membership will tend to mirror the composition of that community. In the limiting case, these "partial societies" will be microcosms of the wider society, and the "canceling out" of opposing interests, which, in Rousseau's "second-best" republic, occurs when the votes of competing factions offset one another, will instead take place within these large and relatively diverse associations themselves. Since associations that encompass divergent interests and outlooks will find it difficult to unite around narrow concerns, the conflict between the association's objectives and the general will be less intense than that which prevails when transparency allows associations to form around more exclusive interests. Finally, while opaque conditions are not favorable to the development of narrow-based interest groups, associations in opaque societies may nevertheless produce a loyal membership because "exit" becomes a riskier option under conditions of uncertainty.

The Civil Society Argument: A Rousseauean View

In contrast to Rousseau, many democratic theorists warmly embrace "partial societies" and, following Tocqueville, look to them to instill in their members a cooperative disposition, an affection for one another, and a wider view of the community's affairs. Within associations, "feelings and ideas are renewed, the heart enlarged, and the understanding developed by the reciprocal action of men upon one another."[97] According to Robert Putnam, one of civil society's most prominent contemporary theorists, intermediate associations "contribute to the effectiveness and stability of democratic government" not only "externally" through " 'interest articulation' and 'interest aggregation,' " but also "internally," as they "instill in their members habits of cooperation, solidarity, and public-spiritedness."[98] In states with a "civic culture," Putnam argues, most citizens "read eagerly about community affairs" and "trust one another to act fairly and obey the law."[99] In addition to these advantages, the proponents of civil society contend that a dense network of secondary associations creates "social capital"—mutual trust—which can be drawn upon to solve a community's collective action problems.[100]

This depiction of a "civic culture," with its emphasis on trust, solidarity, and active participation in civic affairs, bears a close resemblance to Rousseau's model republican state, with its unified, energetic, and public-spirited citizenry. The difference between the two conceptions is that while the "civic culture" model revolves around the voluntary associations within which individuals cooperate for mutual advantage in civil society, Rousseau's conception embraces the entire political community, wherein citizens strive to advance those interests everyone shares in common. From Rousseau's vantage point, trouble arises precisely because the effective organization of special interest groups in civil society comes at the expense of the republic and the common good it is organized to serve. The more successful associations are in organizing particular interests; in creating or reinforcing parochial identities and loyalties; and in influencing the formation of public policy; the more difficult it is to make laws that advance the public interest and call forth the willing obedience of citizens.

The civil society theorist grants that the conditions which favor habits of trust and cooperation are most likely to be fulfilled in smaller groups, but insists that the associations which emerge within civil society pose no serious problems for republican democracy. Rather, many of them affirm, implicitly or explicitly, Tocqueville's view that each citizen will "transfer the concern inspired in him by his little republic into his love of the common motherland."[101] In this version of the civil society argument, the social ties and habits of cooperation formed within secondary associations, far from interfering with the duties of citizenship, are a necessary, or at least a useful, preparation for the tasks of citizenship. Other civil society theorists, like Ernest Gellner, praise the "modular man" of civil society, who "can combine into specific-purpose, *ad hoc*, limited associations, without binding himself by some blood ritual."[102] In this account, civil society does not threaten the vitality of citizenship in a democratic state because associations make very limited demands on the loyalty of their members.

I do not reject these claims out of hand, in part because the alternative of dissociated individuals whose attention and energy are fully absorbed in the life of a republic now seems implausible even for the smallest states. Yet, while Rousseau's model republic is no doubt utopian, he may still have something to teach the enthusiastic admirers of civil society. Most versions of the civil society argument crucially assume that the members of associations will be able to take a wider view of public issues when acting in their role as citizens. According to Putnam, "networks of civic engagement foster sturdy norms of generalized reciprocity," broadening "the participants' sense of self, developing the 'I' into the 'we.'"[103] This claim is put in question, however, once we consider the various ways in which association membership can constrain the thoughts and actions of those belonging to such groups. To begin with, the citizen's understanding of her interests and her relation to the larger society are often shaped by the information that is conveyed through the group, by the pressure for conformity within the group, and by the social standing that is conferred by membership in the group.[104] Associations are successful, in part, because they are able to coordinate the activities of their members around common norms and values, thereby reducing the transaction costs of social exchange. Moreover, this kind of coordination tends to be self-reinforcing, as "social interaction, discussion, and the circulation of ideas within groups will produce shared opinions on matters of common interest such as religion, culture, politics, and morality."[105] Such uniformity of opinion and outlook is likely to be especially thoroughgoing if the association is formed under transparent conditions in which, for example, the inhabitants of a neighborhood or the members of an ethnic group already share common interests, or a common cultural background, and can ascertain one another's cooperative intentions without too much difficulty.

Although transparent commonalities of interest and orientation facilitate association, the groups that populate civil society are not just reflections of preexisting social categories. The shared identity and solidarity that promote intragroup cooperation are often strengthened by "norms of exclusion." Thus, Dennis Chong argues that in some associations the functional role of norms is "to establish difference," and, as such, "they might be most instructively called *norms of particularism, difference*, or *exclusion* rather than of community."[106] In evaluating the force of this argument, it is important to bear in mind that freedom of association entails the right to exclude unwanted membership applicants, and that many associations "labor to preserve their social restrictiveness and pretended distinction, and to claim deference from others."[107] Not all the associations that populate civil society are civic minded. The civil society of Putnam's Italy accommodated not only the development of sports clubs and singing groups, but also the rise of the Fascist Party.[108] Not even the world's greatest practitioner of association is immune from such malignancies; the civic culture of the United States accommodates not only the League of Women Voters, but also the Klu Klux Klan, an organization which, needless to say, does not foster the "generalized reciprocity" and "social trust" that Putnam sees arising, almost as a matter of course, from secondary associations.

For the civil society theorist, associations provide the experience, the skills, and even the energy that propel individuals into the tasks of citizenship. But, as Rousseau observed, the commitments of association members can also drain energy from the public life of a democracy. When citizens join associations, they incur obligations to other members of the group, while also gaining the right to make claims upon their fellow members. These special rights and duties generate benefits for association members that are unavailable to nonmembers. Moreover, these special claims and loyalties will sometimes supersede the claims of other citizens, even citizens in need, who do not belong to the "in-group." Consider the case of parents who become dissatisfied with their local public school and enroll their children in private schools, quitting the public school's parent–teacher association (PTA) and joining the private school's PTA. Although these citizens may become energetic participants in their new PTA, forming the kind of trusting relationships that civil society theorists praise, their new commitments and loyalties are apt to have adverse consequences for the republic. Families who forsake their local public school will, quite naturally, be less inclined to vote for taxes that finance public schools. In addition, when energetic and resourceful citizens withdraw their children from public schools, their departure can initiate a dynamic process wherein the deteriorating quality of public schools and the exit of enterprising parents reinforce one another along the lines we described in explaining the unraveling of association.

This is not, of course, a complete accounting of the costs and benefits that are created by citizens who join an association—a private school and its PTA in this case. The students who transfer to private schools may well get a better education than they were getting in their local public school, and their parents may also profit from their new engagements. In the long run, the public school system might even benefit from competition with private schools. Nevertheless, it is by no means clear whether the "habits of cooperation" and "solidarity" that develop within such associations always redound to the benefit of the republic, rather than advancing at its expense. The emergence of private schools, residential community associations, recreational clubs, private security forces, and other organizations that provide substitutes for public goods doubtlessly create bonds of loyalty and trust among their members. But they also reduce support for the state's provision of public goods, which may bring about a further deterioration of these goods. In the end, Daniel A. Bell asks, "what if associations in civil society begin to seriously undermine attachments to the polity at large," eroding "the basic minimum of social cohesion and trust needed to promote social justice and sustain the democratic process?"[109]

Putnam's praise of associations brings out an important difference between the civil society theorist's implicit view of policymaking as a balancing of competing interests and Rousseau's view of law as an expression of the general will. Putnam stresses the role of associations in "articulating" and "aggregating" interests, but says very little about how these interests should be weighed and evaluated. In Rousseau's conception, the citizen's vote is not to be determined by his or her particular interests and group loyalties, but should express the citizen's opinion about what is the best policy overall, taking account of everyone's interest. Rousseau's point about the adverse effects of "partial societies" on citizenship and civic virtue is well summarized by Simone Weil, who points out that the citizen who belongs to an association will be hard-pressed to "examine the frightfully complex problems of public life while simultaneously being attentive, both to discerning truth, justice, and the public good, and also retaining the attitude appropriate to a member of some group."[110]

Rousseau's vision of independent citizens who resist the pressures exerted by "partial societies" in order to discern the common good is not without its critics. Iris Marion Young, who aims to set forth "the norms and conditions of inclusive democratic communication under circumstances of structural inequality and cultural difference," draws attention to the fact that "social movements mobilizing around experiences and analyses of the oppressive and unequal consequences of social differentiations of gender, race, sexuality, national origin, or religion, along with class, have expressed skepticism about appeals to a common good."[111] Often, Young insists, claims of unity "bias the interpretation of a common good in ways that favor dominant social groups and position women, or indigenous people, or Blacks, or homosexuals, or Muslims as deviant Other."[112] Young's solution to the problems posed by "social differentiations" is a conception of democracy "in which differentiated social groups should attend to the particular situation of others and be willing to work out just solutions to their conflicts and collective problems from across their situated positions."[113] Rather than viewing the claims of "structurally or culturally differentiated social groups as nothing but the assertion of self-regarding interest," these "socially situated interests, proposals, claims, and expressions of experience" should be considered "an important resource," which "can both pluralize and relativize hegemonic discourses."[114]

Young's claim about the strategic use of normative concepts like the "common good" by a dominant group to secure its privileged position would not have been unfamiliar to Rousseau, who described how people with money and power "conceived at length the profoundest plan that ever entered the mind of man," a phony social contract that "imposed new fetters on the poor," "gave new powers to the rich," "eternally fixed the law of property and inequality," and "converted clever usurpation into unalterable right."[115] That said, it must be granted that Rousseau's model republic is not possible for a society which is divided between "dominant social groups" and "deviant Others," where there are "hegemonic discourses" that must be "relativized," and where the "common good" and the notion of "special interests" are merely rhetorical weapons wielded by the powerful to bludgeon the weak. It is ironic, however, that while the polity described by Young is deeply fractured by "structural inequality and cultural difference," she nevertheless expects much more of its citizens than Rousseau demands of his. The citizens of Rousseau's republic are all "similarly situated" and therefore share many interests and values in common. Because laws impose the same burdens on everyone, no one has an interest in proposing oppressive rules, and thus Rousseau can claim that citizens "obey no one but their own will."[116] By contrast, Young hopes to bring forth from a profoundly divided political society a public discussion that "reflects all social experience" so that "discussion participants will be able to develop a collective account of the sources of the problems they are trying to solve," ultimately achieving a "collective critical wisdom," which "enables them to reach a judgment that is not only normatively right in principle, but also empirically and theoretically sound."[117]

Young's depiction of a polity structured by powerful social forces, when combined with her portrait of citizens who can "freely act" in the face of their "group positioning," looks oddly utopian alongside Rousseau's model republic, which could not withstand "the oppressive and unequal consequences of social differentiation," and which is, in fact, designed to preclude the emergence of "structural inequality" and "cultural difference," thereby minimizing the distance each citizen must traverse in order to bring her particular will into concordance with the general will.[118] Of course, Young could respond by insisting that a contemporary theory of democracy must address the actual conditions of our social and political life, which bear little resemblance to the rustic villages of Rousseau's imagination. Fair enough, but while Rousseau's tightly integrated republic is now out of reach, or no longer appealing, his account of the stringent conditions necessary for the success of republican democracy gives us reason to be skeptical about the plausibility of achieving a "collective critical wisdom" within a polity that is divided into conflicting and unequal "partial societies."

Yet, perhaps there is more to be found in Rousseau's reflections on this matter than a bracing dose of realism. Without going into detail, let me suggest that if Rousseau is right in stressing the importance of common interests and shared experience in the creation of citizens who will look beyond their particular concerns, then Young's program of "inclusive democracy" might profit from policies and institutions that bring into being such communal interests and activities. Although proposals for some form of national public service have been advanced mainly by civil society enthusiasts, a program of mandatory public service could further Young's aim of getting citizens to work out solutions "from across their situated positions" by creating a common endeavor and a shared experience, much like that which Rousseau hoped to achieve through the reestablishment of the *corvée* (compulsory community service). In a similar fashion, while national health insurance has been advocated as a way of addressing the medical needs of low- and moderate-income citizens in the United States, it could also be useful in creating common interests among citizens who would otherwise share little in common. Of course, it may be that such initiatives are politically feasible only in states whose citizens already share many interests, values, and beliefs. But this is just to reiterate Rousseau's anti-utopian point about the demanding conditions that must be satisfied if republican democracy is to succeed.

To return to the arguments put forward by the proponents of civil society, it must be acknowledged that historical experience strongly suggests that the prospects for liberty, both public and private, are much better in states with powerful "partial societies" than in states where secondary associations are weak or nonexistent. When one-party states set about destroying every autonomous organization that stands between the citizen and the "common good," we must then take sides with Montesquieu and Tocqueville against Rousseau. But if pursuit of Rousseau's republican ideal, with its absence of "factions," is too dangerous given the great power of the modern state, is it not also true that the narrow outlook of, and sharp inequalities among, associations often block, or distort, public discussion of the common good? When democracies cannot solve problems because they are immobilized by competing factions that forestall any solution disadvantageous to themselves, and when citizens complain about the political power of "interest groups," or about the influence of "political action committees," they are appealing to Rousseauean ideals of democracy and the common good.

"If there are partial societies, it is best to have as many as possible and to prevent them from being unequal."[119] This is good advice. To begin with, it reminds us that associations are not just ramparts against state power. They also influence public debate, and in many instances, go a long way toward determining the content of the laws that are enforced by the state.[120] Insofar as the quality of our citizenship is imperfect, there must be recourse to the logic of countervailing power. Yet this logic might well be applied, not only in thinking through the balance of power between the state and civil society; but also in thinking about the proper balance of power among the associations that constitute civic society itself. Following Rousseau's lead, I have tried to illuminate some additional dimensions of the problem by laying bare the logic of association among citizens whose cooperative quality is transparent or opaque to others. Given the abstract nature of the thought experiments developed earlier, the conclusions I have reached are too general for the purpose of institutional design. Still, it should be reasonably clear from our analysis that if laws are to be more than the outcome of bargaining among competing interest groups, then citizens and their elected representatives must be insulated, in some measure, from the internal and external pressures exerted by such groups, an objective which may be served by such measures as the public financing of election campaigns and by regulations constraining the power associations exercise over their membership.[121] And one may also reasonably conclude from our discussion that, if the egalitarian foundations of a democratic state and the common experience it makes possible are to be secured, then the formation of exclusive "partial societies" that reinforce social and economic inequalities ought to be discouraged, an objective that may require limitations on the right of associations to make membership decisions on the basis of criteria that discriminate against less advantaged groups of citizens.[122]

Rousseau's thoughts on the relationship between citizenship and association provide a unique vantage point from which we can appreciate some of the drawbacks of interest-group democracy, drawbacks which are often neglected in the contemporary celebration of civil society. However, I do not want to conclude this discussion without drawing attention to the utopian premises of Rousseau's own reflections and, by implication, acknowledging the validity of a vital premise in the civil society argument. I am referring to the fact that Rousseau gives serious consideration to the possibility that citizens whose character is formed by the institutions of the republican city-state for the purpose of social cooperation might *not* join together in smaller, "partial societies," to collaborate for mutual advantage. Whereas Rousseau addresses the conflict between the general, and the particular, will as a problem thrust upon us by our *nature*, the question of secondary associations is raised only as a *hypothetical* possibility. When Rousseau introduces the problem of associations with the prefatory remark, "*if* there are partial societies," one must conclude that he has temporarily lost sight of the very logic of association that gives rise to the social contract, itself, and motivates, in large measure, the cooperative endeavors of republican democracy.[123] "Partial societies" are the *necessary* offspring of a civic culture that opens each citizen's character to public view and cheers cooperation for mutual advantage.

CHAPTER FOUR

Opaque Traders and the Invisible Hand

One of the claims I made in chapter two is that the logic of Hobbes's *Leviathan*, which proceeds from rational egoism to the war of all against all to the formation of a sovereign authority, requires as a necessary premise the opacity of human intention. If human beings were transparent to one another, their promises of self-restraint could be taken at face value, and, apart from weakness of will, the problem of compliance would not arise. But in the absence of clear intentions and the mutual assurance they make possible, rational agents must turn to the state to enforce the commitments they make to one another. The argument of the present chapter is that Adam Smith's equally famous chain of reasoning, which shows how the market's "invisible hand" channels the pursuit of self-interest for social benefit, requires as *its* necessary premise the *transparency* of human intention. If this condition is not fulfilled, and Rousseau argued forcefully that human beings lose their transparence in civil society, then some of the advantages claimed for competitive markets collapse as well.

In developing this argument, I begin by sketching Smith's account of the market economy, which shows how competition among buyers and sellers releases individuals from the grip of otherwise powerful interests, and how the impersonal rule of the price system coordinates the self-regarding decisions of a large number of independent agents. Next, I outline Rousseau's opposing view of the marketplace in which trade, like the rest of social intercourse, is marred by a universal deceit, so that we never really know the character of the people with whom we are dealing. In subsequent sections, I draw on the contemporary discipline of information economics to explore the wider implications of Rousseau's criticism, describing some of the complications created by the imperfect transparency of real-world markets and explaining how inequality and low productivity reinforce one another in opaque economies. The various strands of the argument, when woven together, amount to this: the invisible hand's harmonious ordering of economic activity cannot be sustained once opaque men and women intrude upon the marketplace. In the remaining sections, I set forth a Rousseauean critique of the welfare state and its "republic of purses," discuss the main elements of Rousseau's republican political economy, and examine two contemporary specimens of egalitarian thought in light of Rousseau's concerns about opaque interaction and the problems it poses for a "republic of hearts."

The Invisible Hand

In *The Wealth of Nations*, Adam Smith combines into one marvelous conception the *division of labor*, which enhances productivity by allowing each person to specialize in a single task, the *free exchange* of goods, which liberates individuals from the necessity of having to provide for all of their own needs, and the model of a *competitive market*, which automatically directs resources to their most productive uses.[1] This felicitous arrangement was not the product of deliberate human design, but the "gradual consequence of a certain propensity in human nature . . . the propensity to truck, barter, and exchange one thing for another."[2] For Smith, the essence of trade amounts to this: "Give me that which I want, and you shall have this what you want."[3]

Once the market economy takes root, "every man . . . lives by exchanging, or becomes in some measure a merchant, and the society itself grows to be what is properly called a commercial society."[4] The feudal ties between master and servant give way to contractual relationships between legally free individuals who appeal to one another's interests in hopes of reaching agreement on a mutually advantageous course of action. Meanwhile, the whole nation is becoming intertwined in a complex network of unintended interdependence.

It has been more than two centuries since the publication of Smith's masterpiece, and it is difficult to appreciate the arresting novelty of his claim that the unfettered pursuit of self-interest is compatible with, even essential to, the rational organization of a nation's economic resources. The skeptic will point to the problem of "opportunism," that is, traders seeking advantages through subterfuge or dishonesty in their transactions.[5] Smith did not endorse such strategies, but insisted that they pose few problems in a market economy where a large number of firms compete with one another. Simply put, dishonest merchants who promise one thing, but deliver another, will be forced out of business because the customers who buy their products, the firms which provide their materials, and the banks which lend them money will all turn away from unreliable trading partners in the confident expectation that there are many other buyers, sellers, and borrowers waiting the wings.

In addition to the difficulties created by duplicitous traders, it may be asked how trade can work to the advantage of both parties when one commands more resources than the other. Does the more prosperous party not have a bargaining advantage over the less prosperous? Not necessarily; if there are *many* buyers and sellers, then the dependence of the weak on the strong is superceded by a more complex pattern of relationships in which no market participant can easily dominate another. Traders dissatisfied with one offer can turn to other buyers or sellers in search of better terms. Under the pressure of competition, Smith argues, sellers must cater to buyers in order to remain in business, and employers must pay wages commensurate with the productivity of labor in order to attract and retain workers.[6]

It is worth taking notice of the remarkable similarity between Smith's understanding of the liberating potential of competitive markets and Rousseau's depiction of the original social contract as an agreement that obliges us *to no one in particular*. Rousseau characterizes the social contract as an agreement in which "each man, in giving himself to all, gives himself to nobody."[7] Smith may have had Rousseau's words in mind when, in praising markets, he observes that "each tradesman or artificer derives his subsistence from the employment, not of one, but of a hundred or a thousand different customers. Though in some measure obliged to them all, therefore, he is not absolutely dependent upon any one of them."[8] Although Rousseau and Smith both regarded personal dependence as an evil to be minimized in the design of a good society, the solutions they proposed are as contrary as one could imagine: small republican communities united by the general will versus global markets that create multiple trading opportunities.[9] And while Rousseau's scheme requires citizens who know one another and put the public interest ahead of private advantage, Smith's model makes no such exacting demand, for, in his view, the market brings order to the interaction of people who are both strangers to one another and unmoved by the common good.

The market's impersonal rule derives not only from the presence of alternative buyers and sellers, but also from its capacity for self-regulation.

In Smith's informal model, imbalances between supply and demand are reflected in relative prices, and equilibrium is restored by forces internal to the market itself.[10] Smith's reasoning is well-known and may be illustrated by an example. Suppose there is increased demand for lamp oil because the public is reading more at night. In response to this increase in demand, the price of lamp oil will rise, and the profits accruing to lamp oil suppliers will increase. These supernormal profits will draw additional investment into the lamp oil industry. In time the supply of lamp oil will expand, which will reduce its price, thereby eliminating the difference between the rate of profit in the lamp oil industry and the rate of profit in other industries. More generally, competition for profits will direct resources so as to eliminate imbalances between supply and demand, diverting investment from industries where there is excess supply and funneling it into industries where there is excess demand.

The same market mechanism that directs resources to their most valued uses also regulates the incomes of those who cooperate to produce goods and services.[11] Supernormal incomes in one sector of the economy will attract labor and capital from other sectors. The increased supply of workers and equipment will reduce wages and profits in the former, while the diminished supply of productive resources will raise incomes in the latter. This adjustment process is set in motion whenever the incomes received in one industry, or by one factor of production, differ from the earnings of equally productive workers and entrepreneurs in other sectors of the economy. In equilibrium, every person's income must be proportionate to his or her productive contribution.[12]

Although Smith's model of the market was built of words, his successors were able to demonstrate, mathematically, that under certain ideal circumstances, the exchange of goods between agents guided only by their private interests would result in the maximum satisfaction that can be achieved from a given endowment of resources.[13] Under conditions of "perfect competition," the prices of all goods will be such that the quantity demanded is equal to the quantity supplied in each and every market. Moreover, this simultaneous equilibrium is achieved even though no market participant considers the effect of his decisions on the interests of other participants.[14] Rather, every agent, acting solely with her own ends in view, need only take account of market prices in choosing the most efficient means to her ends; the invisible hand of competition takes care of the rest, assuring the harmonious coordination of an enormous number of independent decisions.

Like Rousseau and Hobbes, Smith appreciated the extent to which social intercourse in the modern world involves the interaction of strangers. "In civilized society," Smith writes, "a man stands in need of the cooperation and assistance of great multitudes, while his whole life is scarce sufficient to gain the friendship of a few persons."[15] But whereas Rousseau sought to turn strangers into citizens bound together by ties of loyalty and patriotism; and whereas Hobbes aimed to convince them that their vital interests were best served by submitting to the will of Leviathan; Smith argued that the endeavors of self-regarding strangers were already being effectively organized, without any supervening agency, by a market system that emerged spontaneously from man's propensity to "truck and barter." In Smith's view, neither the tender hand of benevolence, nor the heavy hand of the state is capable of harmonizing the social intercourse of strangers. But neither is necessary, except at the margins, because the market mechanism can organize into a coherent whole the self-regarding choices of millions of strangers—choices undertaken (in principle at least) in a universal equality of freedom constrained only by the freedom of others.

Opaque Goods, Emile's Dinner, and the Limits of Reputation

Smith thought the propensity to "truck and barter" was deeply rooted in human nature, that the haggling of the bazaar was in our bones. Rousseau, who separated himself from the rest of humankind on so many matters, took no such pleasure in trading.

> One must bargain and purchase and often be cheated, paying dear for poor services. I want an article of quality; but my money is sure to obtain a poor one. I pay a lot for a new laid egg and it proves stale; for a ripe fruit, and it is green; for a girl, and she is debauched. I enjoy a good wine, but where can I get it? At a wine merchant's? Notwithstanding all my precautions, he will poison me.[16]

Jean Starobinski regards Rousseau's distaste for the marketplace as another instance of his general disdain for intermediaries, in this case for the merchants who stand between Rousseau's desires and the goods that would satisfy them.[17] Bertil Friden offers a different interpretation, suggesting that Rousseau's disinclination to "truck and barter" was a rational response to the problem of "asymmetric information."[18] The merchants depicted in the *Confessions* know their wares, but Rousseau does not. Uncertain about the quality of commodities offered for sale,

Rousseau is open to disappointment, even exploitation. A prudent response to repeated mistreatment of this kind is to withdraw from the interactions that give rise to it!

Rousseau's exaggerated complaints draw attention to some of the neglected risks inherent in market transactions. To purchase a commodity, a bottle of wine, say, is to take a gamble. Even the wine connoisseur cannot be sure her purchase will yield the expected pleasure. When the quality of a good is not immediately transparent, the buyer who wishes to avoid dissatisfaction must take the time and trouble necessary to discern its real character before making a purchase. For some goods, such as houses, land that is faraway, and secondhand equipment, these information costs can be substantial. Moreover, whether the prospective buyer discovers a defect or not, she incurs a cost that is not included in the price of the good, itself. If, after acquiring information about a commodity's attributes, the buyer still wishes to purchase it, but is unwilling to pay the seller's asking price, she may then decide to incur the costs involved in bargaining with the seller, that is, the time required for negotiation, the anxiety bargaining creates for many people, and so on. And, even after all of this painstaking preparation, there is still no guarantee the buyer's efforts will culminate in a successful trade, either because the buyer and seller cannot settle upon a mutually agreeable price, or because, having acquired the good, the buyer finds that, despite her careful scrutiny, it still does not fulfill her expectations.

In order for an exchange to be advantageous for the buyer, it is not sufficient that the anticipated benefit derived from the good merely exceed its sales price. Rather, the expected benefit must exceed the sum of the good's price, plus any "search costs" incurred in learning about the quality of the good, plus any bargaining costs incurred in reaching a mutually agreeable exchange. Rousseau puts the problem this way: "Suppose I insist on getting what I want. What trouble and embarrassment I must put myself to! I must use my friends and correspondents, give orders, write, go hither and thither, wait; and often I shall be cheated in the end."[19] Of course it is possible to avoid information and bargaining costs altogether if one is willing to risk purchasing defective merchandise, to pay the seller's initial asking price, to accept whatever guarantee is offered, and so on. But this approach to trade, if practiced without exception, would only be prudent in a *transparent* economy, where the character of goods and those who sell them are immediately evident, and bargaining, insofar as it involves bluffing, is impossible.[20]

Emile's Dinner

In *Emile*, Rousseau's treatise on education, the tutor makes an important point about the difference between commodities produced for sale and goods produced for use at home. Wine provides the illustrative example for the tutor's instruction, and he begins by pouring a glass from his land-lord's vineyard and then a second glass from a bottle sold by a wine merchant. Next he adds an alkaline solution to each glass. At the bottom of the glass containing the merchant's wine a layer of lead becomes visible, and Emile is told that wine produced for sale "is rarely free of lead," which is added to counteract the wine's acidity, disguising its poor quality.

To reinforce the lesson, the tutor carefully explains the local origins of a wonderful feast that has been prepared for Emile:

> The white bread that you like so much comes from the wheat har-vested by this peasant. His wine, dark and crude but thirst-quenching and healthy, comes from his vineyards. His clothes come from his hemp, which his wife, daughters and servants spin during the win-ter. The dishes on his tables are prepared by no one outside his own family. The nearest mill and the nearest market are the limits of his world.[21]

The point of Rousseau's pedagogy, apart from its affirmation of self-reliance, is that the quality of goods produced "close to home" is invariably higher than the quality of goods produced by strangers for sale in distant markets. In production for home-use or for trade with neighboring farmers, there is neither the incentive, nor the opportunity, for duplicity. What is gained by making shoddy things for one's family, friends, or neighbors? In producing goods for unknown buyers in faraway markets, by contrast, both the motive and the means of misrepresentation are present. Cutting corners saves time and money, and disappointed buyers will often find it difficult to trace the origin of goods that pass through many hands before the final purchase.

Emile's instruction suggests that Rousseau favored self-sufficiency not only as a means of avoiding psychological dependence—"living in the opinion of others"—but also as a way of avoiding the risks and uncertainty inherent in trading. The trouble with goods produced for sale is not that they are produced by others, but that the producer knows more about the quality of his goods than does the buyer. Whatever the hardships involved in producing the means required for one's own existence, there are no problems of asymmetric information, hence, no need to trouble oneself with the motives and strategies of other traders. In Starobinski's gloss, economic success for Rousseau "consists in meeting all local needs without producing a surplus that might necessitate recourse to sale and exchange, those twin clouds hovering on the horizon of transparency."[22]

The Limits of Reputation

The proponent of unfettered markets will object to Rousseau's criticism on the grounds that dishonest merchants will not remain in business for long because their customers will abandon them in favor of competitors with a reputation for integrity.[23] The logic of this argument has been illustrated by characterizing a two-party exchange as a prisoner's dilemma game in which each trader has a choice between following through on his part of the bargain (cooperating) or not (defecting). If trade is a one-time event, then the dominant strategy is to renege on one's promise to deliver the goods, in which case no mutually advantageous exchange takes place. If, however, trade is an ongoing affair between two parties, then each party will find it advantageous to fulfill his commitments provided the other party does so as well. By adopting a strategy of conditional cooperation, traders can continue trading for mutual benefit. This reasoning has also been extended to the case of multilateral exchange among many traders. In a large market where there is continuous exchange among numerous traders who communicate with one another, it pays to fulfill one's commitments because, even though one may never encounter the same trader twice, a reputation for integrity is necessary in order to maintain and expand one's trading opportunities within the trading network.[24]

The outline of this argument can be found in Smith's *Lectures on Jurisprudence*: "Whenever dealings are frequent, a man does not expect to gain so much by any one contract as by probity and punctuality in the whole, and a prudent dealer, who is sensible of his real interest, would rather choose to lose what he has a right to than give any ground for suspicion."[25] Smith goes on to claim that the high frequency of exchange and the importance of reputation bring a unique kind of moral order to the interactions of self-regarding agents. "When the greater part of people are merchants," Smith writes, "they always bring probity and punctuality into fashion, and these are the principal virtues of commercial nations."[26]

This line of reasoning depends on two premises rarely acknowledged by its proponents: (1) it is a straightforward matter as to whether a commitment has been fulfilled or not; and (2) every trader's reputation is an accurate reflection of whether he or she has honored past commitments. It is precisely this cheery view of commerce that Rousseau challenges, claiming that reputation is the medium, not of transparency, but of opacity, so that "we never know with whom we have to deal."[27]

Rousseau's complaint is of course exaggerated. It is not as though a merchant's honest dealing counts for nothing in the formation of her reputation. And not everyone is as easily duped as Rousseau believed himself to be. Nevertheless, the judgments required in order to determine whether an agreement has been kept are, by no means, always clear cut.[28] Disputes about the quality of goods, the scope of warranties, the promised time of delivery, and many other conditions of sale are commonplace. If we include labor in the list of items exchanged, then the worker's level of effort, as well as the working conditions agreed to by management, may also become issues of dispute. And if we add a financial market, then the quality of a borrower's balance sheet, as well as the terms of a lender's promised line of credit, may come into question. These ambiguities cloud the issue of whether commitments have been honored or not and thereby threaten the viability of conditional cooperation, which requires a clear and faithful account of past behavior. Without an accurate record of the traders' deeds—without transparency—the logic of reputation cannot accomplish the task of transforming unreliable peddlers into trustworthy merchants.[29]

A true accounting of past deeds is not only confounded by the ambiguity of social intercourse, it is also frustrated by the motives of the market participants themselves. If the pursuit of a good reputation is going to weed out untrustworthy traders in large markets, then honest traders must be willing to take the time and trouble necessary to convey their trading experience to others. Yet while traders in general may prefer the greater transparency that would be brought about by such a collective monitoring effort, the rational course of action for each individual trader is to free ride on the reporting efforts of others, in which case there will be little monitoring, and, thus, little light shed upon opaque markets by this kind of collective surveillance.

Even if we ignore the foregoing collective action problem, a further impediment awaits the market participant who does not wish to be hoodwinked. If monitoring is to be effective, then the monitors (buyers in this case) must give an honest account of the quality of the goods they have purchased. Yet such an account will not be forthcoming from the sort of people who are portrayed in Rousseau's *Confessions* and *Discourses*, for their judgments, rather than being based on the real value of the goods, themselves, will instead be calculated to protect, or enhance, the social standing of the person offering the opinion. If a buyer has been duped by a merchant, she risks a diminished stature by admitting it. Moreover, her relative position can be improved if others are duped, which furnishes an additional motive for falsifying her trading experience.[30]

Once reputation enters into the decision calculus of buyers and sellers, the market loses its impersonal character because prices alone no longer convey all of the information that is necessary for rational decision making. Instead of comparing the costs of different goods and choosing the combination that maximizes one's benefits or minimizes one's costs, the market participant is drawn into a strategic environment where she must assess the credibility of her potential trading partners, while at the same time polishing her own reputation. If there were no chasm between appearance and reality, "if the maxims we professed were the rules of our conduct," then we could go about our business without having to decipher the hidden motives of other traders, or being compelled by prudence to consider how our own dealings might be judged or misjudged.[31] But when deeds can be easily misconstrued, traders must take extra care in managing their affairs, and the marketplace begins to look less like Smith's cornucopia of trading opportunities, which liberates traders from dependence on any one buyer or seller, and more like an exacting order in which, like it or not, every trader's livelihood demands that he or she "live in the opinion of others."

Ironically, the possession of a good reputation, *even if it is well-earned*, is inconsistent with the conditions necessary for perfectly competitive markets.[32] Under perfect competition, firms must be small, numerous, and indistinguishable; in short, they must have no identity. If, by contrast, firms stand out from one another, and if buyers consider a firm's reputation in their purchase decisions, then businesses with a good name will have market power, that is, they will have some discretion in pricing their products. Such freedom of maneuver violates one of the essential conditions of perfect competition, viz. the requirement that all firms must sell at prevailing market prices.[33] Put somewhat differently, maintaining a good reputation can only be an effective incentive if it provides the business owner with extra profits (economic rent), which means that prices exceed marginal costs, a circumstance that is inconsistent with the formal model of Smith's market economy.[34]

Let me stress two points in summary. First, while reputation doubtlessly plays a role in limiting misrepresentation, its full effectiveness depends on conditions that are only partially satisfied in real markets.

Accurate information about the quality of goods and merchants is often hard to come by, and collective monitoring efforts are subject to free riding. Moreover, when information about the quality of goods and the merchants who sell them is conveyed by buyers who are preoccupied with their social status, its contribution to market transparency will be limited. Second, the importance of reputation in creating trading opportunities introduces a strategic element into the trader's decision problem, which is at odds with the market's impersonal price system. Perfectly competitive markets require anonymous, price-taking agents and are incompatible with the presence of firms and individuals whose reputation grants them market power.

Unraveling Markets

To develop the general implications of Rousseau's complaints, I am going to describe a hypothetical, and admittedly far-fetched, scenario in which a perfectly transparent market becomes completely opaque, that is, when the quality of goods offered for sale, once known with certainty, can no longer be ascertained by prospective buyers at a cost that justifies the effort. To begin, imagine a perfectly transparent wine market in which two qualities of wine are sold: a low-quality wine that sells for five dollars per bottle and a high-quality wine that sells for fifteen dollars per bottle. Next, assume that it is less costly to produce the low-quality wine than the high-quality wine and that, at the prices of five and fifteen dollars per bottle, the suppliers of low- and high-quality wine, respectively, earn a rate of profit that is just sufficient to induce them to remain in business. Given the assumption of transparency, consumers willing to pay for the high-quality wine will get exactly what they expect, and consumers interested in the lower priced, lower quality wine will get exactly what they expect.

Now let us suppose that, all at once, the wine market becomes opaque so that it is impossible for buyers to differentiate between the two qualities of wine before purchase. Given the (now) uncertain quality of wine, it is reasonable to assume that few, if any, wine consumers will offer to pay as much as fifteen dollars for a bottle of wine of unknown quality. For simplicity, suppose that the price of a bottle of wine, which may be of high- or low-quality, temporarily settles at a price of ten dollars. (For my purpose, it is only necessary for the price to settle at less than fifteen dollars per bottle.) Although the producers of high-quality wine may be willing to sell the wine they have on hand for ten dollars per bottle, they will not produce any new bottles of wine because, given our assumptions, it is not profitable to do so at a sales price below fifteen dollars per bottle. The producers of the low-quality wine, on the other hand, will expand production at any price above five dollars per bottle. As the high-quality wine disappears from the market, and as more low-quality wine is supplied to the market, the average quality of wine will diminish. As wine consumers come to recognize this reduction in average quality, they will reduce the price they are willing to pay. In the long run, only the lower quality wine will be produced, and competition among the producers of low-quality wine will drive its price back down to the original price of five dollars per bottle.[35]

To summarize the results of our thought experiment: when the quality of wine was transparent, every mutually advantageous exchange between wine producers and wine consumers could be exploited. The wine connoisseurs and the better vineyards were able to trade at a price of fifteen dollars per bottle of (high-quality) wine, while the non-connoisseurs and the lower caliber vineyards were able to enjoy mutual benefits at a price of five dollars per bottle of (low-quality) wine. But when the quality of a bottle of wine could no longer be ascertained before purchase, prices and quality spiraled downwards, as wine connoisseurs and their high-grade suppliers could not find one another in the darkness. Thus, the wine market unraveled until only the producers and consumers of low-quality wine found it worthwhile to continue trading.

This process of unraveling does not depend on there being only two qualities of wine. The same sort of market contraction would occur if there were many different qualities of wine, provided that consumers could not distinguish among them before purchase, and that the cost of producing wine increased with the quality of wine produced. Under these conditions, the lowest quality wine will drive out, not only the highest quality wine, but all qualities in between. The point which bears emphasis, and which does not require that there be an actual transition from a transparent to an opaque market, is that *the scope of mutually advantageous exchange can be sharply circumscribed when the quality of goods is opaque.*[36] Although we have reached this conclusion by a consideration of the limiting case in which the quality of particular goods (individual bottles of wine in our example) is completely opaque, we shall see later that whenever one party to a trade has more information than the other, or is even assumed to have such an informational advantage, the market cannot allocate resources in the efficient manner promised by its advocates.

There is another aspect of our unraveling wine market that deserves emphasis. In a transparent market, each producer is held accountable for the quality of goods he or she offers for sale. A high-caliber vineyard that tried to increase its profits by selling a less costly, lower quality of wine for the price of a high-quality wine would suffer the consequences of holding unsold inventory. People will not pay high prices for goods they know to be of poor quality. In an opaque market, by contrast, a winemaker who thrusts low-quality wine upon the market will *not* bear the full consequences of his decision because his decision to sell low-quality wine will affect the average quality of wine on the market, and it is the average quality of goods that forms the basis of decision making in opaque markets. In effect, decisions taken in opaque markets create "information externalities," which influence the terms of trade for everyone. Moreover, as we have seen, these "information externalities" ramify throughout opaque economies, impeding mutually advantageous trade, and constraining the invisible hand's smooth conversion of "private vices" into "public benefits."

Signaling

Our imaginary wine market dealt with the limiting cases of perfect transparency and complete opacity. In the imagined transition between the two, the lower quality wine drove the higher quality wine out of the market. In the real world, by contrast, high-caliber vineyards would not passively accept this outcome, but would take measures to differentiate their wines from lesser wines, putting the chateau's name on the label, disseminating favorable wine reviews, conducting advertising campaigns, and so on. This sort of "signaling" is commonly undertaken by market participants looking for trading partners: manufacturers offer product warranties, job seekers come with favorable references in hand, and entrepreneurs provide prospective investors with promising market analyses.

In Rousseau's view, such "signaling" is not inspired by a desire for transparent exchange, but belongs to the extensive web of mutual deceit called civil society. If we recall Smith's most famous proposition from *The Wealth of Nations*, which reads, "it is not from the benevolence of the butcher, the brewer, or the baker that we expect our dinner, but from their regard to their own interests," then we have reason to believe that Smith, too, would have regarded "signaling" as one of the many market activities that is driven by the pervasive motive of self-interest.[37]

Of course the signaling strategy that is most advantageous *from this perspective* is not necessarily the signaling strategy that conveys to other market participants the real value of the goods or services one has to offer; it is the signal, true or false, that promises the greatest gain.

Consider, in this light, Smith's precept that a man is "more likely to prevail" in gaining the assistance of others "if he can interest their self-love in his favor, and show them that it is for their own advantage to do for him what he requires of them."[38] In this passage, which immediately precedes the more famous one cited earlier, Smith leaves the impression that there is no duplicity involved in such persuasion, that a mutual interest does, in fact, exist and need only be made transparent to the other party.[39] By contrast, Rousseau, who was more attentive to the possibilities of deception, claims that in civil society each person is "perpetually employed in getting others to interest themselves in his lot, and in making them, *apparently at least*, if not really, find their advantage in promoting his own."[40] The essential thing in advancing one's interest is not, after all, the actual existence of a mutual interest, but the other person's *belief* in this common interest. Granted, the task of inducing others to believe in a shared interest will be much easier if one has acquired a reputation for integrity; only fools enter into agreements with people known to be untrustworthy. But here, too, a good *reputation*, regardless of its authenticity, is what really counts.

In a market pervaded by this kind of artifice, one cannot expect to find trading partners by simply announcing to the world that she has valuable goods for sale, as every other trader will be making the same claim! If the owner of quality goods wishes to profit from trade, she must find a means of differentiating her goods from the goods offered by others, and she must do so in a market environment where there is a lot of noise.

What is the significance of this imperative for the workings of a market economy? Let us return to Adam Smith's claim that markets enhance social welfare even though traders are moved exclusively by their own interests. This contention, which we may designate as the "realist" argument in favor of markets, has been supplemented by Smith's successors, who insist that markets are also "informationally efficient," that is, that market prices furnish all the information necessary for rational decision making.[41] In opposition to this view, there is a growing body of economists who argue that these two attributes of a market economy—traders moved exclusively by self-interest and an informationally efficient price system—are in conflict with one another.[42] The trouble is that self-interested agents will not always find it advantageous to convey all they know about matters pertaining to a transaction or contractual agreement, nor can they be counted on to follow through on commitments the fulfillment of which is not easily verified. Two contemporary economists have characterized the change in orientation that has been brought about by a deeper appreciation of opaque markets as follows: "When, instead of traders in the marketplace exchanging homogenous goods and money of costlessly verifiable quality, one looked at agents trading in the face of monitoring costs and asymmetric information, the presumption that the trader would faithfully fulfill his part in an agreed exchange could no longer be maintained."[43]

Simply put, there are market participants with valuable resources who wish to convey this information to others, and there are market participants without such resources who wish to conceal this information from others.[44] Moreover, the strategic problem of deciding what information to communicate to others is made more pressing by the fact that, in peddling one's wares, a trader is nearly always competing against rivals inasmuch as his prospective trading partners will compare his offer against the offers advertised by others. Consequently, the gains of those who are successful in this contest come at the expense of those who are unsuccessful because the information (or what is accepted as such) that establishes the greater worth of some offers simultaneously establishes the lesser worth of others. Traders may be drawn to the marketplace by their propensity to "truck and barter," but the contest that takes place between them does not always resemble the honest competition portrayed in the textbooks, where the quality of goods and services is transparent, and prices are determined by the impersonal forces of supply and demand. There is, in addition to the Smithian search for mutual advantage, a Rousseauean struggle in which individuals contrive to reveal or conceal the true value of their assets, a struggle for relative advantage that will determine each person's position within the distribution of wealth and income and all of the prerogatives and deprivations that follow from it.[45]

Capitalist Authority and the Division of Labor

Adam Smith laid great stress on the progressive division of labor in raising productivity and output. Let us take a closer look at this development from the Rousseauean perspective we have been constructing. It is helpful, albeit somewhat artificial, to split the division of labor into two phases. In the first phase, small-scale producers specialize in the production of those goods for which they have a comparative advantage, a development made possible by the emergence of markets in which each specialized producer can exchange the goods she excels at making for goods that are more efficiently produced by others. In the second phase of the division of labor, the ongoing expansion of markets makes possible a higher degree of specialization, as well as the exploitation of economies of scale both of which are undertaken by entrepreneurs who organize the productive efforts of many workers within large enterprises. We have already discussed some of the difficulties that arise in the initial phase of the division of labor when the quality of goods is less than fully transparent. Let us now consider some of the problems that emerge in the second phase of specialization, when entrepreneurs confront the problem of assembling a workforce of laborers whose individual productivity is often difficult to ascertain.

To begin, suppose that production involves teamwork and that it is difficult to measure each team member's contribution to total output. Insofar as the work is arduous, individual members of the team will be tempted to shirk their responsibilities, secretly free riding on the efforts of other team members. If every team member chooses to shirk, however, their enterprise will eventually go bankrupt, and the team members will have to undertake the costly search for new employment. How can the workers overcome this collective action problem? One alternative is to hire a manager who specializes in monitoring the level of effort put forth by workers and to grant this manager the authority to fire unproductive team members. This solves the problem of slacking workers, but creates a new difficulty: who will keep tabs on the manager? "Who will monitor the monitor?"[46]

According to one school of economists impressed by Smith's stress on self-interested motives, this potentially infinite regress can only be circumvented if there is an owner of the enterprise whose claim on its net income (profit) creates a powerful incentive to manage the enterprise efficiently, thereby obviating the need for further monitoring.[47] From the vantage point of the hard-headed realist, the individual (or small group) that is ultimately responsible for hiring and firing employees must have an immediate and substantial interest in the success of the enterprise if the propensity for shirking is to be held in check, and "the monitoring of monitors" is to be brought to a close without resort to motives that go beyond self-interest. In this chain of reasoning, we can make out the Hobbesian logic according to which self-regarding free agents— workers with a propensity for shirking in this instance—find it prudent to submit to a centralized authority who will bring order and discipline to their otherwise self-defeating endeavors. Like Hobbes's Leviathan state, the capitalist firm, in this account, emerges from individuals' rational desire to avoid the adverse consequences of unfettered self-seeking in circumstances where compliance with promises of cooperation cannot be taken for granted.

It is worth emphasizing that an employment contract is, indeed, one in which the employee agrees to accept the employer's *authority* in the workplace.[48] In this respect, the employment contract differs from a contract to purchase a commodity, for the relationship between the employer and the employee is no longer a market relation, but an authority relation, albeit one of limited scope and duration. Although I have stressed that, according to some of Smith's contemporary followers, the exploitation of scale economies with a complex division of labor requires capitalist authority to solve the monitoring problem, the centralization of productive activities within the factory, *itself*, facilitates the monitoring of the employees' work effort. One of the important advantages Smith found in the organization of the factory is that it makes possible the surveillance of workers who, if they are not concentrated in a single place and around a single task, acquire a "habit of sauntering" and "indolent careless application."[49] Like the sometimes wayward citizens of Rousseau's republic, whose conduct cannot be allowed to "escape the notice and judgment of the public," so, too, the workers who toil in Smith's pin factory are denied the privacy in which they might enjoy the pleasures of indolence.[50]

The authority system of the factory is not, of course, on par with that of the feudal manor which preceded it. In Smith's conception, the competition between capitalists (monitors), coupled with the worker's freedom to quit, limits the control the owner can exercise over his employees. Without transparency, however, the competition among employers for the services of workers is greatly attenuated. If one firm offers the employee of another firm a higher wage or better working conditions, the firm making the offer has reason to expect that the employee's current firm will either match its offer if the employee "is worth it," or will let the employee go if she "is not worth it." Given these potential outcomes, the firm that is thinking about making the offer may well have second thoughts because the employee's present employer is in a much better position to know the worker's skills and traits. The general effect of such asymmetric information, and the kind of reasoning to which it gives rise, is to constrain the competition for workers, thereby weakening the bargaining power of employees.

In addition to this bargaining disadvantage, each worker in a firm only has the power to terminate *his own* contract and "leave the team," whereas the owner has several alternatives from which to choose. Thus, the owner can terminate the employment of *any* team member, employ new team members, or sell the right to the team's income.[51] There is, in short, a significant imbalance in the relationship between the employer and the employee, and it originates in the opaque conditions created by the division of labor wherein unmonitored workers, who have both the motive and opportunity to free ride on the efforts of their coworkers, require an authority who will monitor and, if necessary, compel their industriousness, preventing each one from harming the rest.

The collective action problem facing a team of workers without a supervising authority is analogous to the problem of free-riding citizens in a republican state, which Rousseau proposed to address by encouraging citizens to keep close tabs on one another. Although Rousseau did not specifically address the difficulties confronting a worker's cooperative, such a cooperative association could mitigate the problem of shirking by imposing the republican discipline of mutual surveillance. In fact, given their close proximity to one another and some measure of solidarity, it is not unreasonable to suppose that suitably motivated workers could out-perform managers in maintaining a high level of effort. But to the extent that the members of the cooperative continue to be tempted by the pri-vate benefits of free riding, slacking off or shirking their monitoring responsibilities, the prospects for effective cooperation will diminish as the number of workers in the cooperative increases. If there were only four workers in the cooperative, then each member's share of the group's proceeds might be sufficient to induce a productive work effort. But if there were one hundred members, the cost of any one member's shirking would be borne almost entirely by the other members of the cooperative, hence the appeal of free riding would be much greater. In order to take advantage of scale economies, therefore, the members of a labor cooperative must behave like citizens, working for the common good instead of advancing their private interests.[52] Otherwise, the coop-erative will not be able to compete with firms like Smith's pin factory, which is organized to run efficiently without recourse to the more demanding imperatives of the general will.

For egalitarians who do not share Rousseau's commitment to small-scale, self-sufficient farming, the stakes in this imaginary contest between worker cooperatives and capitalist firms are especially high. If the effec-tive supervision and monitoring of workers can only be accomplished by owners who have an incentive to perform these tasks efficiently, then the capitalist firm will be the most productive form of organization. Moreover, a high concentration of *wealth* will also be more efficient than a more egalitarian distribution, for, unless the ownership of productive enterprise is concentrated in relatively few hands, profits will be too widely dispersed to provide the owners sufficient inducement to keep tabs on their managers.[53] According to the Hobbesian theory of capitalist authority we have been articulating, the large-scale organizations formed to exploit the progressive division of labor also create opaque niches in which employees can enjoy the pleasures of indolence. If workers renounce these pleasures and establish a regime of mutual surveillance to prevent backsliding, then egalitarian forms of enterprise can be at least as productive as more hierarchical forms of enterprise. But if workers lack the necessary self-discipline, then egalitarians must either forego effective control over large-scale enterprise or forswear large-scale production altogether.

Separating, Pooling, and Sharing

Under opaque conditions, the connection between contribution and reward is broken, and the costs of slacking, along with many other kinds of duplicity, are borne by others. If Smith's market system is to effectively channel the pursuit of self-interest for social benefit, then incomes must be closely tied to productive contribution. Yet while transparency promotes productivity by linking compensation to performance and holding each market participant strictly accountable, transparency does not always serve the cause of fairness.

As John Rawls has reminded us, luck has a lot to do with an individual's productive capacities, not to mention many other aspects of a person's life chances. An individual's health risks, for example, are determined in substantial measure by how he or she fares in nature's genetic lottery. To see how transparency can become an obstacle to fairness, suppose that health insurance companies had complete information about every person's genetically determined health risks (a possibility that grows closer by day). Under these circumstances, insurers would separate individuals into different risk categories and offer insurance coverage at premiums that reflected the risk differences across categories. Economists call this a "separating equilibrium" because, when insurers have information about individual health risks, they can separate, or peel away, customers from any competitor that pools low- and high-risk individuals together under the same policy premium.[54] Although transparency produces an efficient outcome in this case, allowing premiums to precisely reflect risks, one is hard-pressed to say it results in a fair allocation of insurance costs, since each person's premium depends on his or her genetic endowments. The lucky ones will pay low insurance rates, and the unlucky ones will pay high rates. It is precisely this kind of undeserved advantage that Rawls wishes to eliminate by means of his "veil of ignorance," which compels the parties in Rawls's original position to choose principles of justice without knowledge of their genetic fortunes among other things.[55]

Although opacity can be an obstacle to effective cooperation in an enterprise, it does facilitate other kinds of social cooperation, such as community risk-pooling. It was during Rousseau's time, when Condorcet and other mathematicians were making great strides in the theory of probability, that the modern theory of risk and insurance came into being.[56] To summarize with extreme brevity, the French probability theorists demonstrated that individuals can effectively pool risks as long as the adverse outcomes to be insured against are independent of one another (i.e., uncorrelated). Thus, a large group of individuals can provide themselves with health insurance if they are unlikely to suffer serious illness at the same time and all agree to come to the aid of those who do suffer ill health. Even purely self-regarding agents will find it advantageous to share the costs of insurance provided they are risk-averse and do not know whether their level of risk is high or low compared with others in the insurance pool. Under these (opaque) conditions, which resemble the circumstances modeled by Rawls's veil of ignorance, people can effectively pool their risks—sharing one another's fate—despite the fact that each person is exclusively concerned with her own fate.[57]

This kind of risk-pooling arrangement will not work, however, if individuals are aware of their own risks, and everyone is offered health insurance at a uniform premium. In this case, people with low health risks will decline to purchase insurance at premiums designed to recover average medical costs. When these low-risk policyholders leave the insurance pool, the existing premiums will not be sufficient to cover the medical costs of the remaining subscribers and, hence, must be raised. But at a higher premium, some additional lower-risk individuals will decline to buy insurance, which will push the per capita medical costs of the covered population still higher. This process of "adverse selection" will thereby limit the extent of mutually advantageous insurance contracts.[58]

In a transparent economy, some costs will only be shared equally if those citizens whose natural assets confer market advantages are willing to combine their assets with the less valuable assets of their fellow citizens. Although opaque economies have many disadvantages, they do make possible egalitarian forms of insurance in which self-regarding individuals find it rational to pool risks across the entire citizenry.[59] When a real-world veil of uncertainty leads rational agents to contemplate the many kinds of misfortune a person might endure, the advantages of risk-pooling are compelling. But when the probable trajectory of each person's life is clearly in view, the pursuit of self-interest is no longer compatible with the sharing of life's misfortunes. If everyone's assets and liabilities are transparent, to themselves and to others, only the general will—the renunciation of private advantage—can move individuals to share one another's fate.[60]

Although the egalitarian sharing of adversity requires will-power sufficient to constrain the pursuit of narrow self-interest, citizens who posses the requisite self-discipline can take advantage of certain kinds of insurance that are unavailable to people moved by purely self-regarding ambitions. Some forms of risk-sharing are impractical because of "moral hazard," the evocative term that was invented to characterize those circumstances in which an insured person can act in ways that increase the insurer's risk without the insurer's knowledge. For example, consider the public grain storehouse Rousseau proposed in order to insure farmers against poor grain harvests.[61] In bad years, farmers could draw on the public stocks, which would be replenished in good years. Such an arrangement would provide social insurance against famine and other harvest-related calamities. This system would not be effective over the long run, however, if farmers were to reduce their exertion in anticipation of drawing upon the public stocks. The greater the farmers' reliance on the public reserve, the sooner it would be exhausted.

There are two solutions to this problem. First, the farmers could monitor one another's efforts, thereby eliminating the possibility of free riding. Second, each farmer could act to advance the common good instead of "gaming the system." More generally, the problem of moral hazard can be eliminated if irresponsible conduct is easily detected, or if those covered by the insurance scheme can be trusted to behave responsibly. In this respect, Rousseau's citizens are doubly blessed: their republic allows no room for the opaque niches that make cheating possible, and, unless corrupted by the temptations of private advantage, they possess the self-discipline necessary to refrain from acting in ways that undermine the system of risk-sharing. Republican citizens are thus able to pool risks that would be uninsurable in societies committed to privacy and the pursuit of self-interest.[62] Granted, a political community in which the more favored citizens willingly pooled risks with the less favored is only conceivable if citizens share a common identity, or are moved by the needs of the less advantaged, or, in Rawls's formulation, regard their genetic gifts as a collective asset and their genetic misfortunes as a collective liability. Nevertheless, if risk-sharing were to be carried out on a massive scale, then we might plausibly imagine, as a prominent theorist of "macro insurance markets" speculates, that "people will see a symbol of reciprocity that is lacking today."[63]

Permanent Inequality and the Logic of Asymmetric Information

Adam Smith's confidence in a relentless wave of economic progress that would lift the poor from their destitution diverged sharply from Rousseau's much more pessimistic outlook. In place of Smith's inexorable advance, which promised to liberate humankind from the bonds of material subsistence, Rousseau beheld the permanent division of society into classes, the poor and the weak dominated by the rich and powerful in ways that could not be easily undone. While Smith was bringing to light the role of the market in expanding the range of choices open to ordinary people, Rousseau had begun to disclose some of the structural features of a market economy that give rise to sharp inequalities of wealth and income.

Rousseau observed that in commercial societies "money is the seed of money," and the first franc is "sometimes more difficult to acquire than the second million."[64] This view is not far removed from Smith's own observation that a man must possess "stock sufficient to maintain him for months or years" before he can invest in tools, land, and materials that will increase his productivity. In the absence of the required savings, a man's income will be "derived from his labor only," this circumstance being "the state of the greater part of the laboring poor in all countries."[65]

Since the purpose of banks, and of the capital markets in general, is to transfer resources from those who possess capital (savers/lenders) to those who can utilize it (borrowers), one might reasonably expect that anyone whose prospects were promising, including ordinary laborers, could acquire productivity-enhancing capital. And, indeed, if the character and wherewithal of potential borrowers could be easily ascertained—if the loan market were *transparent* in other words—credit would be allocated solely on the basis of the borrower's prospects for repayment. Anyone whose income could be increased with the help of investment capital could borrow against future earnings as long as they were known to keep their commitments.[66]

In real-world capital markets, none of which are fully transparent, banks are not inclined to lend to "fringe borrowers" because their creditworthiness cannot be ascertained at low cost.[67] When the repayment of loans is not costlessly enforceable, and borrowers know more about their prospects for success than lenders, banks will require detailed credit histories, collateral, down payments, and other assurances before they are willing to lend. Although such conditions are imposed in the belief that the required collateral will only be forthcoming for the most promising endeavors, their effect is nevertheless to restrict investment opportunities to borrowers who already possess at least a modicum of wealth.

Individuals who own valuable assets are doubly advantaged because, in opaque loan markets, their wealth also provides them favored access to credit. Consequently, they are in a position to undertake projects that require a substantial investment before any income is forthcoming, such as a career in the professions or the launching of a new business. The poor, by contrast, lack the assets necessary to gain entry to the credit market, thus they cannot borrow to finance investment in human, or other forms of, capital. Hence, they remain poor. Reflecting on the many causes of social inequality, Rousseau observed that credit had become "a great instrument of acquisition," but "was inaccessible to those who had nothing."[68] In modern parlance, "it takes money to make money."

The proponent of free markets may object to this contention, advancing Smith's argument that competition among banks "obliges all bankers to be more liberal in their dealings with their customers."[69] Rather than denying credit to borrowers with little wealth, banks will simply charge them higher rates of interest based on their (putatively) greater risk of default. However, this argument fails to take account of the significance of asymmetric information in the loan market in which borrowers know more about their prospects for repayment than lenders. Under these opaque circumstances, the problem of adverse selection is present, so that offers to lend at higher interest rates will attract a disproportionate number of high-risk borrowers whose likelihood of default rises even further *because* of high-interest costs. Knowing this, banks do not typically offer high-interest loans to high-risk borrowers (though "loan sharks" who have special means of forcing repayment sometimes do). Instead banks will ration credit at prevailing (lower) rates of interest, which reduces default losses, but, at the same time, denies credit to many borrowers who would be regarded as acceptable risks in a transparent capital market.

Opaque labor markets also tend to reinforce economic inequality. In a stratified society, skills will not be randomly distributed across the population. Rather, those belonging to privileged groups will convert their advantages into better-than-average productivity. Firms that find it too costly to determine an individual's productivity, but recognize a correlation between productivity and group membership, will find it profitable to hire workers who belong to especially productive (and identifiable) groups, a practice known as "statistical discrimination."[70] Prejudice is not a necessary condition for this practice; productivity differences across groups and the high cost of determining an individual's productive contribution are sufficient to maintain sharp inequalities in employment opportunity.[71]

In opaque labor markets, the competition between firms will not eliminate invidious forms of discrimination as some of Smith's followers have claimed.[72] According to their argument, firms will hire the most skilled workers available, regardless of their race, class, or gender because hiring the most productive workers at prevailing wages will maximize the firm's profits. But if the individual worker's productive potential is not transparent, and there are observable productivity differences across groups, firms may find it profitable to hire on the basis of group productivity even if management is unprejudiced.[73] And if individual workers who belong to disadvantaged groups believe their wages are based on the average productivity of their group rather than on their own productivity, they will have little incentive to exert high levels of effort or to invest in training and education. Consequently, the group's low productivity and low wages are self-reinforcing.

The role played by opaque labor and capital markets in generating inequalities of wealth and income lends support to Rousseau's view that the sharp disparity between rich and poor has little to do with differences in natural ability. In addition to tracing the origin and development of inequality to a constellation of circumstances that included the establishment of private property, the division of labor, and the loss of man's natural independence, Rousseau also had an intuition about the primary mechanism through which the powerful gain at the expense of the weak. Unlike many defenders of laissez faire, who implicitly assume that the benefits of exchange are divided more or less equitably between the trading parties, Rousseau regarded the terms of trade, not as the outcome of impersonal market forces, but as the consequence of hard bargaining, of a test of wills. Moreover, in negotiating an exchange, an individual's bargaining power does not depend solely on what he is capable of contributing to a cooperative undertaking, but also on how long he can "wait." In Rousseau's account, "it is always the less eager party who dictates to the other."[74] Beneath the haggling over prices in Smith's marketplace, there is a tug of war between those who can hold out for more favorable terms and those who run short of life's necessities and must accept whatever terms are offered.[75] Bearing in mind the credit constraints facing the less advantaged in opaque capital markets, and the obvious manner in which these constraints limit their ability to hold out for better terms, we can again see how the structure of opaque economies reinforces economic inequality.

Rousseau's anxieties about unequal exchange were most pronounced regarding "trade in agricultural products." If farmers were to hold their own in a "system of commerce," then "profits would have to be shared equally between the merchant and the tiller of the soil." But that, according to Rousseau, "is the very thing that cannot be; for the bargaining of the one [the merchant] being always free, and that of the other [the farmer] always forced, the former will always dictate to the latter a relationship which, by destroying the balance, cannot lead to a solid and permanent state of affairs."[76]

There are many contingencies that could diminish a person's capacity to hold out for better terms. For Rousseau's citizen-farmers, who must produce some goods for sale, if only to pay taxes, a bad harvest or a sharp decline in commodity prices could be the beginning of the end, as assets, even land, may have to be sold to meet financial obligations or other urgent needs. Rousseau stresses the point that when poor Corsicans could not pay their taxes, they were "stripped of their most necessary utensils, their furniture, their poultry," which were "sold at less than a tenth of the true value: with the result that, for lack of money, they paid the tax tenfold."[77] One of the purposes of the public grain stocks Rousseau advocated was to forestall the forced sale of farmers' limited assets. But, it may be added, a transparent capital market would serve the same purpose, allowing farmers to smooth out their income stream over good harvests and bad.

Once a segment of the community loses its independence, the gulf between the "haves" and the "have-nots" will widen through a dynamic, self-reinforcing process the essence of which is based on Rousseau's simple insight that the terms of trade are dictated by the party who can afford to hold out the longest. The logic runs as follows: the wealthier a man becomes, the longer he can hold out in bargaining; the longer he holds out, the more favorable terms he is able to command;

the more favorable his terms of exchange, the more wealth he acquires. This self-reinforcing process is symmetrical: the poorer a person becomes, the sooner her bargaining position collapses, the less she receives in exchange for her goods and services, and the poorer she becomes.[78] Eventually, "those who grow rich in commerce" invest "in landed properties which others cultivate for them; thus the whole nation finds itself divided into rich idlers, and wretched peasants, who starve while tilling it."[79]

Opaque Markets and the Invisible Hand:
The Critique Summarized

Beneath the chaotic surface of the marketplace, Adam Smith discovered a rational order in which countless decisions are efficiently coordinated "as if by an invisible hand." In Smith's conception, the system of market prices continuously transforms the self-centered choices of market participants into a mutually consistent scheme of action. Remarkably, the unfettered market economy is able to achieve this result even though no market participant intends it. It is not necessary for individuals to consider the effects of their choices on others because the social consequences of these choices are already reflected in the prices people pay for the goods and services they use.[80] Nor is it necessary for market participants to undertake any strategic reasoning, imagining how other agents might react to their decisions, because a competitive market, by definition, includes no agents powerful enough to affect the terms of trade. All that is required for rational decision making on the part of the consumer is a knowledge of his or her own needs and the relatively few prices bearing on their satisfaction. All that is required for rational decision making on the part of the producer is a knowledge of the costs of producing different outputs and the prices at which they can be sold. The market mechanism assures that the totality of these decisions will yield the greatest possible satisfaction given the constraint that all exchanges are voluntary.

Rousseau was impressed by a different aspect of trade and reached a less favorable judgment about the nature of exchange relations. When we trade, Rousseau complained, "we never know with whom we have to deal," for a person's reputation, assuming it is known to us, is not always a true reflection of his character. Rousseau attributed this condition, in large measure, to the size of the modern city and the duplicity of people who live entirely "in the opinion of others."

Although Smith gave less emphasis to deliberate deception, he, too, observed that in a market economy most trade takes place between strangers. But Smith denied that this lack of familiarity mattered. Quite the contrary, he counted as one of the market's great virtues its capacity to bring into harmonious equilibrium the decisions of millions of people who know nothing of one another.

The shortcomings of the market described above, which develop some of the implications of Rousseau's complaint that "we never know with whom we have to deal," show that Smith's invisible hand cannot achieve the perfectly efficient coordination of decisions if traders are opaque. The effective organization of economic activity by means of competitive markets requires transparency. If the price system is to accomplish its task, then it must be relatively easy for market participants to ascertain the quality and durability of goods offered for sale, the skill and energy of workers seeking employment, the prudence and wherewithal of borrowers applying for loans. Real-world economies do not fully satisfy these criteria: it is not always easy to identify faulty merchandise, indolent workers, reckless entrepreneurs, or unreliable borrowers. This seemingly inconsequential inconvenience—*that the qualities of goods and people are not immediately transparent*—impairs the functioning, and restricts the effective range, of Smith's invisible hand, which cannot perform its work effectively in darkness.[81]

In opaque economies, where costs must be incurred in order to determine the real attributes of goods and services, supplying others with goods of a desired quality is only one of several avenues for advancing one's interests. Alternatively, one may mislead, conceal, embellish, and dissemble, for, in Rousseau's view, "there is no legitimate profit so great that it cannot be greatly exceeded by what may be made illegitimately."[82] When markets lose their transparency, the trader's decision calculus becomes much more complicated than when prices supply all the information necessary for rational decision making. In opaque markets, traders must think strategically about what information to disclose to others and what knowledge to keep to themselves. And they must act with the understanding that others are also choosing, with an eye to *their* advantage, what to reveal and what to conceal.[83]

The consequences of these strategic requirements are not limited to the occasional disappointments of those who buy defective merchandise; they ramify throughout opaque economies. Uncertainty about the quality of goods favors the least reliable producer; resources are wasted in elaborate efforts to communicate one's value, real or contrived, to potential trading partners; firms successful in gaining a reputation for integrity also gain a degree of monopoly power; the feasible range of cooperation through enforceable contracts is constrained by the limited extent of commonly observed behavior; decisions often create information externalities the adverse consequences of which are ignored by self-interested traders; many kinds of insurance, which would allow people to pool risks, are foreclosed by adverse selection or moral hazard; inequalities of wealth and income are reinforced by opaque labor and capital markets, which allocate the best employment and training opportunities, and the most favorable terms of credit, to the most advantaged classes.

If human beings were transparent to one another, each person's real intentions plainly visible, everyone's private information disclosed just for the asking, then the pathologies of strategic interaction could give way to the impersonal rule of the price system. In reality, these pathologies, the bitter fruit of deception and defense against deception, are the cost that must be borne by rational agents with the ability to manage their public identity.

A Republic of Purses: The Limits of
Egalitarian Liberalism

There is a contemporary school of thought whose adherents, having assumed a vantage point alongside the impartial spectator described in Adam Smith's other great book, *The Theory of Moral Sentiments*, criticize the inequalities of income generated by competitive markets as unfair, unjust, or simply non-welfare maximizing.[84] One prominent strain of liberal thinking, impressed by the freedom of choice and economic efficiency claimed for competitive markets, favors an institutional arrangement in which resource allocation is left mainly to the invisible hand, while the state assumes the responsibility of achieving a more equitable distribution of income.[85] In this conception, government raises the living standards of the poor by taxing high-income households and making transfer payments to low-income households. Individuals remain free to choose their occupation, level of effort, rate of saving, and the like, while regulated markets continue to do the work of coordinating these choices in a more or less coherent fashion.

This is not the institutional arrangement favored by Rousseau, who was interested in a virtuous state rather than a welfare state; a state where "public affairs encroach on private in the minds of citizens"; a state where the legislator's task is to see to it that the fatherland is constantly before the eyes of its citizens, "in their laws, in their games, in their homes, in their mating, in their feasts"; a state where citizens do not have "an instant of free time that they could call their own."[86] Does the republic envisioned by Rousseau demand too much of its citizens? No doubt, but let us consider a question that is less frequently asked. Can the objectives of *egalitarian* liberalism be achieved in states where citizens are primarily, if not exclusively, concerned with "private business"?

From the Rousseauean perspective we have been developing, there are ample reasons for skepticism. Most importantly, the institutional design of the egalitarian liberal state is not "incentive compatible," to borrow an awkward term from information economics. It requires considerable optimism to suppose that citizens who devote all of their time and energy to private interests and pursuits will readily set these preoccupations aside on those occasions when they are called upon to make sacrifices for the common good.[87] The danger is that the wealthy will resist "confiscatory taxes," and the poor, if offered subsidies, may resist gainful employment.[88] As a consequence, progressive tax policies are apt to be under constant pressure from the privileged, while generous welfare benefits can erode the level of effort put forth by those who are eligible for public subsidies.

Some of the problematic aspects of the welfare state originate in the same circumstances that hamper the functioning of markets, in particular, the troublesome combination of self-interested motives and opaque conditions, which allow self-regarding agents to advance their private interests without worrying about how their decisions affect others. To appreciate these difficulties from our vantage point, it is useful to regard the welfare state as an extensive scheme of social insurance that pays benefits to citizens in adverse circumstances, for example, when a citizen becomes ill, is injured, loses a job, or cannot earn a living wage even if employed.[89] This arrangement, like private insurance, is subject to the problems of moral hazard and adverse selection. Thus, the more expansive the insurance coverage offered by the state, the weaker is the citizen's incentive to refrain from actions that reduce the likelihood of ill health, injury, joblessness, and poverty (the problem of moral hazard). And whenever tax rates are increased to fund additional benefits, after-tax incomes will fall, further tipping the balance of advantages against productive endeavor (the problem of adverse selection). If citizens choose to reduce their work effort, saving, or investment, the tax base will shrink, and tax rates will have to be raised in order to collect the same amount of revenue. These problems are compounded by "globalization" because, in a worldwide network of markets, firms and investors can more easily transfer their resources to states with lower tax rates and less extensive welfare benefits.[90]

Let me reiterate my theoretical point, which is that the combination of (1) citizens who make choices without regard to the wider consequences of their decisions; and (2) opaque circumstances, are necessary conditions for the presence of both moral hazard and adverse selection. The egalitarian liberal is not well equipped to deal with these problems, which must be addressed either by transforming self-regarding individuals into community-regarding citizens, or by an intrusive discipline of surveillance, or by some combination of the two. Although it is easy to appreciate the liberal's desire to sidestep Rousseau's demand that citizens not have "an instant of free time that they could call their own," and substitute in its place a "moral division of labor" that allows "everyone to be publicly egalitarian and privately partial," to borrow Thomas Nagel's felicitous phrase, the issue is whether the egalitarian liberal can have her cake and eat it too, maintaining an egalitarian distribution of income in a state that leaves citizens free to pursue their own interests.[91]

The Transparent Economy of
Rousseau's Model Republic

I have argued that many of the shortcomings of real-world markets, as well as some of the problems that beset states which transfer income from the advantaged to the less advantaged, arise when self-regarding agents within stratified societies can pursue their interests behind a cloak of anonymity. In the model republic envisioned by Rousseau, the circumstances and motives of action are different, and so, consequently, are the outcomes.

Rousseau begins the *Social Contract* by promising to "take men as they are" and "to unite what right sanctions with what is prescribed by interest."[92] Measured against this criterion, the programmatic centerpiece of egalitarian liberalism—the continuous transfer of income from the advantaged to the less advantaged—seems unstable if not utopian. Instead of calling upon the wealthy to sacrifice on behalf of the poor, Rousseau stresses the importance of foreclosing the division of society into classes by maintaining a rough equality of property holdings and preventing an "extreme inequality of fortunes."[93] Rousseau's maxim is that "everyone should make a living, and no one should grow rich."[94] In a property-owning republic, the conflict of interest between the "haves" and "have nots" gives way to a commonality of circumstances among citizens who have "the same tastes and interests" and therefore find it "easy to unite in pursuit of the same objects."[95] These common circumstances reduce the gap between the individual's particular will and the general will, so that, in deciding which policies will advance the common good, each citizen can make a good start by asking which policies would advance her own interests. This is not to say that there would be no conflicts among citizens with equal property holdings, but rather that, beneath such conflicts, there would be a broad overlapping of interests, which, we may reasonably suppose, would alleviate, though not eliminate, the problem of "incentive compatibility," since the laws would advance the interests shared in common by citizens whose circumstances were similar if not uniform.[96]

In drawing attention to Rousseau's aim of bringing the particular will and the general will into closer alignment by "homogenizing" the interests of citizens, I do not mean to claim that a general will could be achieved without considerable self-restraint, if not self-denial. Quite the contrary, there are countless occasions when what is best for everyone conflicts with what is best for me. Yet Rousseau does not expect the general will to emerge *ex nihilo* (in the manner of Kant's categorical imperative); it is both disciplined by, and expressed within, the demanding public life of the citizen. On the one hand, this public life is intended to foster solidarity so that citizens "might at length come to identify themselves in some degree with this greater whole."[97] On the other hand, the public life envisioned by Rousseau incorporates a scheme of mutual surveillance that circumscribes the scope of anonymity and therewith the citizen's ability to advance narrower objectives at the expense of the republic. Thus, the design of Rousseau's republican state aims to strengthen the citizen's commitment to the common good by creating common interests and a shared identity, while at the same time making sure that neither vice nor virtue can "escape the notice and judgment of the public."

Although Rousseau's aims in designing a model republic were, for the most part, noneconomic, his proposed scheme of institutional arrangements has several promising economic implications. To begin with, communities without sharp inequalities of wealth and income can probably sustain higher levels of trust than societies which are divided into classes with conflicting interests.[98] And trust, in turn, creates opportunities to cooperate for mutual advantage that are not available to conflict-ridden societies in which mutual confidence is a scarce commodity, and business must be conducted through contracts rather than through less formal agreements. Moreover, on those occasions when citizens must resort to contracts, their agreements will be easier to negotiate and simpler to write because their base of common understanding will be broader than that found in more stratified societies, and because compliance with contractual obligations is more easily verified when so much of life is conducted in public.[99]

Recall that the combination of opacity, or private information, and self-interest creates economic relations in which self-regarding choices generate adverse externalities: slacking workers drag down average productivity and the wages that are based upon it; irresponsible behavior drives up the cost of health insurance, whether it is provided privately or publicly; imprudent risk-taking, which leads to loan defaults, can also result in tighter credit constraints, and so forth. The institutions of Rousseau's republican state, by reinforcing loyalty and solidarity at the expense of narrow self-interest, and by arranging society so that citizens can keep tabs on one another, provide the groundwork for a more transparent and more altruistic economy, which is less exposed to these unwanted externalities. Citizens who monitor each other's conduct and are moved by common interests and objectives can take advantage of cooperative opportunities that would otherwise be unattractive or infeasible because of moral hazard, adverse selection, credit rationing, and many other unfortunate side effects of self-seeking behavior under opaque conditions.[100]

The next point I wish to make is that opaque conditions, which, to some extent, are part of the human condition, cause more problems in societies where the distribution of wealth is very unequal than in societies where property ownership is less concentrated. Let me begin by taking note of the fact that a great deal of the economic behavior that is crucial to productivity is either impossible, or too costly, to monitor and therefore cannot be fully specified in an enforceable contract. Consequently, workers, managers, and entrepreneurs cannot capture all of the productivity gains that would be available to them under conditions of complete transparency, an ideal that, admittedly, lies beyond even Rousseau's model republic. Of course, owners can devote additional resources to monitoring, or reorganize production activities so that employees can be more easily observed, when it is profitable to do so. Nevertheless, overall productivity could be enhanced if resources could be shifted from monitoring to more fruitful activities.

We have already explained how an increase in transparency can expand the range of mutually advantageous exchange.[101] Let us now add the proposition that *a more equal distribution of wealth would also alleviate some of the principle-agent problems that plague opaque economies.* Consider the following examples of how the concentration of wealth, of asset ownership, gives rise to principal-agent problems. When a firm hires workers, it must monitor their level of effort because the workers, themselves, have no incentive to toil in a manner that maximizes the firm's profits, as these accrue to the firm's owners. When a landowner leases acreage to a tenant farmer for a fixed sum, the farmer will work productively because the crops grown on the farm belong to the farmer, but the farmer does not have an incentive to maintain the land's long-term productivity, as this aspect of the land's value is retained by the landowner.

In these examples, temporary use of an asset, machinery or land, is separated from the right to residual income. The workers receive no share of the firm's profits, and the tenant farmer has no enduring claim on the value of the land she rents. By contrast, in a more egalitarian economy, where workers own capital and farmers own land, the individual worker or farmer has an incentive both to put the capital or land to productive use and to maintain its longer term value, as these "owner-agents" have a legal right to both the current income their property generates as well as to its long-term capital value. Widespread ownership thereby eliminates many principal-agent problems because there are no longer two parties with conflicting interests, one of whom must devote resources to monitoring the other. Consequently there is an efficiency gain insofar as the resources devoted to monitoring can be redirected toward productive activities.[102]

The productivity-enhancing effects of a deconcentration of wealth flow from the premise that opacity—our ability to conceal information from others—has more adverse consequences in an economy where wealth is unevenly distributed than in an economy where property holdings are more equally apportioned. If a society is divided into capitalists and workers, the former must devote considerable resources to the surveillance of the latter. If the housing market is populated by landlords and tenants, the former will find it prudent to keep tabs on the conduct of the latter. If there are lenders and borrowers, the former will want to know a great deal about the latter before granting a loan and accepting the risk of default. But if wealth were spread more equally among citizens, then there would be more small businesses and fewer employees, more homeowners and fewer renters, more qualified borrowers and fewer credit-constrained households. As a consequence of these changes, there would also be fewer principal-agent problems and fewer resources devoted to the monitoring of propertyless citizens.[103]

Critics of such egalitarian arrangements argue that if wealth were equally distributed, there would be less saving and less risk-taking than occurs when wealth is concentrated in fewer hands.[104] It is, after all, the wealthy who can afford to save and to invest in projects that may be unsuccessful. Moreover, the small-scale production implied by the equal distribution of assets forecloses the exploitation of scale economies, which allow goods to be produced at lower cost. Whatever their merits, these are not objections that would have moved Rousseau, who cared nothing about efficiency, productivity, or economic growth. Quite the contrary, Rousseau would have been quite content with a property-owning democracy whose citizens were endowed with roughly equal property holdings and the independence it sustains.[105] However, for those of us who count prosperity among the proper ends of political economy, it is important to include among the benefits of equality some mitigation of the principal-agent problems that emerge when society is divided between those who own valuable assets and those who do not, as well as the economic advantages that accrue to citizens who can conduct a good deal of their business on the basis of trust rather than contract.

In addition to universal property ownership—"asset egalitarianism"—there is another contemporary approach to political economy that, I believe, Rousseau would have found appealing. According to this view, the equalization of money incomes is less important than the preservation of a common life shared by all citizens, rich and poor alike.[106] Bearing in mind Rousseau's distaste for hierarchical social relations, consider George Orwell's description of revolutionary Spain in December 1936, where "waiters and shopwalkers looked you in the face and treated you as equal," where "servile and even ceremonial forms of speech had temporarily disappeared," where "tipping had been forbidden by law," where "many of the normal motives of civilized life—snobbishness, money-grubbing, fear of the boss, etc.—had simply ceased to exist . . . One had breathed the air of equality."[107]

If this is the kind of equality that is most essential to a republican state, then perhaps strict economic equality is not so important, for, even under Republican rule, Spain remained a country where wealth and income were by no means equally divided. To create and maintain this kind of egalitarian atmosphere and the social solidarity that comes with it, it may not be necessary to level incomes completely, provided that those areas of life in which money confers power are circumscribed and the domains in which it does not hold sway are enlarged and protected. The egalitarian's proper objective, in this view, is not to redistribute income, but to create a noneconomic sphere of life—a public, community sphere—in which money is powerless and the logic of the market economy is supplanted by the equality of citizenship.[108]

Although Rousseau detested the drive for superior status, *amour-propre*, as well as the division of society into rich and poor, he was willing to tolerate a modicum of social stratification provided that it did not interfere with the common life of the republic. For example, Rousseau urged the Poles to have "frequent open-air spectacles in which different ranks would be carefully distinguished, but in which, as in ancient times, all the people would take equal part."[109] Rousseau was prepared to accept distinctions of rank, provided they were based upon service to the republic. What he opposed were inequalities that destroyed the common life of the republic and the competition for relative position that leads us to "find our advantage in the misfortunes of our fellow-creatures," an outlook fatal to the general will.[110]

Rousseau's aim was to sustain the presence of the republic in the hearts of its citizens, while recognizing that citizens will always be tempted to advance their private interests. There are many aspects of Rousseau's model republic that embody this spirit, but none more than his proposed reestablishment of the *corvée* wherein citizens, instead of paying taxes, use "their labor, their arms and their hearts, rather than their purses, in the service of the fatherland."[111] From the standpoint of efficiency, the *corvée* is, by no means, the best method for constructing public works. Rather than compelling skilled craftsmen to build roads, it would be more efficient to allow them to ply their specialized trades, pay taxes on the income received therefrom, and then use the tax revenue to hire common laborers for road building. Rousseau is prepared to grant all this, but for one premise—that taxes collected from citizens will flow *without leakage* to fund public works. Instead, he insists that "the means of payment"—money—introduces "an infinity of measureless abuses and of evils greater and more unlimited than those which can result from this form of constraint [the *corvée*]."[112] Why? Because money "can be readily hidden from public inspection."[113]

If the *corvée* is to reinforce the egalitarian spirit of the republic, then "let the magistrate himself, though occupied with other cares, show that the rest are not beneath him, like those Roman consuls who, to set an example to their troops, were the first to put their hands to the construction of field works."[114] By substituting, as far as possible, the labor of citizens for the levy of taxes, the republic will increase its "moral treasure," for the payment of taxes "gives only the appearance of service, since the will cannot be bought."[115] Paying taxes amounts to a kind of anonymous citizenship, for money is the primary instrument of opacity. Once "it leaves the hand of the man who pays it over," it "vanishes from sight." By contrast, working alongside fellow citizens to build public works creates a daily reminder of their common effort, a transparent manifestation of the general will.[116]

Rousseau had no interest in enhancing the market's power to coordinate the innumerable choices of strangers, nor even in softening the sharper edges of the market economy. Nonetheless, one can find in his critique of civil society, in his complaint that "we never know with whom we have to deal," a recognition of the importance of asymmetric information in the actual operation of a market economy, where the impersonal rule of the price system has been overthrown, supplanted by the strategic interaction of agents who often command vastly unequal bargaining power. Rousseau's model of republican political economy is not intended to enhance "the wealth of nations," but to preserve the independence, solidarity, and virtue of their citizens. The task of designing institutional arrangements to secure these ends must begin by "taking men as they are," that is, human beings who are sometimes tempted by private advantage and whose motives are not always transparent. Whether or not we share Rousseau's disdain for material progress, we may at least admire his ingenuity in seeking to pool risks, to minimize free riding, and to preserve an extensive public sphere of equal rights and obligations. And while few of us would be willing to exchange the material comforts generated by the division of labor for a humble self-sufficiency, we ought to recognize that the markets in which we trade are not nearly transparent enough to perform in the manner advertised by their most aggressive advocates.

Appendix   Citizen and State:
The Republic and the Principal-Agent Problem

Rousseau begins his "Discourse on Political Economy" by drawing a distinction between the economy of the family or household, where "a father can see everything for himself," and "*general* or *political* economy," "where the chief sees hardly anything save through the eyes of others."[117] In states, as contrasted with families, rulers must rely on their lieutenants for the information necessary to conduct the operations of government. In addition to this difference between families and states, there is another, even more important, distinction, for while the father naturally looks after the interests of the family, "the chief is so far from having any natural interest in the happiness of [his subjects] that it is not uncommon for him to seek his own in their misery."[118] Hence, where the "personal interest and passions of the ruler" take precedence over "the public interest and the laws," "abuses are inevitable and their consequences fatal."[119]

Rousseau was one of the first democratic theorists to stress the potential conflict of interest between the citizens of a republic and those who administer the organs of government on their behalf. In *The Social Contract*, he emphasizes that those charged with the administration of government are the people's deputies and may be replaced at any time; "the depositaries of executive power are not the people's masters, but its officers . . . [the people] can set them up and pull them down when it likes."[120] To ensure the fidelity and accountability of the people's "officers," Rousseau urges the institution of "periodical assemblies," which should always begin their deliberations with the following question, "Does it please the people to leave its administration in the hands of those who are actually in charge of it?"[121]

In the lexicon of information economics, Rousseau is grappling with a "principal-agent problem," which may be defined as a relationship in which there is a potential conflict between a "principal," whose interests are to be advanced, and an "agent," who is hired to act on the principal's behalf. In this regard, Rousseau laments the fact that "public money [must] go through the hands of the rulers, all of whom have, besides the interests of the State, their own individual interests, which are not the last to be listened to."[122] The relationship between principal and agent is also made problematic by the fact that the principal cannot directly observe all of the agent's conduct and, hence, cannot costlessly determine whether the agent is looking after the principal's interests or simply advancing her own. (It is again worth calling attention to the fact that the pursuit of self-interest is not a sufficient condition for the presence of a principal-agent problem; some degree of opacity, or private information, is also necessary.)

Much of the contemporary work on the principal-agent problem deals with the inherent conflict between the managers of a corporation and its shareholders.[123] Shareholders are interested in the value of the company's stock, while company managers may be tempted by the emoluments of office. Although incentive contracts may be helpful in bringing management interests into line with shareholder interests, the direct monitoring of managerial performance is also necessary because the value of a firm's stock depends on many factors besides the quality of management.[124] Shareholders whose wealth is concentrated in a single company's stock may find it worthwhile to take the time and trouble necessary to determine the quality of managerial effort. But since most investors diversify their holdings across many companies, few shareholders will find it rewarding to closely monitor the activities of management. Moreover, because all shareholders benefit from whatever monitoring efforts are undertaken, individual shareholders may choose to free ride on the efforts of other stockholders, which, in turn, results in too little oversight.

Like the investor who owns a diversified portfolio, the liberal citizen has a stake in a variety of associations, which may include a professional organization, sports club, neighborhood group, church, and so forth. Because the conduct of government is but one of many things that affect his welfare, the liberal citizen will not find it worthwhile to carefully monitor the behavior of public officials except on those infrequent occasions when his rights or basic interests are threatened.[125] By contrast, Rousseau insisted that the republican citizen's "investments" of time, energy, and commitment must be concentrated in the political community so that its affairs are given the attention they require.[126] Citizens will only "fly to the assemblies," where laws are made and the performance of those charged with administering the laws is judged, if they are discouraged from acquiring a "diversified portfolio" of interests wherein the citizen's concern with public matters merely takes its place alongside many other, private interests.[127]

Let me quickly enumerate some of the specific means by which Rousseau planned to address the principal-agent problem in his republic. First, he emphasizes the importance of restricting the size of the republic, both the number of its citizens as well as its geographic area.[128] The fewer the number of citizens, the greater is the importance of each citizen's vote, hence the more time and effort it is rational to spend attending to the issues facing the community.[129] In addition, there is a closer fit between the citizen's capacity for understanding and the range of practical problems confronting the community when its territory is circumscribed and its population small and relatively homogenous. Thus, Rousseau praises republics whose geographic reach is "proportionate to human faculties" and whose population is small enough that citizens know one another by name. Within such close-knit communities, it is relatively easy to become informed about the issues of the day, to observe the conduct of administration, to take part in the deliberations of the "periodical assemblies," and to intelligently decide whether the people's administration should be left "in the hands of those who are actually in charge of it." Moreover, small states allow the people's administrators to "see for themselves the harm that is being done and the good that is theirs to do and can look on as their orders are being executed."[130]

Besides giving citizens an incentive to monitor the conduct of their agents, Rousseau also sought to make the conduct of administration, itself, more transparent. The opacity of government derives in large measure from the character of money. "Where money is used," Rousseau complains, "it is easily diverted and concealed, what is intended for one purpose is utilized for another; those who handle money soon learn how to divert it—and what are all the officials assigned to keep watch on them, except so many more rascals whom one sends to go shares with them?"[131] Paying the people's deputies in money is "the weakest and least dependable engine I know of for driving the political machine toward its object, the strongest and surest for sending it off on a tangent."[132]

What is the alternative? Follow Switzerland, Rousseau advises, which pays its officials "in kind, that is, in the form of tithes, wine, wood, privileges, both utilitarian and honorific."[133] Granted, such methods of payment entail "waste and extravagance" and are "clumsy to administer." Nevertheless, it is worth the extra cost because of the "multiplicity of evils it prevents." "Try as a man may to make off with something, he still cannot do it—not, at least, without someone seeing him." Unlike pecuniary rewards, "which disappear as soon as they are conferred," honorific rewards "address themselves constantly to the peoples' eyes and hearts." Giving administrators goods and honors instead of money will assure that they cannot "move about *incognito*."[134] And when the conduct of the people's officers is made visible to the people, themselves, the opportunities for malfeasance and corruption will be sharply diminished.[135]

CHAPTER FIVE

The Ring of Gyges, the Perfect Shield, and the Veil of Ignorance

I have deployed the dichotomy of transparent and opaque relations for several purposes: to construct a Rousseauean typology of social interaction that draws out the political implications of various kinds of interpersonal relations; to describe different patterns of association and dissociation and their ramifications for the character of civil society; and to contrast the nature of transparent markets in which traders are fully informed and Adam Smith's impersonal price system rules with opaque markets in which strategy and bargaining power assume a central role in the allocation of resources and the distribution of income. Having explored the practical logic that governs the interaction among transparent and opaque agents, as well as some of the consequences of this logic for human association, my aim in this chapter is to see whether the vantage point afforded by our inquiry can shed any light upon the political thought of three contemporary thinkers: David Gauthier, Bruce Ackerman, and John Rawls.

Social Contract Theory and the Ring of Gyges:
From Glaucon to Gauthier

The idea of a social contract goes back at least to Book II of Plato's *Republic* where Glaucon challenges Socrates's depiction of justice as the intrinsic good of both the polis and its individual members.[1] Against this view, Glaucon advances the notion that justice is only a prudent compromise among men who are too weak to pursue their interests without restraint. This compromise, or *modus vivendi*, emerges from the recognition that while there are benefits to be gained by wrongdoing, there are greater harms to be suffered as a victim of wrongdoing. Hence, Glaucon argues, men find it prudent to accept a compromise whereby each one forswears unfettered self-aggrandizement in exchange for the security afforded by mutual restraint.

It is important not to overlook the asymmetry between the gains enjoyed by the wrongdoer and the losses suffered by the victim of wrongdoing, for, in Glaucon's account of the social contract, these gains and loses do not cancel out (or sum to zero if we conceive of them as numerical values). Rather, the costs suffered by the victim of wrongdoing greatly exceed the benefits accruing to the offender. This asymmetry is significant for the following reason. Suppose that each person had an equal chance of being either a wrongdoer or a victim of wrongdoing. Since the gains accruing to the former are not as large as the losses suffered by the latter, the expected payoff to anyone who plays the game of self-aggrandizement *and is equally likely to be the perpetrator of wrongdoing or its victim* will be negative. Facing these prospects, we can surmise that people will relinquish self-aggrandizement in favor of self-restraint.

But what about the person who believes she has *a better than even chance* of becoming a successful perpetrator of wrongdoing as opposed to a victim of wrongdoing, perhaps even a much greater than equal chance? Such a person will only elect to forego the opportunities of wrongdoing if the harms she might suffer on those few occasions when she is the victim of wrongdoing are very damaging indeed. In simple algebra, if we let B stand for the benefits of wrongdoing, C for the costs suffered by the victim of wrongdoing, p for the probability of being a successful wrongdoer, and $(1 - p)$ for the probability of being a victim of wrongdoing, then a person will only choose a life of transgression if its expected benefits exceed the expected benefits of self-restraint, that is, if $pB > (1 - p)C$. If a *duplicitous* wrongdoer is going to forego wrongdoing, then the more skilled she is at deception (i.e., the greater the value of p), the greater must be the costs she suffers as a victim of wrongdoing (i.e., the greater the value of C) on those occasions when her duplicity falters, and she is vulnerable to the transgressions of others.

If a person can get away with everything while at the same time being invulnerable to any aggression by others, then of course it does not matter how great the cost of being victimized might be, for one can count on never being a victim. What would it be like to have such power? For Glaucon, this kind of prerogative need not flow from the sort of brute force that, in Thrasymachus's conception of "justice," permits the strongest man to define "justice" in a manner that advances his own interest.[2] Instead, Glaucon invokes the mystical Ring of Gyges, which allows its wearer to become invisible at will, to show what it would be like to be a man who could get away with every wrongdoing, to "fearlessly help himself to anything he wanted, enter houses and sleep with any woman he chose, set prisoners free and kill men at his pleasure."[3] In this, the limiting case, the probability of being a successful wrongdoer, p in our little equation, rises to one (unity), so that a person in possession of Gyges's Ring would have no reason to renounce wrongdoing no matter how great were the costs of being a victim of wrongdoing.

Glaucon puts Gyges's Ring in the hands of a just man in order to demonstrate that it is the risk of being found out, as opposed to the appeal of justice, itself, which compels men to act with self-restraint. If justice were an intrinsic good, as Socrates claims, then it should be valued even when it brings none of the material rewards and friendships that accrue to the respected man of virtue. Although Glaucon began his argument with the limiting case of a just man possessed of the supernatural power to become invisible at will, he proceeds to the more familiar case of someone skilled in the art of deception. Thus, he asks Socrates to consider the advantages enjoyed by the unjust man who has achieved "the highest pitch of injustice," that is, "to seem just when you are not," to maintain "a spotless reputation for virtue while committing the blackest crimes."[4] Glaucon has here picked up the thread of Thrasymachus's cynical attack on "what is called 'justice,' " yet it is not the latter's boorish self-assertion that poses the greatest threat to virtue, but rather the strategy of *sophisticated* self-aggrandizement, practiced with the arts of duplicity and deception, which most threatens the case for self-restraint.

Although Glaucon's original account of why men accept the compromise embodied in the social contract turned on the claim that the costs suffered by the victim of wrongdoing exceed the benefits enjoyed by the wrongdoer, he concludes his argument with the claim that the self-restraint required by the social contract is forthcoming *because human beings are more or less transparent.* Unlike the Lydian Shepherd who came into possession of Gyges's ring, human beings with ordinary powers cannot perpetually succeed in pretending to comply with society's rules while actually breaking them for personal advantage. It is human transparency that compels us to affirm the social contract and to abide by its terms, for, if we were opaque, then, leaving aside Socrates's claim about the intrinsic value of justice, we would have no reason to act with self-restraint.

Glaucon's contention that self-aggrandizement is an irresistible force in human conduct, and that political society rests on an implicit agreement to renounce unrestrained freedom of action in favor of mutual restraint, finds modern expression in Hobbes's *Leviathan*, which also contemplates a political order without virtue. Although Hobbes gives us a much more extensive account of the strategic considerations that lead men to relinquish unfettered self-assertion in return for mutual security, Hobbes's reasoning lacks an essential premise, a premise that must do the work of Gyges's ring or its real-world surrogate—the ability "to cover one's tracks." This comes out clearly when, having explained the advantages of a state-enforced *modus vivendi*, Hobbes confronts the "foole," who believes it is profitable to break promises, to borrow without intending to repay one's debts, and, in general, to extract whatever one can by failing to keep one's "part of the bargain."[5] Hobbes's reply to the "foole" is that a man who fails to follow through on his commitments cannot expect to be received into society because rational individuals concerned to further their own interests will not enter into agreements with people who are known to be unreliable cooperation partners.

Hobbes's advice to the "foole" is, of course, consistent with Glaucon's conception of the social contract as a mutually advantageous compromise among people who cannot get away with wrongdoing. It is not, however, entirely consistent with Hobbes's own justification of the contract that establishes the sovereign, for if it is rational to keep promises *even without the threat of punishment*, then what is the need of a coercive state? If cooperation for mutual benefit is more advantageous than a life of exile, and if promise-keeping is the credential necessary for admission to the scheme of social cooperation, *then this scheme is self-enforcing and needs no authority to punish defectors.*

Hobbes is caught in the following dilemma. His reply to the "foole" regarding the advantages of promise-keeping will only be persuasive if the "foole's" conduct is transparent. But if the behavior of the "foole," and of human beings in general, is transparent, then there is no need for a coercive state to punish untrustworthy promise-makers because there is nothing to gain from promise-breaking.[6] On the other hand, if the "foole" and the rest of the human race are opaque, if, to borrow Glaucon's words, they have achieved "the highest pitch of injustice" and are capable of maintaining "a spotless reputation for virtue while committing the blackest crimes," then not even a Leviathan state could assure that their promises would be kept. Thus, while Hobbes assumes that human beings are more or less transparent in his reply to the "foole," he must assume a more opaque disposition in order to justify voluntary submission to a sovereign authority. Combining these two ill-fitting assumptions together, we must conclude that Hobbes's version of the social contract only gains traction if men and women are not so transparent that their character and conduct can be accurately discerned at first glance, yet not so opaque that their words bear no connection to their deeds.

According to David Gauthier, who accepts many of Hobbes's premises while rejecting his conclusions, a compelling reply to the "foole" must demonstrate that only those people who are disposed to keep their commitments will be afforded opportunities to cooperate for mutual advantage.[7] The crucial premise in Gauthier's argument is that each person's disposition, whether cooperative or not, is immediately transparent to others.[8] Given this assumption, Gauthier is able to show that the rational egoist will do best by cultivating a disposition to comply with mutually advantageous agreements, that is, to become a "constrained maximizer" as opposed to a "straightforward maximizer," who does not comply with such agreements, that is, defects in a prisoner's dilemma game. Since constrained maximizers keep their promises, they need no state to enforce them. By simply grafting the premise of transparency onto Hobbes's rational egoists, Gauthier is able to dispense with Hobbes's Leviathan.

We encountered transparent beings in Rousseau's primitive communities, where innocent men and women have no conception of how they appear to others and, hence, cannot disguise their real intentions. But, of course, Rousseau insisted that this kind of naïve social intercourse is not possible among "civilized" men and women who have learned to carefully manage their public identities. One need not accept all the details of Rousseau's unflattering portrait of civilized men and women to grasp the limits of Gauthier's "morals by agreement." The sheer anonymity of urban life makes it difficult to ascertain with confidence the character of the many strangers we encounter in the course of our lives. For the rational egoist, who is the *dramatis personae* in Gauthier's postmodern morality tale, the most effective strategy is that of Hume's "knave," for whom "honesty is the best policy" *except on those occasions when it pays to be dishonest.*[9]

In some interactions, a failure to follow through on one's promises will pay dividends even though one is not anonymous. For example, the rational egoist gains nothing by fulfilling commitments to people who are disposed to cooperate regardless of what they expect others to do. In such interactions, Gauthier's "constrained maximizer" has no reason to restrain herself because restraint is not necessary in order to elicit the collaboration of the "*unconditional* cooperator."[10] As long as other "constrained maximizers" know that she will meet her commitments *when they demand reciprocity*, she foregoes no cooperative opportunities by taking advantage of unconditional cooperators. Transparency may be a necessary condition of reciprocal cooperation, but it is not always sufficient.

In fact there are circumstances in which transparency can actually hinder cooperation. Put yourself in Rousseau's autobiographical shoes and imagine that you are, as Rousseau believed himself to be, an unconditional cooperator whose kind disposition cannot be hidden from others, including all the men and women who are ready to take advantage of your generous nature. In this case, transparency simply announces your readiness to be exploited. Moreover, your easily discerned disposition to cooperate without reciprocity causes problems not only for other unconditional cooperators, but also for Gauthier's more prudent, "constrained maximizers" (conditional cooperators). The trouble is that the greater the number of transparent unconditional cooperators there are, the greater will be the opportunities awaiting the "straightforward maximizer" (unconditional defector). And if, in light of these opportunities, there are more "straightforward maximizers," either as a result of evolutionary pressures or strategic decisions, then the lower will be the expected returns to conditional cooperation. By contrast, if these good-natured souls, who cooperate unconditionally, were able to keep their disposition secret, if they could remain opaque, in other words, then "straightforward maximizers" would find fewer prey and, consequently, would be fewer in number. In this case, opacity of a limited kind actually increases the prospects for mutual cooperation by reducing the expected benefits that accrue to "straightforward maximizers."

Interactions with strangers we will never see again, or with unconditional cooperators, are not the only forms of social intercourse in which it pays to defect. In exploring Rousseau's conception of civilized society, we came across vainglorious men and women whose concern with relative position ruled out cooperation except under conditions of hyper-transparency. Interestingly, Gauthier does not remove the threat posed by vainglorious individuals to his scheme of mutually advantageous cooperation by insisting on such ultra-transparency. Rather, he eliminates it by ruling out *any* concern with relative position. Mutual defection on the part of men and women striving for preeminence does not arise in Gauthier's account because vanity and envy (as well as sympathy and compassion) have been banished by stipulation. Once we take account of all Gauthier's special premises, it turns out that "constrained maximization" proves to be a suboptimal strategy, not only for individuals who live in opaque cities, or who encounter unconditional cooperators, but also for people with other-regarding motives, whether these are benign or not.[11]

In the end, Gauthier confirms Glaucon's claim that a person in possession of Gyges's ring would have no reason for self-restraint. And since Gauthier denies that trustworthiness, loyalty, honor, or virtue can be ends in themselves, and, in addition, allows no scope for compassion or any other fellow feeling, the entire burden of his argument for "constrained maximization" rests on his assumption that the intentions of promise-keepers and promise-breakers are equally transparent. By contrast, the more one is persuaded by Rousseau's account of the opaque city and its duplicitous "citizens," the less convincing Gauthier's "morals by agreement" becomes.

If we think in terms of two simple dichotomies: (1) whether you can, or cannot, conceal your intentions from others; and (2) whether others can, or cannot, conceal their intentions from you, then we can make out the four possibilities shown in table 5.1.[12]

We have seen variations of these modes of interaction before. To live in a society where you and everyone else can conceal your intentions, cell (1) in table 5.1, is to dwell in circumstances not dissimilar from Hobbes's state of nature, where social interaction is risky, and trust is in exceedingly short supply. This condition, like that depicted in the *Leviathan*, is infused by a kind of equality, or symmetry at least, viz. a universal capacity to dissimulate. In such an environment, the prudent

Table 5.1   Symmetrical and asymmetrical modes of interaction

	Others can conceal their intentions from you	*Others cannot conceal their intentions from you*
You can conceal your intentions from others	(1) Symmetrical opacity (Rousseau's Paris; Hobbes's state of nature)	(3) Asymmetrical opacity (an individual in possession of Gyges's Ring)
You cannot conceal your intentions from others	(2) Asymmetrical transparency (Rousseau's self-understanding)	(4) Symmetrical transparency (Rousseau's republic; Gauthier's "morals by agreement"

course of action may not be, as Hobbes suggests, a preemptive strike against one's suspicious-looking neighbor, but rather a self-imposed isolation, or, less dramatically, a Tocquevillian "withdrawal into a small circle of family and friends." In either case, however, the ultimate political outcome may be the same. For Hobbes, uncertainty about the character of others leads men to establish a sovereign who will enforce the promises they make to one another. But a lack of confidence in the motives of others, which induces individuals to turn away from one another, can also create the conditions most favorable to a powerful centralized authority with predatory ambitions, which is *not* the outcome desired by rational egoists. As Montesquieu observed, vast spaces between people, whether measured in miles, misunderstanding, or moral distance, tend to produce despotic regimes because nothing stands between the state and its disconnected subjects, who have been scattered across the political landscape by the centrifugal forces of opacity.[13]

Of course you would be even worse off if you could not hide your intentions while all those around you could conceal theirs [cell (2) in table 5.1]. From the testimony of Rousseau's *Confessions*, we may infer that this is how Jean-Jacques understood his own place in the world, a transparent soul surrounded by opaque wolves. Unlike the symmetrically opaque scenario, where a perverse kind of equality in deceptive powers prevails, in this case the transparent soul is vulnerable to everyone around him, and therefore may find it prudent to follow Rousseau's example, retreating as far as possible from the men and women whose dark dispositions have become a threat to his happiness, if not to his survival.

Cell (3) in table 5.1 is the home of the Lydian Shepherd who came into possession of Gyges's Ring, and, in fact, one cannot easily imagine this possibility—that *one man only* could conceal his intentions—without recourse to a supernatural device. In the absence of such a powerful technology, which in Glaucon's arresting example, allows the ring's wearer to conceal his actions as well as his intentions, it is difficult to envision how anyone could attain such power. As long as a person's deeds eventually come to light, and as long as the victims of his duplicity are inclined to share their experience with others, predators must be perpetually on the lookout for new victims who are ignorant of their predatory character. In the real world, a recalcitrant double-dealer must become a rootless vagabond, who, like the generous and transparent soul who must withdraw from society for the sake of self-preservation, is deprived of genuine fellowship.

I have located both Rousseau's transparent republic and David Gauthier's quasi-libertarian "morals by agreement" within the Cell (4) of table 5.1.[14] The presence of these two divergent conceptions within the same conceptual location is jarring because, apart from the premise of transparency, the two conceptions share very little. If Rousseau is right in insisting that transparency among civilized men and women is a hard-won achievement that requires an elaborate and intrusive scheme of mutual surveillance, then Gauthier is chasing a pipe-dream by supposing that transparent cooperation can be attained in the absence of a sociopolitical regime that exposes each person's conduct and character to continuous public scrutiny. And if Gauthier is right in assuming that human beings are so constructed that our true aims are spontaneously expressed and easily discerned, then we can dispense with all of Rousseau's republican trappings, for they are not necessary conditions of cooperation for mutual advantage, but only the superfluous lineaments of a collectivist state.

Transparency and "Perfect Transactional Flexibility" in Ackerman's Liberal State

Fantastic technologies, if I may characterize Gyges's ring as such, have also been employed by contemporary thinkers as a way of illuminating important social and political issues. In *Social Justice in the Liberal State*, Bruce Ackerman develops a conception of justice through a series of dialogues in which no participant is permitted to claim superiority for herself or her vision of the good.[15] The entire conversation takes place onboard an imaginary spaceship that is headed toward an uninhabited planet. The ship has a powerful computer that is capable of answering all empirical questions, and a "master designer" who is able to design "perfect technologies of justice," thereby dispensing with issues of second-best. For our purposes, we may pick up the dialogue at a point where the spaceship travelers have just agreed to equal shares of wealth ("manna") and are trying to decide the form in which it should be distributed. If the "manna" is distributed piecemeal, one bit to each citizen, and costs must be incurred to combine these bits, then individualist conceptions of the good will be favored over collectivist conceptions. On the other hand, if the "manna" is distributed in "lumpy" packages to groups, and costs must be incurred to separate the "manna" into individual pieces, then collectivist conceptions of the good will be favored over individualist conceptions.[16] The problem, therefore, is to find a form of property rights that is neutral between these opposing visions of the good.

It is in response to this dilemma that Ackerman develops "the liberal ideal of perfect *transactional flexibility*."[17] Specifically, Ackerman asks us to imagine an "ideal transmitter" that would allow each person to costlessly communicate to all members of the community (or any subset thereof) the terms on which the citizen is willing to cooperate with others, combining their "manna" for common purposes. Given universal possession of this imaginary device, "manna" could be distributed in individual bits to each citizen without putting communitarian citizens at a disadvantage because, once in possession of the "transmitter," they could combine their resources and efforts without cost. Although Ackerman does not insist that only "good faith" offers of cooperation be communicated via the "transmitters," it is obvious that this requirement must be satisfied if the "transmitters" are going to play the role Ackerman assigns to them. Otherwise citizens pursuing collectivist aims would have to assess the veracity of cooperative offers, and even if these citizens were never fooled, they would still incur costs that more individualistic citizens would not. In fact, this "no-additional-cost" criterion can only be satisfied if everyone *knows in advance* that every offer made will be made in good faith. Thus, Ackermanian neutrality between collectivist and individualist conceptions of the good requires a kind of "super-transparency" wherein the communication of cooperative offers must be costless, truthful, and known to have been made in good faith.[18]

If Ackerman's ideal "transmitters" are to function effectively, then citizens must also have sophisticated "receivers," which, to protect them from being overwhelmed by millions of offers, must be equipped with a filter that selects the kinds of cooperative offers the citizen wishes to consider, while screening out all others. Without the help of Ackerman's "master designer," the architecture of such a filter would pose formidable problems. For example, how could citizens decide which kinds of offers to screen in, or out, without knowing the sort of offers that might be forthcoming? Even the design of a "sampling filter," which would admit a variety of messages for preliminary review, would be difficult to program without knowing the nature of the offers to be sampled. These are, in fact, instances of a well-known problem in information economics, viz. the impossibility of determining the optimal amount of information to acquire before actually acquiring it. Opacity, it turns out, is not the only obstacle to effective cooperation; too much information can be as great an impediment to collaboration as too little.

Although perfectly tuned "transmitters" and "receivers" combined with guaranteed veracity, or "super-transparency" as I have called it, remove important obstacles to cooperation, such lucidity is not necessarily compatible with every conception of the good. For civic republicans, in particular, the trouble with "super-transparency" is that it facilitates the formation of "partial societies" within the republic. Indeed, it is hard to imagine anything *more* favorable to the organization of special interests than a technology that permits the costless communication of cooperative offers to any identifiable subgroup within the community. And insofar as these "partial societies" compete for the citizen's time and loyalty, they drain the reservoir of civic virtue that is necessary to sustain a republic. Hence, a contemporary Rousseauean might complain that a communications technology which affords "perfect transactional flexibility," that is, the right of unfettered combination plus costless, truthful communication, favors liberal democracy, with its proliferation of interest groups, at the expense of republican democracy, which thrives in the absence of these secondary associations.[19]

Of course the Ackermanian liberal is apt to dismiss this communitarian complaint, insisting that no one has a right to decide whether a polity should be organized around the liberal model of civil society in which individuals combine to advance their private interests, or around the civic republican model, which discourages the formation of such groups. Rather, this liberal argument continues, every person has a right to enter into cooperative associations with whoever is willing to join them, and the result, *whatever it turns out to be*, is legitimate just insofar as it is the outcome of these unfettered choices. This reply is not, however, fully satisfactory because it says nothing about the circumstances in which such voluntary agreements are made. We have seen that the composition and character of associations depend on the kind of information that is available to the citizens contemplating membership in associations. The issue is whether the outcome of choices made by individuals in possession of Ackerman's transparency-enhancing technologies of "perfect transactional flexibility" has greater legitimacy than the outcome that would result from the choices of citizens who lacked these idealized devices. (It is interesting to note, in this regard, that John Rawls, who also aims to develop liberal principles of justice, relies on an *"opacity-enhancing* technology"—the veil of ignorance—which we shall consider in the next section.)

Ackerman is able to sidestep this question because he does not say very much about the kind of social setting in which his marvelous technologies might be employed. Yet, once we leave behind Ackerman's exceedingly sparse scenario, it is easy to see that the kind of information which is available to individual choosers does, in fact, bear upon the moral quality of the mutual agreements they enter into. To take an example from one of our own thought experiments: when citizens possess unequal resources and these differences are easily discerned, then those citizens with greater advantages may form exclusive groups among themselves, which will amplify their advantages over time. By contrast, if the well-endowed cannot easily identify one another, then associations will be more heterogeneous in composition and less likely to generate self-reinforcing inequalities.

In addition to the issue of whether "super-transparency" necessarily confers legitimacy upon the social arrangements arising from voluntary agreements, Ackerman's scheme is subject to collective action problems. While each person may prefer to use his or her "transmitter" to communicate offers of cooperation only to those who share the same interests or beliefs, the collective outcome of these individual decisions, for example, a fragmented society composed of internally homogenous groups, may be less appealing to these same individuals than the kind of society that might emerge in the event they had all adjusted their "transmitters" and "receivers" to allow at least some of the random interaction that occurs under more opaque conditions. Although there is nothing in Ackerman's scheme that prevents a person from making such an adjustment, the potential gains from it may only be realized if a threshold number of citizens chooses to interact under more opaque conditions. In a similar fashion, while each person, acting separately, may prefer to join one of the homogenous associations that arise under transparent conditions, he or she may, nevertheless, find that the politics and policy outcomes which result from the participation of homogenous interest-groups in the democratic process are inferior to the politics and policy outcomes which would result from the participation of heterogeneous groups in this process.

In the twenty-five years since Ackerman proposed to clarify the liberal conception of justice by recourse to his fantastic machinery, there have been great advances in communications technology, which have brought Ackerman's "perfect transactional flexibility" closer to realization. Although the political consequences of these new technologies are not yet clear, some of the emerging possibilities are discouraging. For example, in *Republic.com*, Cass Sunstein draws attention to the fact that the increasingly popular Internet allows each citizen to create a kind of personalized newspaper, "the Daily Me," which includes only those topics a person is interested in, while screening out all that is uninteresting or irritating. While this power is entirely consistent with "perfect trans-actional flexibility," it provides a striking illustration of how narrowly programmed receivers can produce narrow-minded citizens.[20] When deployed in pluralistic societies with diverse "speech communities," Sunstein argues that the Internet increases "people's ability to hear echoes of their own voices and to wall themselves off from others," not a good thing for anyone interested in creating citizens who will participate in the common life of the community.[21]

In addition to this hardening of boundaries between citizens, "an individually filtered speech universe" will produce a suboptimal supply of what Sunstein calls "solidarity goods," that is, "goods whose value increases with the number of people who are consuming them."[22] Such goods are especially important to republics because "people who would otherwise see one another as quite unfamiliar" may become inclined, through the nonexclusive sharing of solidarity goods, "to regard one another as fellow citizens with shared hopes, goals, and concerns."[23] In this respect, the "transactional flexibility" afforded by the Internet works at cross-purposes with the aspirations of communitarians.

Ackerman completes the specification of his liberal utopia by introducing a perfect "shield" that can be used by citizens to protect themselves and their "manna" from the unwanted side effects that may be generated by the activities of other citizens.[24] This impenetrable shield also has the power to "screen in" activities "originating in [the citizen's] space which he wants to keep private."[25] In terms of our cate-gories, Ackerman's "shield" allows every citizen to determine which aspects of their lives will be transparent to others and which aspects of their lives will remain opaque to others.

Except for exhibitionists, voyeurs, and perhaps those who believe that the personal is always political, most people feel that such control is essen-tial to the conduct of life. This view is forcefully articulated by Thomas Nagel, who argues that "the boundary between what we reveal and what we do not, and some control over that boundary, are among the most important attributes of our humanity."[26] Furthermore, Nagel contends that the more we are called upon to reveal our thoughts and to justify our personal conduct, the more we will try to conceal or mask our real aims and feelings, becoming hypocrites in the process. If we are not subject to such imposing demands, if we are allowed to keep these thoughts to ourselves, to remain opaque as it were, then we will enjoy the benefits of a "smoothly fitting public surface," which "protects one from the sense of exposure without having to be in any way dishonest or deceptive, just as clothing does not conceal the fact that one is naked underneath."[27]

As appealing as Ackerman's "shield" and Nagel's "smoothly fitting public surface" are to anyone who values their privacy, it is not clear whether they are consistent with the requirements of transparent cooperation. In a society littered with personal "shields," specially programmed "transmitters," and narrowly tuned "receivers," it is hard to predict what kinds of interaction would be feasible. It seems that a society with so many opaque spaces would be incompatible with one of the premises that is necessary to maintain neutrality between individualistic and communitarian conceptions of the good, viz. the assurance that every cooperative offer will be made in good faith. It is worth recalling that, for Rousseau, this requirement can only be satisfied through an intrusive regime of mutual surveillance, which is designed to penetrate the "smoothly fitting public surface" that conceals the intentions of the virtuous and the vicious alike. But even if we leave Rousseau's illiberal solution aside, could it be that the "natural, frank, and open" relations Tocqueville found in nineteenth-century America, a kind of "easygoing transparency," was a necessary condition of the highly developed science of association he also found in the new democracy?[28] Put the other way around, is it possible for people who are adept at "managing what appears on the surface" to cooperate without ever having to worry whether promises made will be promises kept?[29]

I do not wish to deny the obvious appeal of Ackerman's shields, which, after all, resemble Gyges's ring in allowing us to become opaque, if not invisible, to others. But when everyone possesses this power, the moral is not the one Plato had in mind.[30] The temptation for the shield-owner is not the exercise of power with impunity, but rather the extension of personal control over public space. In Ackerman's liberal utopia, if a citizen finds displeasing things in his environment, he can simply turn on his "shield" to effect a costless exit from the problem. But once we leave this fantasy world and put in its place a real-world example, such as the declining fortunes of urban public schools; and once we replace the costless exit afforded by the "shield" with, say, retreat to the suburbs; then Ackerman's "transactional flexibility" loses some of its appeal because the consequences of such "flexibility" in this real-world example are by no means entirely benign. When resourceful families, who have considerable, if not perfect, flexibility, abandon a public school, their exit can set in motion a cascade effect that draws increasing numbers of such families out of public schools, with unfortunate consequences for those families who, having very little flexibility, are left behind.

I am not arguing that an Ackermanian policy which, in general, aims to reduce the cost of "exit," will pay no dividends whatsoever.

Rather, my point is that if, inspired by Ackerman's "shields," you reduce the cost of "exit," you will also reduce the propensity toward "voice." And while "exit" may often be attractive to individuals acting separately, the collective result of many such choices can sometimes be less appealing than the "no exit" option in which everyone's "shields" are "turned off."

Although Ackerman's fantastic technologies are useful in pushing the ideas of privacy, free exchange, and neutral forms of property to their logical limits, they are less helpful when it comes to real-world trade-offs among these and other values. I am referring to difficult problems in "the theory of second best."[31] Put simply, when one requirement of a model scheme is not satisfied in its real-world counterpart, for example, the presence of externalities in real-world market economies, it is often very difficult to figure out how, in light of this imperfection, other aspects of the real-world scheme should be modified in order to achieve the "second best" arrangement overall. For example, suppose we lack the Ackermanian "shields" that would allow each person to determine the level of air quality around his or her body, and, as a consequence, we must make a collective decision about the quality of the air we all breathe. In theory, it is possible to discover the optimal level of investment in public goods by asking each citizen how much he or she would be willing to pay for them. The appropriate level of public expenditure for such goods is then determined by totaling these notional amounts. There is a hitch, however. Unless individual citizens are taxed according to their expressed "willingness to pay," they will have an incentive to lie about their preferences, for example, exaggerating their desire for clean air, since their expressed preference does not affect their share of the cost. Where "exit" is not a feasible option, the efficient level of expenditure on public goods thus requires a kind of civic virtue, that is, the expression of honest preferences. Hence, the civic republican may argue, the "second best" institutional arrangement must be one that promotes (at least) this minimal kind of civic virtue, which, in turn, may require modifications in the remaining components of Ackerman's "transactional flexibility."

Once we move closer to reality and accept the fact that we lack the kind of power that would allow each of us, individually, to control the quality of our immediate environment, we may want to impose some restrictions on the citizen's use of his or her "transmitter" and "receiver." If collective decisions about "the commons" are going to be made democratically, then citizens must take an interest in, and become informed about, the basic facts, competing viewpoints, and policy alternatives pertaining to our shared environment. Most likely this kind of engagement will only be forthcoming if citizens program their "receivers" to admit a variety of viewpoints and set aside some time to evaluate the competing arguments and policy options. In other words, if our "shields" are not powerful enough to give each of us complete control over the environment surrounding our bodies (among other things), then other aspects of our "transactional flexibility," for example, the ability to screen out arguments that challenge our beliefs, may require modification.

The point of Ackerman's "perfect transactional flexibility" is to maximize the scope of individual choice, but this goal is achieved at the cost of undermining the conditions in which personal autonomy is most likely to flourish. Choices are made among possibilities, and if these possibilities are sharply circumscribed by narrowly tuned "receivers," "individually filtered speech communities," and the like, then the choices that emerge from this constricted environment will, in the absence of special considerations, carry less weight than the choices that would emerge from a more open-minded orientation to the world around us. In a similar fashion, if citizens remain opaque to one another, and ignorant of public concerns and issues, because their "receivers" block out all messages except those which are "echoes of their own voices," then the quality of their citizenship is open to question, especially if they are free riding on the efforts of citizens who have programmed their Ackermanian technologies in ways that facilitate an informed engagement in public affairs. In order to create the conditions in which individual and collective choices will be most highly valued and worthy of respect, it is not implausible to suppose that the citizen's "transactional flexibility" will have to be restricted in some measure, which is, in effect, to put forward a modest version of Rousseau's claim that, sometimes, "men have to be forced to be free."[32]

The Uses of Opacity: John Rawls's Veil of Ignorance

John Rawls introduces *A Theory of Justice* with these words, "My aim is to present a conception of justice which generalizes and carries to a higher level of abstraction the familiar theory of the social contract as found, say, in Locke, Rousseau, and Kant."[33] Rawls's own version of social contract theory is built around a thought experiment in which "free and rational persons concerned to further their own interests" reach an agreement that specifies "the kinds of social cooperation that can be entered into and the forms of government that can be established."[34] Although Rousseau characterizes his conception of the social contract somewhat differently, seeking to find "a form of association . . . in which each, while uniting himself with all, may still obey himself alone, and remain as free as before," both thinkers assume the parties to the agreement aim to advance their own interests, which is a fair reading of Rousseau's promise to take "men as they are" and "to unite what right sanctions with what is prescribed by interest."[35] The premise of self-regarding parties creates two challenges for the social contract theorist: (1) how are these self-interested persons to reach agreement given the likelihood that at least some of their interests will be in conflict? and (2) once these self-regarding agents have reached an agreement, how will they be motivated to comply with its terms? My aims in this section are twofold: (1) to consider how transparency and opaqueness bear on Rawls's answers to these questions, comparing his replies at certain points with Rousseau's; and (2) to suggest how various kinds of real-world opacity might be drawn upon to improve the prospects for realizing Rawls's conception of justice.

Transparency and Opacity in Rawls and Rousseau: *The Veil of Ignorance and the General Will*

We have seen that, for Rousseau, opaque social relations have many adverse consequences, including uncertainty, mistrust, and, most importantly, conditions unfavorable to the maintenance of civic virtue. Rawls, by contrast, makes brilliant use of a special kind of opacity—ignorance of one's place in the distribution of social and natural advantages—to derive his two well-known principles of justice. Rawls begins with an account of "the original position" in which the principles that are to govern the basic structure of society are chosen by rational, self-regarding agents from behind a "veil of ignorance," which deprives each person of the information that would be required in order to tailor the principles to his advantage. Although the parties choosing the principles of justice aim to further their own interests, no one can improve his prospects by holding out for better terms because no one knows which principles would be most favorable to his interests. Furthermore, Rawls goes on to point out, "the same holds true for coalitions: if a group were to decide to band together to the disadvantage of the others, they would not know how to favor themselves in the choice of principles," a conclusion reminiscent of our own findings regarding association under opaque conditions.[36]

Rawls argues that the principles chosen under these conditions must be fair because no one has the kind of knowledge that is necessary to further her particular interests at the expense of others. Rather, each person must consider whether she could willingly affirm a particular set of principles no matter what her social position and natural endowments turned out to be. In addition to guaranteeing a fair outcome, Rawls also claims that the opaque circumstances embodied in the original position yield principles which are compatible with individual autonomy. In describing some of the Kantian features of "justice as fairness," Rawls claims that, for Kant, "a person is acting autonomously when the principles of his action are chosen by him as the most adequate expression of his nature as a free and equal rational being."[37] Such principles cannot be dictated by a person's "social position or natural endowments," for "to act on such principles is to act heteronymously."[38] The veil of ignorance is crucial, in this regard, because it deprives the parties in the original position of "the knowledge that would enable them to choose heteronymous principles."[39] Once the veil is lifted, citizens can express their nature as free, equal, and rational agents by meeting their obligations as members of a political society that is governed by the principles of justice.[40] In Rawls's theory, then, opacity of a special kind supports the notion of "justice as fairness" while also making it possible for citizens to conduct their lives as autonomous beings.

Rawls views Kant's moral philosophy as an attempt to deepen and extend Rousseau's conception of freedom as obedience to self-given law. In his discussion of the veil of ignorance, Rawls refers to a paragraph in *The Social Contract* where Rousseau defines the general will as a will that "comes from all," "applies to all," and seeks "the happiness of each one."[41] The circumstances in the original position capture the first two of these requirements, since the principles of justice must be agreed to by all the parties, who are, in turn, all subject to the rules agreed upon. But whereas Rawls is able to ensure that his self-regarding parties will take account of everyone's interests by making them choose principles from behind the veil of ignorance, Rousseau's conception of the general will demands that citizens, whose own interests are fully transparent to themselves and to others, advance the interests of all alike by an act of *will-power*—that is, a disciplined renunciation of narrow self-interest in favor of the common good. Moreover, the general will can only achieve its objective if social conditions are sufficiently transparent to allow citizens to develop informed opinions about what course of action would promote "the happiness of each one."

Although the information necessary to determine which laws will advance the interests of "each one" would seem to be extensive, and the motivational imperatives of the general will equally demanding, both of these requirements are eased considerably by Rousseau's insistence upon a rough equality of property. A community of small property owners, and, to be more specific, a community of small property-owning farmers, will quite naturally share many interests in common. And since all these citizen-farmers are similarly situated, every law, assuming it is an "authentic act of the general will," will, according to Rousseau's understanding, favor or bind "all the citizens equally."[42]

At first thought, this conclusion seems overly optimistic, in part, because we have become suspicious, perhaps even cynical, about "formal equality." A law prohibiting everyone from "sleeping under a bridge" is a great deal more constraining for the poor than for the wealthy. But it is important to remember that the social differentiation, cultural pluralism, and economic inequality, which are characteristic of contemporary societies and which, in Rawls's version of social contract theory, are suppressed by the veil of ignorance, are absent from Rousseau's socially homogeneous and economically egalitarian republic. Consequently, the many conflicts of interest and belief that emerge when societies are vertically stratified and horizontally fragmented do not arise either. Thus, whereas Rawls requires the veil of ignorance in order to compel the parties in the original position to consider everyone's interest, Rousseau is able to achieve a similar result without the introduction of an opaque curtain by merely requiring that each citizen submit to "the conditions he imposes on others," a constraint that can be effective in "generalizing" the self-regarding wills of individual citizens, even under transparent circumstances, provided that each citizen is *similarly situated*, and therefore bears the same costs and enjoys the same benefits of whatever rules are adopted.[43] If the parties seeking to reach agreement have diverse and conflicting interests and beliefs, then they must either ignore their differences, for example, through the artifice of Rawls's veil of ignorance, or put themselves into one another's shoes in order to achieve an impartial weighting of everyone's interests, which, roughly speaking, is what utilitarianism requires of us, or bargain their way to an accord in the manner proposed by Gauthier and others.

We are now in a position to see that while both Rousseau and Rawls aim to formulate a social contract that will secure the freedom of the parties to the agreement, their proposed solutions to the problem are quite different. Rawls relies on the opaque circumstances of the original position to derive principles of justice that are unaffected by such contingent matters as the parties' particular positions within the distribution of social and natural advantages. Citizens who comply with the principles chosen under these conditions will be acting autonomously because these principles are, Rawls argues, the best expression of our nature as free and equal persons. By contrast, Rousseau can claim to have found a mode of association in which each person, "while uniting himself with all, may still obey himself alone, and remain as free as before," because, in Rousseau's contract theory, all citizens share a common set of circumstances and therefore every law consistent with the general will must advance the interests of each citizen, who, therefore, obeys no one but himself. Although a full account of the two conceptions would be a good deal more complicated, this simple comparison is useful in drawing attention to the fact that Rawls, because he effectively suppresses our particular interests in the choice of principles, must later confront a larger obstacle in achieving compliance with his principles. Rousseau, on the other hand, faces a more manageable problem in achieving compliance with the general will because it originates in the broadly overlapping interests shared by all citizens.

The Difference Principle

Rawls argues that the parties in the original position, not knowing their place in the distribution of social and natural advantages, would choose the "Difference Principle," which specifies that economic inequalities are just only insofar as they work to the long-run advantage of the least well off. At one point Rawls explains the parties' choice of the Difference Principle as "the maximin solution to the problem of social justice."[44] The maximin rule instructs decision makers to rank alternatives by their worst possible outcomes and to select the alternative in which the worst outcome is superior to the worst outcome of the others. One of the reasons Rawls gives in favor of the parties using the maximin rule is that the veil of ignorance is super-opaque; the parties in the original position do not even know the average or median income in the society for which they are choosing principles of justice. Some critics argue that the original position is *too* opaque, that there is nothing rationality can grab hold of. It would be more appropriate, according to this view, to allow the parties enough information to assign probabilities to the possible positions they might occupy, in which case, this argument runs, some form of utilitarianism would be the most attractive principle.[45] It is worth emphasizing that the whole question of which principles would be chosen in the original position depends, in large part, on whether the idealized circumstances of choice should be transparent or opaque! Complete opacity (plus some other assumptions) leads the parties to adopt the Difference Principle. Affording the parties probabilistic knowledge drives them toward some form of utilitarianism. And granting the parties knowledge of their own endowments tends to produce bargaining "solutions" that favor the more advantaged.[46]

In addition to being the most prudent choice, Rawls also characterizes the parties' selection of the Difference Principle as "an agreement to regard the distribution of natural talents as a common asset and to share in the benefits of this distribution whatever it turns out to be."[47] As Rawls famously says, "No one deserves his greater natural capacity nor merits a more favorable starting place in society."[48] Instead of accepting these contingencies, "men agree to share one another's fate."[49] Thus, "those who have been favored by nature, whoever they are, may gain from their good fortune only on terms that improve the situation of those who have lost out."[50]

Although Rawls, himself, does not put it this way, the choice of the Difference Principle may also be characterized as a decision to pool the risks associated with nature's genetic lottery.[51] Thus, instead of accepting the natural distribution, in which some people do very well and some very poorly, the parties, by choosing the Difference Principle, effectively "trade" this distribution, with its wide variance of outcomes (i.e., high risk), for a much narrower distribution (i.e., lower risk), which is brought about through a scheme in which those favored by nature compensate those who are less fortunate. Later, we shall see that this kind of risk-pooling arrangement may be used to enhance the appeal of Rawls's conception of justice to self-regarding citizens whose interests are not completely obscured by a veil of ignorance.

The Problem of Compliance

Let us now turn to the problem of compliance and ask whether it is reasonable to suppose that agents whose particular attributes were opaque at the moment of choosing would then act in accordance with the chosen principles once their particular advantages became transparent to themselves and to others.[52] To put the question as some of Rawls's communitarian critics have phrased it: is it plausible to expect that citizens, whose identities are not intimately bound up with one another and with the political community to which they belong, would nevertheless willingly comply with their duties even when it was costly for them to do so?[53] In particular, could we reasonably expect the most well-endowed citizens to view their social advantages as unfair and their natural endowments as a "collective asset," and, on the basis of this self-understanding, embrace laws and institutional arrangements that would eliminate these advantages, while harnessing their productive capabilities in the service of the least fortunate as required by the Difference Principle?[54] And, similarly, could we reasonably expect citizens who would be eligible to receive generous income subsidies in a Rawlsian state to nevertheless work productively, doing their part within the overall scheme social cooperation?

In thinking about these questions, it is important to bear in mind that Rawls does not claim that the citizens of a just state willingly meet their obligations *only* because they accord with the principles of justice. On the contrary, in a remark that paraphrases Rousseau, Rawls says that a readiness to comply with just laws and to do one's part in just social and political arrangements is "no mere moral conception formed from the understanding alone, but a true sentiment of the heart, enlightened by reason, the natural outcome of our primitive affections."[55] In chapter eight of *A Theory of Justice*, Rawls outlines his theory of moral psychology and explains how a sense of justice develops naturally from our disposition to reciprocate, "a psychological law" that Rawls says he has "drawn from *Emile*."[56] In brief, we come to care about the good of persons and institutions that advance our good. Thus, according to Rawls's account, the individual members of a cooperative association governed by a fair assignment of rights and duties will spontaneously develop ties of friendship and loyalty, and, recognizing that they and those whom they care about are the beneficiaries of the association, will be moved to fulfill their public responsibilities.[57] "In due course the reciprocal efforts of everyone's doing his share strengthens one another until a kind of equilibrium is reached."[58]

I think it is fair to say that Rousseau was not nearly so optimistic regarding the likelihood that citizens can be made to readily turn away from their private interests in order to fulfill their public obligations, even when they have been constrained and cajoled in ways that would be unacceptable to a liberal thinker like Rawls. In Rousseau's view, citizens will always be tempted to shirk their responsibilities, either because they believe their individual defection will impose only a small cost upon the republic, or because they cannot be assured that others will refrain from free riding on their efforts, or, finally, because they simply lack the self-discipline necessary to forego the pursuit of private advantage. And the psychological law Rawls extracts from *Emile*, wherein we come to advance the good of those who advance our good, is a law that exerts a much more powerful force within smaller bodies than in larger ones, which is to say that many, if not most, of us typically have a stronger attachment to our families, friends, and perhaps even some of our "partial societies," than to our country. It is because of these tendencies that many of Rousseau's meditations on the republican state focus upon the problem of transforming "men into citizens" and then reducing the chances of backsliding. This is the point of his emphasis on the education of compassionate citizens (like Emile), his injunction against "partial societies," his egalitarian economic policies, and the discipline imposed by the scheme of mutual surveillance that pervades his model republic.

For better or worse, none of these mechanisms is available to Rawls. In the first place, a compassionate identification with others and a willingness to make sacrifices on their behalf is a demand too severe to provide a solid foundation for a just state, a judgment that comes across clearly in Rawls's criticism of utilitarianism.[59] Second, whereas Rousseau insists on preventing inequalities of wealth from arising in order to preserve the common interests essential to the formation of the general will, Rawls proposes to use economic inequalities as an incentive to induce the most productive citizens to create wealth that will redound to the advantage of the least fortunate. Third, the "partial societies" Rousseau would discourage are, for Rawls, the natural consequence of one of the most basic liberties, freedom of association, the protection of which is accorded priority in Rawls's conception of justice. And, finally, this same commitment to individual liberties and the privacy rights that protect them precludes the introduction of a Rousseauean scheme of collective surveillance, which could ensure that every citizen is meeting her obligations under the principles of justice.

Realizing Rawls: The Further Uses of Opacity

Bearing these liberal constraints in mind, let us see whether, by extending Rawls's notion of a veil of ignorance beyond the original position, we can find some effective mechanism which would increase the likelihood that liberal citizens would affirm the Difference Principle, or at least a modest semblance thereof. Our problem arises because, once a citizen's assets and liabilities come into full view, those with a generous allotment of resources, talents, social connections, and the like may find it exceedingly difficult to support policies that would transfer a significant share of their income to those less favored. It is one thing to choose principles of justice without knowing whether one is rich or poor. It is quite another to willingly comply with principles that leave one significantly worse off than one could have been under an alternative, and not implausible, set of principles.[60] Moreover, insofar as Rawls's Difference Principle provides a generous income subsidy to the least advantaged citizens, it creates the potential for moral hazard because citizens who slack off will not bear the full cost of their lack of effort.

Earlier I suggested that the kind of risk-sharing which leads the parties to choose the Difference Principle might have application beyond the original position. To see why, we may begin by taking note of the fact that while, in real life, we do not have to make important decisions in complete ignorance of our prospects, that is, from behind a completely opaque veil of ignorance, the possibilities awaiting us are almost never completely transparent either, especially when we are making decisions for the long run. Many people manage this uncertainty, or at least a small part of it, by purchasing insurance against such adverse events as an automobile accident, or a home-destroying fire, or a prolonged illness. In addition, the citizens of many countries share the risks of natural disaster, medical emergencies, and short-term unemployment.

Yet the risks we share at present are, in fact, only a fraction of the risks that could be shared, even by purely self-regarding persons. To appreciate this point, consider the stock market, which affords investors the opportunity to diversify their holdings across many firms. In fact, investors can spread their holdings over many different sectors of the economy and even over many countries. Such diversification reduces the variance (risk) of the investor's total portfolio. Yet, while stock markets allow the holders of existing wealth to spread their assets widely, effectively hedging their risks, corporate profits amount to no more than 10 percent of national income, which means that 90 percent of the average citizen's income is subject to uninsured risks. These risks include such events as an unexpected deterioration of the local, regional, or national economy, sectoral demand shifts that increase wages in some occupations, while reducing them in others, a collapse of local housing values, and so on. Robert Shiller, an expert in this field, contends that "most of the risk that individuals face about their lifetime well-being is not shared."[61] Indeed, Shiller insists that, "we allow our standards of living to be determined substantially by a game of chance."[62]

This is a remarkable observation, which implies that our future prospects are much more opaque than most of us realize. To begin with, the major demographic and socioeconomic variables that affect our economic prospects—age, years of school, years of work experience, parents' level of education, occupation, and income—*taken together*, account for only one-fifth to one-third of the variation in annual incomes across individuals in the United States.[63] In addition to these factors, our incomes can be affected by the pace and direction of technological change, which can eliminate whole categories of human labor; macroeconomic shocks, which can create unemployment, plunging asset values, and pension-destroying bankruptcies; "career breaks," which may involve nothing more than "being in the right place at the right time"; and countless other variables over which we have little control.[64]

Some of these risks could, in fact, be shared. For example, consider the case of home values, which vary much less over the country as a whole than in the various regions that comprise the whole. Insofar as changes in regional housing prices are unexpected, which, for simplicity, I shall assume throughout, homeowners could enter into "insurance" contracts wherein they would receive a payment in the event housing values in their region increased by less than the national average, but would pay a premium if property values in their region increased by more than the national average. (This scheme is, of course, much oversimplified. Since only *un*expected price changes can be insured against, a more complicated set of price indices would be required to implement this kind of insurance.)[65] Another area of potential risk-sharing concerns occupational risk, that is, the risk that future wages in one's occupation could turn out to be lower than expected. Insurance against this risk is feasible because the average income of all occupations varies by less than the average income of particular occupations. In this case, people could "trade" the future variability of the average wage in their particular occupational group for the much smaller variability of the average wage over all occupational groups, bearing in mind that only the risks associated with unexpected changes in relative wages can be shared. More specifically, individuals working in occupations where wages fell in relation to the overall average wage would receive payments from individuals working in occupations where wage increases exceeded the overall average. These forms of insurance are feasible for self-regarding persons, in part, because they are not subject to moral hazard. In both cases, the insurance payout is tied to a broad index rather than to a particular value that could be affected by an individual's behavior, such as a person's own wage or the market value of one's own home.

The upshot of this discussion may be summarized as follows: (1) there is a moderately opaque, real-world veil of ignorance that clouds our economic prospects (2) this uncertainty is due to unpredictable trends and events, which are analogous, in a general way, to the "natural lottery of talent" that Rawls draws attention to in his justification of the Difference Principle; and (3) a substantial part of the risk implied by this uncertainty could, in fact, be pooled by rational, self-regarding individuals who agreed to "share one another's fate," exchanging the wide variability of a relatively narrow market (a regional housing market or a segment of the labor market in our examples) for a less variable, less risky, range of outcomes (the price or wage change in the national housing and labor markets). The point I now wish to make is that the sharing of these risks, like the sharing of risks associated with nature's genetic lottery by the parties in Rawls's original position, would reduce the variance of wealth and income across all citizens because the "winners" in these lotteries would compensate the "losers." In other words, individuals insuring their personal incomes against unpredictable risks by pooling these risks would, at the same time, bring about a more equal distribution of income.

The forms of risk-sharing just described are rare partly because human beings do not behave as rational utility-maximizers who attach well-informed probabilities to possible outcomes before making a decision. Research has shown that we rely too heavily on recent experience and that we tend to exaggerate our prospects for success, while ignoring many important risks altogether.[66] In other words, we underinsure because we think our future is more transparent than it really is, and the result is a more unequal distribution of income than would prevail if we had a better understanding of how opaque our prospects actually are.

Our self-regarding interest in social insurance, the unintended consequence of which is to reduce economic inequality, would be even greater if our future prospects were, *in fact*, a good deal less certain than they are at present. For example, suppose there were an equal chance that a person's income would be either $20,000 or $60,000. Faced with this prospect, many risk-averse citizens would likely favor a tax-financed insurance scheme under which their after-tax income plus insurance payout would be either $30,000 or $50,000.[67] Of course, support for such a program would be much weaker among those who earned $60,000 last year if they also had a high probability of earning the same income many years into the future, and, for good measure, were confident that their children also had a high probability of earning a good income.

Suppose, however, the second part of Rawls's second principle of justice, which requires "fair equality of opportunity," were successfully implemented. Then the economic prospects of every citizen, as well as the prospects of their children, would become much less certain because competition for the best jobs would be more intense. If public schools were as good as the very best private schools, if a great deal more money were invested in job training programs for the less advantaged, if any citizen wishing to attend college could do so, then today's more favored citizens would face greater competition, and, consequently, their prospects would be less clear. Insofar as these citizens could not confidently foresee their economic fate, nor that of their children, many of them might well favor a social insurance scheme that provided a generous income subsidy to citizens who fell upon hard times. In other words, an effective program to increase economic opportunities would create a semi-opaque, real-world veil of uncertainty which, leaving citizens less sure about their prospects, would enhance the appeal of social insurance programs that transferred income from "winners" to "losers," thereby reducing the variance, which is also to say, the inequality, of income across all citizens.

It almost goes without saying that Rousseau would not have approved of institutions and policies that left everyone uncertain about their economic prospects. "Nothing is more fatal to morality and the fate of the Republic," Rousseau argues, "than the continual shifting of rank and fortune among the citizens."[68] The civic virtue of a small, socially undifferentiated republic will be threatened when the prospects for advancement are distracting citizens from their duties, and the public gaze is constantly shifting. Of course Rousseau had no reason to search for solidarity in the opaqueness of the unknown future, for the citizens of his model republic are interconnected by common interests and powerful loyalties in the here-and-now. But if this kind of citizenship is no longer possible for us; if we cannot keep the community constantly "before our eyes"; then we might want to take a closer look at the considerable role that chance plays in determining our separate fates. For even self-regarding citizens will find it advantageous to share many risks if their future is sufficiently opaque.

CHAPTER SIX

Conclusion

Good science fiction creates dream worlds that give us a novel look at ourselves, drawing attention to aspects of human life that usually go unnoticed. Perhaps it is not surprising, then, that political thinkers have occasionally turned to fantastic technologies in order to frame a particular question or issue in an especially penetrating light. Plato invokes the story of Gyges's Ring in order to strip away all of the ancillary benefits that accrue to the person who has a reputation for being virtuous, forcing us to consider whether ethical conduct is good in itself, while, at the same time, inviting us to contemplate whether we could resist the temptation of absolute power exerted with complete impunity. For those who reject Plato's argument in favor of self-restraint and its appeal to intrinsic goodness, the Ring's supernatural powers simply cast into bold relief the crucial importance of visibility in keeping our propensity for self-aggrandizement in check. For one of our contemporary Hobbesians (David Gauthier), who rejects the very idea of intrinsic goodness, it is *only* our visibility, our *transparency*, that stands between us and the nightmare depicted in the *Leviathan*.[1]

In an altogether different flight from reality, John Rawls's veil of ignorance transforms us momentarily into rational agents without any knowledge of our particular ends, our interests, our place in society, or our natural endowments, in short, into rational agents without an identity. For some of Rawls's admirers, this piece of fiction is useful in showing how individuals who aim to further their own ends might nevertheless agree on fair principles that would allow them cooperate for mutual advantage. Although the main purpose of Rawls's fictional device is to prevent the parties in the original position from tailoring principles around their own particular ends and interests, the veil of ignorance also rules out the possibility of bargaining, which requires that the sources of one's bargaining power be at least partially transparent *to others*. In the absence of this knowledge, in conditions of symmetrical or universal opacity, we must consider how things look from a variety of social positions because, once the veil is lifted, we will occupy one of these positions ourselves. Whereas the opaqueness made possible by Gyges's Ring allows its wearer to turn his back on the interests of others, the veil of ignorance compels us to take them into account as if they were our own. For some of Rawls's critics, on the other hand, this opaque curtain carries us too far from the real conditions of human life to provide any useful guidance in evaluating alternative conceptions of our political possibilities.[2] According to these critics, the essence of the human condition lies in the fact that our identities and interests are transparent to us in a way that precludes the possibility of attaining a "view from nowhere," that is, a detached vantage point from which we might impartially judge alternative institutional arrangements.[3]

If we possessed Ackerman's visionary technologies of "transactional flexibility"; if each of us could find our most perfectly matched "cooperation partners" without having to sort through a multitude of unattractive offers; if, being fully transparent, we could instantaneously reach agreement on the terms of our joint endeavors, these terms being enforceable at no cost; if each person could shield herself from the unwanted side effects of actions taken by others in pursuit of their ends; then the scope of civil society and the market economy would extend without limit, while the agenda of government, and the significance of democracy, would become vanishingly small. Although Ackerman's aim is to reveal the essence of liberalism—what the world would look like if every interaction were voluntary—one might just as easily take away from his thought experiment the inescapable inference that, in the real world, despite our most determined efforts, we are often opaque to one another, that each of us has limited control over even our immediate surroundings, that we cannot shield ourselves from many things we wish to, that social life is pervaded by "externalities" in the broadest sense of the word.

Rousseau knew a thing or two about being vulnerable to the harms that can be inflicted by other people, particularly when their "demeanor does not proclaim at first glance their true disposition." Although he did not invoke supernatural technologies to bring out the distinctive aspects of modern society, Rousseau's conjectures about the natural history of humankind perform much the same service. Thus, he speculates that, before "art had moulded our behavior," human beings enjoyed the confident security afforded by the ability "to see through one another," a power which, like a kind of Gyges's Ring in reverse, once prevented our descent into Hobbes's war of all against all. Of course Rousseau's conjectures about our distant past will only be persuasive if we can recognize ourselves in these speculations, or can at least envision some lineage connecting their circumstances to ours. When Rousseau conjures up primitive beings whose lack of a *persona* precluded the possibility of deception, we may doubt the relevance of such natural transparency for our predicament because these creatures lacked self-consciousness and a conception of themselves as the object of another's judgment, attributes, which, arguably, are features essential to the human form of life.

While Rousseau's unreflective primitives may be too distant from us to shed much light on our circumstances, surely he was onto something in drawing attention to the fact that transparent intentions facilitate cooperation, even when the agents involved are exclusively interested in their own gains. It takes just a moment's reflection to realize that those interactions in which we immediately apprehend the intentions of the other person are quite different from those encounters in which the other remains more or less opaque to us. It is easier to make plans and coordinate actions when we are confident in our assessment of one another's aims and character. And surely Rousseau was not misguided in pointing out that the degree to which one person can rely on another depends on the social setting in which they interact. Citizens who share many of the same values, beliefs, and interests, and who interact within a dense social network that allows them to monitor one another's behavior while keeping the community constantly "before their eyes," will find it easier to cooperate for mutual advantage than citizens who inhabit large, socially stratified, and culturally diverse societies, and encounter one another as strangers. If we now regard Hobbes as the first thinker to clearly formulate the circumstances in which the universal pursuit of self-interest is self-defeating, and if contemporary game theorists deserve credit for discovering the theoretical solution to the problem of cooperation in the strategy of conditional cooperation, or tit-for-tat, let us then recognize Rousseau as a thinker who gave us a vivid description of the social conditions in which cooperative strategies are most likely to succeed.[4]

By the same token, Rousseau did not fully appreciate the implications of transparent conditions, particularly for the kind of republic he urged upon his readers. I have tried to drive the logic of transparency to its limit, where we find two disconcerting results: associations of the most well-endowed citizens whose advantages are compounded by their combination within exclusive groups; and the decomposition of the public into secondary associations that advance the particular goals and interests of their members. As long as transparency is a function of social distance, and people find it easier to "see through" those who belong to the same class, religion, ethnic group, and the like, freedom of association will, as a matter of course, create a fragmented polity of "partial societies," which, while they provide an antidote to "individualism," nevertheless make it very difficult to formulate a common good around which citizens might reach agreement, and for the sake of which they might attenuate at least some of their commitments to the groups that advance their more parochial interests.

In his reflections on the modern predicament, Rousseau found that people were strangers to one another because they hid their real ambitions behind the mask of reputation. And since these ambitions often involve the pursuit of gains at another person's expense, Rousseau regarded the dawn of opacity and the struggle for superiority as two sides of the same coin. Leaving aside for the moment the *necessary* connection Rousseau claims to find between opaqueness and inequality, I think he had a deep insight into at least one important aspect of this relationship. When it comes to social interactions of the prisoner's dilemma variety, the combination of opaque intentions and an interest in relative position (*amour-propre*) is fatal to cooperation. People who prefer preeminence to mutual respect and cannot read one another's intentions are likely to find themselves in a condition of mutual hostility. On the other hand, people who are less preoccupied with social status, or who are more transparent to one another, or who possess both of these traits, are more likely to enjoy the benefits of cooperation, whether in pursuit of material gains or in sustaining a social environment conducive to self-respect. Which of these patterns prevails within a society will go a considerable distance in shaping the political possibilities that are open to its citizens. Like Montesquieu before him, and Tocqueville after him, Rousseau taught us a great deal about the political ramifications of different kinds of "interpersonal relations."

In lamenting that "we never know with whom we have to deal," Rousseau was onto something that economists have only recently come to appreciate—that the nature of trade is very different when markets are opaque than when, as in the older textbooks, there are no secrets and, hence, no need to defend against duplicity. Of course there is no gainsaying Adam Smith's magnificent insight: there is an "invisible hand" at work in the market economy and it does impose a modicum of order upon activities that are undertaken with the narrowest objectives in mind. In the limiting case, where prices convey all the information necessary for decision making, Smith's "invisible hand" can efficiently coordinate the choices of millions of free and rational agents, the income of each one being proportionate to his or her productive contribution. But this is not the marketplace in which we actually conduct our business. Self-interested merchants will not always find it profitable to reveal all they know about their goods, workers do not announce that they are going to "take it easy" for awhile, and borrowers may not reveal the weaknesses in their balance sheets. Although these oversights seem to be of relatively minor importance, it turns out that this kind of asymmetric information pervades real-world economies and precludes the efficient operation of the "invisible hand," which can only bring harmony to the self-interested choices of market participants under transparent conditions.

In regarding opaqueness and inequality as parts of a seamless whole, Rousseau also missed important dimensions of modernity. One of the defining transformations of the modern world was the liberation of individuals from the traditional roles and obligations characteristic of premodern communities. When people are no longer constrained by the duties of their station, but make their own way in life, their behavior is much less predictable.[5] This lack of predictability is compounded in an urban setting that affords everyone a measure of anonymity. In these respects, the opaqueness that is manifest in our uncertainty about the intentions of those with whom we interact is both the natural consequence of the birth of the modern self and a precondition of its survival. Thus, while Rousseau insists that the social contract must be the product of each person's willing consent, he seems not to recognize that real autonomy requires reflection on the given, and that this kind of reflection is only possible if we are granted a measure of protection from the gaze of others. Although there are places in Rousseau's work where he acknowledges this requirement, for example, in recommending that votes should be cast in private, in general, the regime of republican surveillance works against it.

The point of mutual surveillance in Rousseau's model republic is to allow each citizen to do her part in a cooperative undertaking with the assurance that everyone else is doing theirs. Of course it must be acknowledged that the same kind of watchfulness is likely to play a very different role in a large, highly differentiated, multicultural state. The necessary foundations of Rousseau's model republic—a small, unified community whose citizens share a common conception of the good— have disappeared. And when a shared understanding of what human life is about gives way to a variety of conceptions, that is, when the central premise of Rousseau's republic of virtue is supplanted by the pluralism that confronts Rawls and Ackerman, a new source of opacity emerges— the difficulty of communicating across a diversity of "life worlds." Under these conditions, surveillance is not likely to be mutual, nor is it apt to produce transparent relations among the inhabitants of these disparate worlds. While a regime of mutual watchfulness and accountability may be congenial, or at least tolerable, to a people who share common criteria of judgment, it will seem oppressive, and may often be so, to those segments of a pluralistic society which do not affirm, nor perhaps even accept, the criteria according to which they are being judged.

For those who value the opaque spaces of modernity and the privacy they protect, there is one device, above all, that symbolizes the threat posed by society's judgmental gaze—Bentham's Panopticon, the model prison which is arranged in a circle so that every prisoner can be observed at all times.[6] Michel Foucault, who, like Rousseau, was a self-conscious outsider, developed the implications of Bentham's Panopticon with great ingenuity in order to construct a theory of modernity and its distinctive mode of "discipline." In Foucault's understanding, the civilizations of ancient Greece and Rome sought "to render accessible to a multiple of men the inspection of a small number of objects" through the classical "architecture of temples, theatres and circuses."[7] But the idea of Rome during the Enlightenment harbored two images. "In its Republican aspect, it was the very embodiment of liberty; in its military aspect, it was the ideal scheme of discipline."[8] For Foucault, it was Roman discipline, not Roman citizenship, which was reborn, albeit in a form that was more extensive and reached much deeper than anything the Romans could have imagined. We now live in a "panoptic machine" where power is "like a faceless gaze," which transforms "the whole social body into a field of perception . . . thousands of eyes posted everywhere, mobile attentions ever on the alert."[9] "Our society is not one of spectacle," Foucault concludes, "but of surveillance."[10]

How is it possible that Rousseau, who also drew inspiration from Greece and Rome, could be aligned with what Foucault calls a "society of surveillance"? We know the answer to this question, but before we repeat it, let us take note of the fact that Foucault, like Rousseau, seizes upon the contrast between the "predominance of public life" in the civilization of antiquity and the division of modern society into "private individuals," on the one side, and "the state," on the other.[11] Rousseau's aim was, in some measure, to recreate the ancient republic, not by reliance upon public spectacle alone, which would have been inadequate given the ambitions of "private individuals," but by a scheme of mutual surveillance that would prevent citizens from free riding on the efforts of their neighbors, while at the same time providing each citizen with the assurance that everyone else is doing their part as well. Of course things look very different if we accept Foucault's view of moral distinctions as arbitrary categories. From this vantage point, we can easily appreciate the desire not to be judged, or be subjected to a disciplinary mechanism "that coerces by means of observations," a mechanism that casts "a normalizing gaze" and renders "a normalizing judgment."[12] If this is your understanding of our predicament, then Ackerman's "shield" is just the ticket. But if moral categories like "free rider" are not arbitrary, if "cooperation for mutual benefit" is not just an empty phrase, then freedom from the judgments of others, which is conferred upon the citizens of opaque societies, may be a mixed blessing.

NOTES

Preface

1. Jean Starobinski, *Jean-Jacques Rousseau: Transparency and Obstruction*, trans. Arthur Goldhammer (Chicago: University of Chicago Press, 1988), p. xii, emphasis in the original.
2. Jean-Jacques Rousseau, "The Social Contract," in *The Social Contract and Discourses*, ed. and trans. G. D. H. Cole (New York: E. P. Dutton, 1950), p. 26.
3. Jean-Jacques Rousseau, "A Discourse on the Origin of Inequality," in *The Social Contract and Discourses*, ed. and trans. G. D. H. Cole (New York: E. P. Dutton, 1950), p. 198.
4. The idea of "rational reconstruction" is elaborated in Edna Ulmann-Margalit, *The Emergence of Norms* (Oxford: Oxford University Press, 1977), pp. 1–5.

Chapter One   Introduction

1. Jean-Jacques Rousseau, "A Discourse on the Arts and Sciences," in *The Social Contract and Discourses*, ed. and trans. G. D. H. Cole (New York: E. P. Dutton, 1950), pp. 148–149.
2. Rousseau, "Discourse on the Arts and Sciences," p. 148.
3. Ibid., p. 164.
4. Jean-Jacques Rousseau, "A Discourse on the Origin of Inequality," in *The Social Contract and Discourses*, ed. and trans. G. D. H. Cole (New York: E. P. Dutton, 1950), p. 241.
5. Ibid., p. 247.
6. Jean-Jacques Rousseau, "Considerations on the Government of Poland," in *Jean-Jacques Rousseau: Political Writings*, ed. and trans. Frederick Watkins (Madison: University of Wisconsin Press, 1986), p. 231.
7. Rousseau, "Discourse on the Origin of Inequality," p. 177.
8. Jean Starobinski, *Jean-Jacques Rousseau: Transparency and Obstruction*, trans. Arthur Goldhammer (Chicago: University of Chicago Press, 1988), p. 38.
9. See especially Starobinski, *Jean-Jacques Rousseau*; Marshall Berman, *The Politics of Authenticity* (New York: Atheneum, 1980); Ronald Grimsley, *Jean-Jacques Rousseau: A Study in Self-Awareness* (Cardiff, Wales: University of Wales Press, 1961); Patrick Riley, ed., *The Cambridge Companion to Rousseau* (Cambridge: Cambridge University Press, 2001), especially the essays by George Armstrong Kelly, Patrick Riley, Jean Starobinski, and Robert Wolker; Christopher Kelly, *Rousseau as Author: Consecrating One's Life to Truth* (Chicago: University of Chicago Press, 2003); Elizabeth Wingrove, *Rousseau's Republican Romance* (Princeton, NJ: Princeton University Press, 2000); Clifford Orwin and Nathan Tarcov, eds., *The Legacy of Rousseau* (Chicago: University

of Chicago Press, 1997); and Mira Morgenstern, *Rousseau and the Politics of Ambiguity* (University Park, PA: Penn State Press, 1996).

10. See Ludwig Wittgenstein, *Philosophical Investigations*, trans. G. E. M. Anscombe (Oxford: Blackwell, 1958); and Greg Hill, "Solidarity, Objectivity, and the Human Form of Life," *Critical Review* (Fall 1997): 550–580.

11. Plato, *Republic*, trans. by Francis MacDonald Cornford (Oxford: Oxford University Press, 1945), 359c–360b.

12. We may add that, in Jean-Jacques Rousseau's *Confessions*, trans. J. M. Cohen (Harmondsworth, UK: Penguin, 1954); and Jean-Jacques Rousseau, *The Reveries of a Solitary Walker*, trans. and ed. C. Butterworth (Harmondsworth, UK: Penguin, 1964) the question becomes, "what kind of life can I, Jean-Jacques, lead when everyone *else* possesses a ring like Gyges'?"

13. Rousseau, "Considerations on the Government of Poland," p. 231, emphasis added.

14. David Brin, *The Transparent Society* (New York: Perseus, 1999), p. 5. It has been reported that the average Londoner is caught "on screen" more than sixty times a day.

15. For contrasting views on the proper boundary between public and private, see Amitai Etzioni, *The Limits of Privacy* (New York: Basic Books, 1999); Jeffery Rosen, *The Unwanted Gaze* (New York: Random House, 2000); and Thomas Nagel, *Concealment and Exposure* (Oxford: Oxford University Press, 2002).

16. Brin, *Transparent Society*, p. 9.

17. Jean-Jacques Rousseau, "A Discourse on Political Economy," in *The Social Contract and Discourses*, ed. and trans. G. D. H. Cole (New York: E. P. Dutton, 1950), p. 299.

18. It is worth remembering that Bentham also deflected criticism of his Panopticon by insisting that everyone could come and observe the observers, the building being open "to the great tribunal of the world," quoted in Michel Foucault, *Discipline and Punish* (New York: Vintage, 1979), p. 207.

19. Foucault, *Discipline and Punish*.

20. Adam Smith, *The Wealth of Nations* (Oxford: Clarendon Press, 1976).

21. See, e.g., Michael J. Sandel, *Democracy's Discontent* (Cambridge: Belknap Press of Harvard University Press, 1996).

22. See, e.g., Joseph E. Stiglitz, *Whither Socialism?* (Cambridge: MIT Press, 1994).

23. Rousseau, "Discourse on the Origin of Inequality," p. 177.

24. Alexis de Tocqueville, *Democracy in America*, ed. J. P. Mayer, trans. by George Lawrence (Garden City, NY: Anchor Books, 1969), vol. II.

25. Rousseau, "Discourse on the Arts and Sciences," p. 149.

26. David Gauthier, *Morals by Agreement* (Oxford: Oxford University Press, 1986).

27. Bruce A. Ackerman, *Social Justice in the Liberal State* (New Haven: Yale University Press, 1980).

28. John Rawls, *A Theory of Justice* (Cambridge: Harvard University Press, 1971).

Chapter Two   Transparency and Opacity in Nature, Society, and State

1. Charles De Secondat Montesquieu, *Spirit of the Laws*, ed. Ann M. Cohler (Cambridge: Cambridge University Press, 1989), book III.

2. Raymond Aron, *Main Currents in Sociological Thought* (London: Transaction, 1998), vol. 1, p. 27.

3. Jean-Jacques Rousseau, "A Discourse on the Origin of Inequality," in *The Social Contract and Discourses*, ed. and trans. G. D. H. Cole (New York: E. P. Dutton, 1950), p. 222.

4. Rousseau, "Discourse on the Origin of Inequality," pp. 222–223.

5. Ibid., p. 270.

6. For example, see Gregory S. Kavka, "Hobbes's War of All Against All," in *The Social Contract Theorists*, ed. Christopher W. Morris (New York: Rowman & Littlefield, 1999), p. 3. Other game-theoretic interpretations of Hobbes's argument can be found in Edna Ullmann-Margalit,

The Emergence of Norms (Oxford: Oxford University Press, 1977), pp. 62–73; Jean Hampton, *Hobbes and the Social Contract Tradition* (New York: Cambridge University Press, 1986); and Gregory S. Kavka, *Hobbesian Moral and Political Theory* (Princeton: Princeton University Press, 1986). For a different view, see David Gauthier, *The Logic of Leviathan* (Oxford: Oxford University Press, 1969); and David Gauthier, "Hobbes's Social Contract," in *The Social Contract Theorists*, ed. Christopher W. Morris (New York: Rowman & Littlefield, 1999), pp. 59–72.

7. For reasons that will become clear shortly, the payoffs are expressed in subjectively valued units or utility.

8. Kavka, "Hobbes's War of All Against All," p. 3, emphasis in the original.

9. According to this interpretation of Hobbes, an enforceable contract, not just a coordination agreement, is necessary to secure the benefits of peace. See Gauthier, "Hobbes's Social Contract," pp. 59–72. For the coordination view, see Jean Hampton, "The Failure of Hobbes's Social Contract Argument," in *The Social Contract Theorists*, ed. Christopher W. Morris (New York: Rowman & Littlefield, 1999), pp. 41–58; and Hampton, *Hobbes and the Social Contract Tradition*.

10. Thomas Hobbes, *Leviathan*, ed. C. B. Macpherson (Middlesex: Penguin, 1968), p. 196.

11. Jean-Jacques Rousseau, "A Discourse on the Arts and Sciences," in *The Social Contract and Discourses*, ed. and trans. G. D. H. Cole (New York: E. P. Dutton, 1950), pp. 148–149.

12. In the context of these first primitive societies, where social interaction is still sporadic, to "cooperate" simply means to act with restraint; it does not initiate an ongoing social relationship.

13. See David Gauthier, *Morals by Agreement* (Oxford: Oxford University Press, 1986), chap. 6. For a different, but still sympathetic, treatment of conditional cooperation as a rational strategy within a single-play prisoner's dilemma game, see Nigel Howard, *Paradoxes of Rationality* (Cambridge, MA: MIT Press, 1971); and Robert Nozick, *The Nature of Rationality* (Princeton: Princeton University Press, 1993). For an even-handed assessment of the issues surrounding the strategy of conditional cooperation, see Shaun P. Hargreaves Heap and Yanis Varoufakis, *Game Theory* (London: Routledge, 1995), pp. 162–164.

14. Hobbes's own view is actually more complicated. See David Gauthier, *Moral Dealing* (Ithaca, NY: Cornell University Press, 1990), pp. 129–149.

15. This version of the prisoner's dilemma game can be formalized by adding the requirement that, when asked what kind of player one is, i.e., a conditional cooperator or an unconditional defector, the player always gives an honest answer. See Leslie Burkholder, "Theorem 1," in *Modeling Rationality, Morality, and Evolution*, ed. Peter A. Danielson (New York: Oxford University Press, 1998), pp. 137–160. Alternatively, we could suppose that players are programmed by nature to reveal their intentions through involuntary facial expressions and the like. See Robert H. Frank, *Passions within Reason* (New York: W. W. Norton, 1988), chap. 6.

16. This objection is raised in Hargreaves Heap and Varoufakis, *Game Theory*, pp. 162–164.

17. Rousseau, "Discourse on the Arts and Sciences," p. 148. Jason Andrew Neidleman, *The General Will Is Citizenship* (New York: Rowman & Littlefield, 2001), p. 43, interprets Rousseau's nostalgic longing for a time when "the outward countenance was always the image of the heart's dispositions" simply as a critical comment on the corrupt disposition of the civilized heart, which is infected by *amour-propre*. But it is, in addition to this, a complaint about the pervasive deception characteristic of civilized life.

18. See Frank, *Passions within Reason*, chap. 6.

19. See Eleanor Ostrom, "Collective Action and the Evolution of Norms," *Journal of Economic Perspectives* 14:3 (Summer 2000): 137–158.

20. For simplicity, I ignore the inadvertent "exploitation" that occurs when only one conditional cooperator mistakes another for an unconditional defector.

21. To compute the threshold probability of recognition at which conditional cooperation becomes the rational strategy, we begin by writing the equations that give the expected utility payoffs of the two strategies. The expected payoff to the strategy of unconditional defection is given by the following [1].

$$UD = pM + (1 - p)rM + (1 - p)(1 - r)N \;[1]$$

Where,

UD = Expected payoff of unconditional defection

p = Probability of interacting with another unconditional defector

M = Payoff to each player in mutual defection outcome

1 − p = Probability of interacting with a conditional cooperator

r = Probability that a conditional cooperator will recognize the strategic disposition of the other player

1 − r = Probability that a conditional cooperator will not recognize the strategic disposition of the other player

N = Payoff to player who defects when the other player cooperates

The expected payoff to the strategy of conditional cooperation is given by the following [2].

$$CC = (1 - p)rS + (1 - p)(1 - r)M + prM + p(1 - r)T \;[2]$$

Where,

CC = Expected payoff of conditional cooperation

1 − p = Probability of interacting with a conditional cooperator

r = Probability that a conditional cooperator will recognize the strategic disposition of the other player

S = Payoff to each player in the mutual cooperation outcome

1 − r = Probability that a conditional cooperator will not recognize the strategic disposition of the other player

M = Payoff to each player in the mutual defection outcome

p = Probability of interacting with an unconditional defector

T = Payoff to the cooperating player when the other player defects

The threshold probability of recognition is that value for r, i.e., the probability of accurate recognition in [1] and [2], such that CC exceeds UD by a marginal amount. (Bear in mind that, given the stipulation in note 20, the value of r is the same in both equations.)

22. Given the equations in note 21, it is *necessarily* the case that the expected payoff to conditional cooperation increases as the probability of recognition increases. To remain faithful to Rousseau's account of simple souls who do not calculate, we require something like the process of natural selection, which might plausibly favor a behavioral template that includes both conditional cooperation and transparent intentions. Alternatively, people might have acquired these traits through a learning process in which successful patterns of behavior were unself-consciously emulated. An evolutionary argument of this kind can be found in R. L. Trivers, "The Evolution of Reciprocal Altruism," *Quarterly Review of Biology* 46 (1971): 35–57. The same result will be achieved when interactions are correlated, so that conditional cooperators are more likely to interact with one another than with unconditional defectors, who, in turn, are more likely to interact with one another than with conditional cooperators. See Brian Skyrms, *Evolution of the Social Contract* (Cambridge: Cambridge University Press, 1996).

23. Strictly speaking, the population of conditional cooperators will rise as the probability of interacting with conditional cooperators increases. See Skyrms, *Evolution of the Social Contract*.

24. It may also be noted that a population of conditional cooperators is evolutionarily stable in that it cannot be successfully invaded by unconditional defectors as long as the players' intentions remain sufficiently transparent. See John Maynard Smith, *Evolution and the Theory of Games* (Cambridge: Cambridge University Press, 1982); and Peter Ockenfels, "Cooperation in the Prisoner's Dilemma," *European Journal of Political Economy* 9 (1993): 567–579.

25. Hobbes also points to uncertainty in explaining why people in the state of nature renounce self-restraint in favor of self-assertion. See Hobbes, *Leviathan*, chap. 13. It may be noted that Kavka's emphasis on the logic of "anticipatory violence" presupposes opaque intentions insofar as the element of surprise is essential to the advantage gained by striking first (see note 8 earlier).

26. It is important to add that the disutility of violent death cannot be infinite if we are to be able to compute the expected utility payoffs of alternative strategies. By the same token, while equating violent death with infinite negative utility may seem attractive at first glance, it implies that human beings never risk this outcome, which is contrary to the facts. If the disutility of violent death is not infinite, then, strictly speaking, people do not have to be *perfectly* transparent, if by this we mean their intentions can *never* be misconstrued, in order for conditional cooperation to be a rational strategy.

27. I assume, as before, a population equally divided between conditional cooperators and unconditional defectors.

28. Some degree of transparency is, of course, essential for the existence of social life, itself.

29. This point is developed in considerable detail in John Charvet, *The Social Problem in the Philosophy of Rousseau* (Cambridge: Cambridge University Press, 1974). Also see N. J. H. Dent, *Rousseau* (Oxford: Basil Blackwell, 1988), chap. 6; and Roger D. Masters, "Rousseau and the Rediscovery of Human Nature," in *The Legacy of Rousseau*, ed. Clifford Orwin and Nathan Tarcov (Chicago: University of Chicago Press, 1997), pp. 110–142.

30. Rousseau, "Discourse on the Origin of Inequality," p. 223, note 2.

31. Loyal Rue, *By the Grace of Guile* (New York: Oxford University Press, 1994), pp. 121–124.

32. See G. H. Mead, *Mind, Self, and Society* (Chicago: University of Chicago Press, 1934). Cf. Richard Noble, *Language, Subjectivity, and Freedom in Rousseau's Moral Philosophy* (New York: Garland Press, 1991), p. 87, note 14, and pp. 138–140.

33. The role of judgments in language acquisition is emphasized in Ludwig Wittgenstein, *On Certainty*, ed. G. E. M. Anscombe and G. H. von Wright, trans. G. E. M. Anscombe (Oxford: Blackwell, 1969).

34. See Ludwig Wittgenstein, *Philosophical Investigations*, trans. G. E. M. Anscombe (Oxford: Blackwell, 1958), paragraph 244.

35. Arguably, this is precisely what Rousseau assumed, especially with regard to the first human languages, which emerged as spontaneous expressions of natural sentiments. See Jean-Jacques Rousseau, "Essay on the Origin of Languages," in *Discourses and Essay on the Origin of Languages*, ed. and trans. Victor Gourevitch (New York: Harper & Row, 1990); cf. Noble, *Language, Subjectivity, and Freedom in Rousseau's Moral Philosophy*, pp. 109–132. Noble characterizes Rousseau's conception of man's original language as one "suited only to the expression of primal passions such as love and pity, or jealously and fear," while denying "him the capacity to deceive others about himself or his desires" (pp. 138–139). Whether this was Rousseau's view or not, it seems wrongheaded. Languages do not come in modular units: one module for doing work, one for expressing emotions, another for deceiving others, and so on. Learning to express jealousy goes hand-in-hand with learning how to recognize feelings of jealousy, learning how a jealous person is regarded by others, learning how to conceal one's jealousy, and so forth. See Rush Rhees, *Wittgenstein and the Possibility of Discourse*, ed. D. Z. Phillips (Cambridge: Cambridge University Press, 1998).

36. Wittgenstein, *Philosophical Investigations*, paragraphs 244 and 246.

37. This possibility is envisioned in Rue, *By the Grace of Guile*, pp. 138–145.

38. Alexis de Tocqueville, *Democracy in America*, ed. J. P. Mayer, trans. George Lawrence (Garden City, NY: Anchor Books, 1969), vol. II, part 3.

39. Michael Taylor, *Anarchy and Cooperation* (London: John Wiley, 1976); Michael Taylor, *The Possibility of Cooperation* (Cambridge: Cambridge University Press, 1987); and Robert Axelrod, *The Evolution of Cooperation* (New York: Basic Books, 1984).

40. See Axelrod, *Evolution of Cooperation*, pp. 10–21; and Elliot Sober, "Stable Cooperation in Iterated Prisoners' Dilemmas," *Economics and Philosophy* 8 (1992): 127–139.

41. This lack of foresight is essential to understanding the game-theoretic logic underlying Rousseau's depiction of a deer (stag) hunt, "Discourse on the Origin of Inequality," p. 238, which runs as follows: "If a deer was to be taken, every one saw that, in order to succeed, he must faithfully abide by his post: but if a hare happened to come within reach of any one of

them, it is not to be doubted that he pursued it without scruple, and, having seized his prey, cared very little, if by so doing he caused his companions to miss theirs." If we assume that all the hunters prefer to share a deer as opposed to each one having a hare to himself, and also assume that this preference ordering is common knowledge, then, all else being the same, each hunter would have reason to "faithfully abide by his post." This preference ordering would be upset, however, if the hunters were "perfect strangers to foresight," so that each one prefers a hare "now" to sharing a deer "later." Given this preference ordering, each hunter can be expected to defect if the opportunity arises, i.e., abandon his post if a hare should happen by.

42. Ibid.
43. Ibid., p. 244.
44. Ibid., p. 248.
45. Cf. Zev M. Trachtenberg, *Making Citizens: Rousseau's Political Theory of Culture* (London: Routledge, 1993), chap. 3.
46. See, e.g., Marshall Sahlins, *Stone Age Economics* (Hawthorne, NY: Aldine de Gruyter, 1972).
47. See Richard A. Posner, *The Economics of Justice* (Cambridge, MA: Harvard University Press, 1981), pp. 146–174. It is worth noting that in Rousseau's Geneva, "the good citizens were themselves derelict in their duty if they did not notify the Consistory when a neighbor violated [the citizen's] solemn obligations," William H. Blandshard, *Rousseau and the Spirit of Revolt* (Ann Arbor: University of Michigan Press, 1967), p. 1.
48. Rousseau, "Discourse on the Origin of Inequality," pp. 233–247. Cf. Adam B. Seligman, *The Problem of Trust* (Princeton, NJ: Princeton University Press, 1997), who stresses the role of social differentiation and "role indeterminacy" in creating "the opaqueness of [the] other's intentions," p. 43.
49. The consequences of imperfect monitoring are examined in Jonathan Bendor and Dilip Moskherjee, "Institutional Structure and the Logic of Ongoing Collective Action," *American Political Science Review* 81 (1987): 129–154.
50. The consequences of shirking are explored in Rudolf Schuessler, "Threshold Effects and the Decline of Cooperation," *Journal of Conflict Resolution* 34 (1990): 476–494.
51. This is a prominent theme in many of Rousseau's works, but particularly in his "Discourse on the Arts and Sciences"; and the "Letter to M. D'Alembert on the Theatre," in *Politics and the Arts*, ed. and trans. Allan Bloom (Ithaca: Cornell University Press, 1960). Jean Starobinski discusses Rousseau's use of the contrast between rural and urban life in *Jean-Jacques Rousseau: Transparency and Obstruction*, trans. Arthur Goldhammer (Chicago: University of Chicago Press, 1988), pp. 346–349.
52. Cf. Peter M. Blau, *Exchange and Power in Social Life* (London: Transaction, 1986), pp. 44–46.
53. See David Hirshleifer and Eric Rasmusen, "Cooperation in a Repeated Prisoners' Dilemma with Ostracism," *Journal of Economic Behavior and Organization* 12 (1989): 87–106.
54. Rousseau, "Discourse on the Origin of Inequality," p. 270. In the "Letter to M. D'Alembert on the Theatre," pp. 34–47, Rousseau complains that Moliere's plays have raised the costs of being regarded as an innocent dupe.
55. The effect of unconditional cooperators on the strategic environment is explained in Peter A. Danielson, *Artificial Morality* (London: Routledge, 1992).
56. The economics of acquiring costly information about the character of one's prospective collaborators is formalized in Frank, *Passions within Reason*, appendix.
57. "Discourse on the Arts and Sciences," p. 149. While I have stressed the consequences of deception for those who are deceived (given my focus on the instrumental aspects of transparency and opacity), Rousseau is, of course, also interested in the deceiver's self-inflicted wounds. Consider, e.g., Rousseau's characterization of the actor who, while specializing in the "traffic of oneself," in actuality "annihilates himself" in the "Letter to M. D'Alembert on the Theatre," pp. 79–81. Also, see Jean-Jacques Rousseau, *Emile*, trans. Allan Bloom (New York: Basic Books, 1979), p. 244. For a different view, see Frank, *Passions within Reason*, chaps. 4–6.

58. The human capacity not only to conceal, but also to explain away, or rationalize, defection casts doubt on optimistic accounts of the prospects for spontaneous cooperation. A similar point is made in Howard Margolis, *Selfishness, Altruism, and Rationality* (Chicago: University of Chicago Press, 1982), p. 185, f.n. 18. Cf. Arthur M. Melzer, "Rousseau and the Modern Cult of Sincerity," in *The Legacy of Rousseau*, ed. Clifford Orwin and Nathan Tarcov (Chicago: University of Chicago Press, 1997), pp. 274–295; and Erving Goffman, *The Presentation of Self in Everyday Life* (Woodstock, NY: Overlook Press, 1973), pp. 8–9, where Goffman contends that we are better at seeing through attempts to deceive us than we are at successfully deceiving others.

59. This is, of course, a prominent theme in Jean-Jacques Rousseau's *Confessions*, trans. J. M. Cohen (Harmondsworth, UK: Penguin, 1954).

60. When there are many players, an additional problem arises, for each player will only have direct knowledge about the past behavior of a small fraction of the total population. See Michael Hechter, *Principles of Group Solidarity* (Berkeley: University of California Press, 1987), pp. 75–76; and Gary J. Miller, *Managerial Dilemmas* (Cambridge: Cambridge University Press, 1992), pp. 184–186.

61. Accurate recognition is also necessary for the success tit-for-tat.

62. It may be noted that a population of unconditional defectors is evolutionarily stable in that it cannot be successfully invaded by conditional cooperators as long as the players' intentions remain sufficiently opaque.

63. I use the term, "rational egoist," loosely here and mean by it people moved by *amour de soi*.

64. Rousseau, "Discourse on the Origin of Inequality," p. 274.

65. Ibid., p. 248.

66. Ibid.

67. See Taylor, *Possibility of Cooperation*, chap. 5.

68. As Rousseau puts it, "every intended injury becomes an affront; because besides the hurt . . . the party injured was certain to find in it a contempt for his person," "Discourse on the Origin of Inequality," p. 242.

69. See note 21.

70. Michael Oakeshott, *Rationalism in Politics* (Indianapolis: Liberty Press, 1991), p. 307.

71. I assume these individuals would not purchase the goods in question expect for status reasons.

72. See Robert H. Frank, *Choosing the Right Pond* (New York: Oxford University Press, 1985); Robert H. Frank, *Luxury Fever* (New York: Free Press, 1999); and Fred Hirsch, *Social Limits to Growth* (London: Routledge and Kegan Paul, 1977).

73. Judith N. Shklar, *Montesquieu* (Oxford: Oxford University Press, 1987), p. 80.

74. See Paul Benichou, *Man and Ethics* (New York: Anchor, 1971), pp. 48–52.

75. Roughly speaking, this is the difference between Hobbes's and Montesquieu's aristocracy.

76. Rousseau, "Discourse on the Arts and Sciences," p. 149; and "Discourse on the Origin of Inequality," p. 249.

77. Rousseau, "Discourse on the Origin of Inequality," p. 225.

78. Rousseau, *Emile*, p. 224.

79. Cf. Tocqueville, *Democracy in America*, pp. 561–565.

80. Rousseau, "Discourse on the Origin of Inequality," p. 223.

81. See Taylor, *Possibility of Cooperation*, pp. 112–121.

82. This conclusion necessarily follows from the game-theoretic definitions we have given to *amour-propre* and compassion in relation to *amour de soi*.

83. See note 21 earlier.

84. We have been focusing on transparent intentions, but compassion, if it is to be effective, also requires "transparency of feeling." To sympathize with another person, we must, to use a contemporary expression, "feel their pain," and this requires either that people's feelings are easily understood, or that our powers of imagination are especially well-developed, or a combination of the two. See Rousseau, "Essay on the Origin of Languages," p. 261. The relationship

between compassion and transparency may also run in the other direction if we suppose that a compassionate person has a better than average chance of discerning a person's intentions from his or her demeanor. In this case, compassion, itself, makes a contribution to transparency.

85. See Tocqueville, *Democracy in America*, vol. II, part III, chap. 1.

86. Hannah Arendt, *On Revolution* (New York: Viking, 1963), pp. 74–85.

87. This worry is expressed by Jean Hampton, "Two Faces of Contractarian Thought," in *Contractarianism and Rational Choice*, ed. Peter Vallentyne (New York: Cambridge University Press, 1991), pp. 31–55. See also David Gauthier, *Morals by Agreement* (Oxford: Oxford University Press, 1986), p. 11.

88. See Martha C. Nussbaum, *Upheavals of Thought* (Cambridge: Cambridge University Press, 2001), pp. 399 ff.

89. Rousseau, "Discourse on the Origin of Inequality," p. 267.

90. George Armstrong Kelly concludes that "Rousseau may have been the greatest realist of all." See George Armstrong Kelly, "A General Overview," in *The Cambridge Companion to Rousseau*, ed. Patrick Riley (Cambridge: Cambridge University Press, 2001), p. 45.

91. Jean-Jacques Rousseau, "The Social Contract," in *The Social Contract and Discourses*, ed. and trans. by G. D. H. Cole (New York: E. P. Dutton, 1950), pp. 17–18. See also ibid., p. 103. Cf. Ullmann-Margalit, *Emergence of Norms*, pp. 27–29 on "generalized PD-structured situations" where there are many players involved, and the "condition of individual insignificance" prevails.

92. Jean-Jacques Rousseau, "A Discourse on Political Economy," in *The Social Contract and Discourses*, ed. and trans. G. D. H. Cole (New York: E. P. Dutton, 1950), p. 299.

93. Rousseau, "Letter to M. D'Alembert on the Theatre," pp. 58–59 and 127.

94. See Frank, *Passions within Reason*, pp. 266–269.

95. In addition to this solution, which is discussed later, Rousseau also recommends an education that will enable citizens to penetrate the guises of their neighbors. In particular, he commends the study of history, for the best historians pursue a person everywhere, leaving "no moment of respite, no nook where he can avoid the spectator's piercing eye," in *Emile*, p. 240.

96. Ibid., p. 237.

97. Rousseau, "Letter to M. D'Alembert on the Theatre," pp. 58–59.

98. Ibid., p. 59.

99. Quoted in Jean Starobinski, "The Political Thought of Jean Jacques Rousseau," in *Rousseau's Political Writings*, ed. Alan Ritter and Julia Conaway Bondanella (New York: Norton, 1988), p. 231.

100. Jean-Jacques Rousseau, "Considerations on the Government of Poland," in *Jean-Jacques Rousseau: Political Writings*, ed. and trans. Frederick Watkins (Madison: University of Wisconsin Press, 1986), p. 244. See also Mark Hulling, "Rousseau, Voltaire, and the Revenge of Pascal," in *The Cambridge Companion to Rousseau*, ed. by Patrick Riley (Cambridge: Cambridge University Press, 2001), pp. 73–74; and Patrick Riley, "Rousseau's General Will," in *The Cambridge Companion to Rousseau* (Cambridge: Cambridge University Press, 2001), pp. 78–93.

101. Rousseau, "Discourse on the Origin of Inequality," p. 177. Compare the following description of life in a kibbutz, "everyone here judges, everyone is judged, and no weakness can succeed in escaping judgment," quoted in Hechter, *Principles of Group Solidarity*, p. 155.

102. Rousseau, "Considerations on the Government of Poland," p. 253.

103. Ibid., p. 245.

104. Ibid., p. 263.

105. Rousseau quoted in Bertil Friden, *Rousseau's Economic Philosophy* (Dordrecht: Kluwer, 1998), p. 121.

106. Rousseau, "Considerations on the Government of Poland," p. 179.

107. It is important to bear in mind that Rousseau's reference to the *feeling* of being watched is an exception. Typically, Rousseau does not mention the mere feeling of being observed when

he is describing the conditions favorable to civic virtue. For example, he recommends that young Polish nobles should grow up "*under the eyes* of their fellow citizens," that administrators should act "*under the eyes* of the legislator," and that the representatives of the people should conduct the state's business "*under the eyes* of their constituents," in Starobinski, "Political Thought of Jean Jacques Rousseau," p. 231, original emphasis.

108. A good explanation of this phenomenon can be found in Richard Wollheim, *The Thread of Life* (Cambridge: Harvard University Press, 1984), chap. 7. An alternative account of a similar process, in which the self takes the view of a "generalized other" that represents "the attitude of the whole community," is provided in Mead, *Mind, Self, and Society*, pp. 152–164. See also Bernard Williams, *Shame and Necessity* (Berkeley: University of California Press, 1993), chap. 4.

109. Quoted in Starobinski, *Jean-Jacques Rousseau*, p. 95. Cf. Michael J. Sandel, *Democracy's Discontent* (Cambridge: Belknap Press of Harvard University Press, 1996), p. 320, where Sandel argues that the "republican ideal seeks to collapse the distance between persons so that citizens stand in a kind of speechless transparence, or immediate presence to one another."

110. Starobinski, *Jean-Jacques Rousseau*, pp. 96–97, emphasis in the original.

111. Ibid., p. 97. Cf. C. Fred Alford, *The Self in Social Theory* (New Haven: Yale University Press, 1991), p. 156, who claims that "Rousseau wishes to eliminate difference per se—that is, the otherness of the other, the existence of other wills." See also H. D. Forbes, "Rousseau, Ethnicity, and Difference," in *The Legacy of Rousseau*, ed. Clifford Orwin and Nathan Tarcov (Chicago: University of Chicago Press, 1997), pp. 226–228.

112. Rousseau, "Considerations on the Government of Poland," p. 245.

113. I am alluding to Rousseau's distinction between the "general will" and "the will of all," *The Social Contract*, pp. 26–28. The general will is portrayed as a solution to the problem of collective action in W. G. Runciman and A. K. Sen, "Games, Justice and the General Will," *Mind* (October 1965): 554–562. For a contrary view, see David Schmidtz, *The Limits of Government: An Essay on the Public Goods Argument* (Boulder: Westview Press, 1991), pp. 171–173.

114. Rousseau, "Discourse on Political Economy," p. 307. Rousseau's conception of citizenship extends beyond a solution to collective action problems; the education of citizens is not just a matter of teaching people how to cooperate in order to best achieve their antecedent ends. Rather, Rousseau's civic education is intended to give rise to new, common interests, which people acquire as they come to regard themselves as citizens. The difference between these two kinds of interest is discussed in Charles Taylor, "Cross-Purposes: The Liberal–Communitarian Debate," in *Liberalism and the Moral Life*, ed. Nancy L. Rosenblum (Cambridge: Harvard University Press, 1989), pp. 168–170.

115. Jean-Jacques Rousseau, "Geneva Manuscript," in *Jean-Jacques Rousseau, On The Social Contract*, ed. Roger D. Masters, trans. Judith R. Masters (New York: St. Martins, 1978), p. 160. In the "Letter to M. D'Alembert on the Theatre," p. 24, Rousseau asks, "What more advantageous treaty could one conclude than one obliging the whole world, excepting himself, to be just, so that everyone will faithfully render unto him what is due him, while he renders to no one what he owes?"

116. In fact, extensive monitoring of citizen conduct effectively transforms the canonical prisoner's dilemma game, in which defection pays the greatest dividend, at least under opaque conditions, into an "assurances game," in which cooperation is the individually best strategy so long as each player is assured that others will cooperate as well. The distinction between the two types of games parallels the distinction between "the will of all" and "the general will." In the case of the prisoner's dilemma game, each player acts on the basis of what is most advantageous to himself and the result, "the will of all," is the Pareto-inferior defect/defect outcome. The assurances game differs from the prisoner's dilemma game in that, if everyone else cooperates, the individual prefers to cooperate himself, otherwise he prefers to defect as in the prisoner's dilemma game. The point of mutual surveillance is to provide mutual assurance on precisely this point. See Runciman and Sen, "Games, Justice and the General Will."

117. Cf. John Rawls's conception of a "well-ordered society," in *A Theory of Justice* (Cambridge: Harvard University Press, 1971), pp. 453–462.

118. See Michael Suk-Young Chwe, *Rational Ritual: Culture, Coordination, and Common Knowledge* (Princeton, NJ: Princeton University Press, 2001), chap. 2.

119. The surveillance state as a "design of subtle coercion" is developed in Michel Foucault, *Discipline and Punish* (New York: Vintage, 1979), pp. 221–214. See also Thomas Nagel, *Concealment and Exposure* (Oxford: Oxford University Press, 2002), chaps. 1–3; and Jeffery Rosen, *The Unwanted Gaze* (New York: Random House, 2000).

120. Foucault, *Discipline and Punish*, p. 217.

121. Unlike many of the thinkers Foucault criticizes, Rousseau cannot be accused of being committed only to "formal equality."

122. Rousseau, "Considerations on the Government of Poland," p. 244. Rousseau's anxiety provides the right context in which to appreciate Rene Girard's observation that "Stendhal, Flaubert, and Tocqueville describe as 'republican' or 'democratic' an evolution which we today would call *totalitarian*," *Deceit, Desire, & the Novel*, trans. Yvonne Fressero (Baltimore: Johns Hopkins, 1965), p. 137, emphasis in the original.

123. Foucault, *Discipline and Punish*, p. 183.

124. Ibid., p. 184; see also Geraint Parry, "Emile: Learning to be Men, Women, and Citizens," in *The Cambridge Companion to Rousseau*, ed. Patrick Riley (Cambridge: Cambridge University Press, 2001), pp. 247–271.

125. Quoted in James Miller, *Rousseau: Dreamer of Democracy* (New Haven: Yale University Press, 1984), p. 197. The "terror" experienced by Rousseau was, perhaps, precisely what Robespierre had in mind when he concluded that without terror, "virtue is impotent," quoted in Miller, p. 157. This line of interpretation is pursued in J. L. Talmon, *The Origins of Totalitarian Democracy* (New York: Praeger, 1960); and Simon Shama, *Citizens* (New York: A. Knopf, 1989), chap. 15. Cf. Neidleman, *General Will as Citizenship*, pp. 109–110.

126. Cf. Neidleman, *General Will Is Citizenship*, p. 109, who summarizes the choice this way: "Whereas the drive toward transparency makes hypocrisy a crime, the preservation of a private sphere neutralizes hypocrisy, allowing it to exist within the confines of a democratic system." Neidleman, p. 110, defends Rousseau against critics who stress the continuity between Rousseau's thought and Robbespiere's edicts by emphasizing that "Rousseau restricts the sphere of politics to that which pertains to the common good," whereas Robespierre "recognizes no distinction between public and private matters." Rousseau's heavy reliance on mutual surveillance complicates this line of defense.

127. Hobbes's own account, with its vainglorious agents, is probably closer to our fourth type, interaction between opaque agents moved by *amour-propre*.

128. I use the phrase, "deeply compassionate," because even the deceitful person retains some compassion according to Rousseau.

129. See W. Michael Reisman, *Law in Brief Encounters* (New Haven: Yale University Press, 1999), p. 3.

130. See Rousseau , *Emile*, p. 229, where, among other things, Rousseau suggests that "when one has suffered or fears suffering, one pities those who suffer; but when one is suffering, one pities only oneself."

131. Tocqueville, *Democracy in America*, p. 564.

132. See notes to table 2.4.

Chapter Three   Association and Civil Society in Transparent and Opaque Communities

1. See Don E. Eberly, ed., *The Essential Civil Society Reader* (Oxford: Rowman & Littlefield, 2000); Amy Gutmann, ed., *Freedom of Association* (Princeton: Princeton University Press,

1998); Amitai Etzioni, ed., *The Essential Communitarian Reader* (Oxford: Rowman & Littlefield, 1998); Simone Chambers and Will Kymlicka, eds., *Alternative Conceptions of Civil Society* (Princeton: Princeton University Press, 2002); Mark E. Warren, *Democracy and Association* (Princeton: Princeton University Press, 2001); Robert D. Putnam, *Making Democracy Work: Civic Traditions in Modern Italy* (Princeton: Princeton University Press, 1993); Robert D. Putnam, *Bowling Alone: The Collapse and Revival of American Community* (New York: Simon & Schuster, 2000); John A. Holt, ed., *Civil Society* (Cambridge: Polity Press, 1995); and Ernest Gellner, *Conditions of Liberty: Civil Society and Its Rivals* (New York: Penguin Press, 1994).

2. Don E. Eberly, "The Meaning, Origin, and Applications of Civil Society," in *The Essential Civil Society Reader*, ed. Eberly (Oxford: Rowman & Littlefield, 2000), p. 13.

3. Jean-Jacques Rousseau, "The Social Contract," in *The Social Contract and Discourses*, ed. and trans. G. D. H. Cole (New York: E. P. Dutton, 1950), pp. 26–27. For a sweeping historical account of the ideas behind republican democracy, see Samuel Beer, *To Make a Nation* (Cambridge: Harvard University Press, 1993), part II. For a critique of the role the "common good" can play in suppressing the legitimate claims of disadvantaged groups, which may be characterized as "special interests," see Iris Marion Young, *Inclusion and Democracy* (Oxford: Oxford University Press, 2000), chap. 3.

4. Alexis de Tocqueville, *Democracy in America*, ed. J. P. Mayer, trans. George Lawrence (Garden City, NY: Anchor Books, 1969), pp. 506–509.

5. Albert O. Hirschman, *Exit, Voice, and Loyalty* (Cambridge: Harvard University Press, 1970).

6. Jean-Jacques Rousseau, "Discourse on Political Economy," in *The Social Contract and Discourses*, ed. and trans. G. D. H. Cole (New York: E. P. Dutton, 1950), p. 299.

7. Rousseau, "Social Contract," p. 3.

8. Rousseau quoted in Jean Starobinski, "The Political Thought of Jean-Jacques Rousseau," in *Rousseau's Political Writings*, ed. Alan Ritter and Julia Conaway Bondanella (New York: Norton, 1988), p. 231; and Jean-Jacques Rousseau, "Discourse on the Origin of Inequality," in *The Social Contract and Discourses*, ed. and trans. G. D. H. Cole (New York: E. P. Dutton, 1950), p. 177.

9. The formation of associations does require that individuals no longer possess the self-sufficiency they enjoyed in Rousseau's state of nature.

10. Rousseau, "Discourse on Political Economy," p. 291.

11. Ibid.

12. A contemporary account of the implications of this proposition can be found in Mancur Olson, Jr., *The Logic of Collective Action* (New York: Schocken, 1968).

13. Rousseau, "Discourse on Political Economy," pp. 291–292.

14. Ibid., p. 291.

15. Rousseau, "Social Contract," p. 26.

16. This interpretation is set forth in Bernard Grofman and Scott Feld, "Rousseau's General Will: A Condorcetian Perspective," *American Political Science Review* 82 (1988): 567–576. See also Jeremy Waldron, *Liberal Rights* (Cambridge: Cambridge University Press, 1993), pp. 392–421. For different interpretations of Rousseau's argument, see Hilail Gilden, *Rousseau's Social Contract: The Design of the Argument* (Chicago: University of Chicago Press, 1983), chap. 3; and Jason Andrew Neidleman, *The General Will Is Citizenship* (New York: Rowman & Littlefield, 2001), chaps. 2 and 3.

17. Rousseau, "Social Contract," p. 27.

18. Ibid.

19. We can explicate this notion (without claiming to be faithful to Rousseau's own intentions) by drawing on the "law of large numbers," or, as it is known in everyday parlance, the "law of averages." According to this law, idiosyncratic factors tend to "average out," or be "averaged away," as the number of trials increases. For example, the more times a coin is tossed, the more likely the effects of wind and other random variables will "average out," so that the number of

"heads" and "tails" approaches the true distribution of "fifty-fifty." In analogous fashion, as the number of voters increases, the idiosyncratic interests of individual voters, e.g., one citizen grows wheat and another corn, will be "averaged away," or "cancelled out," leaving only the common interests shared by all citizens. This process only works, however, if each coin flip, or each vote, is independent of the rest. Just as the results of a few coin tosses are less likely to reveal the true probability distribution of "heads" and "tails" than are many tosses, so a small number of independent votes is less likely to reveal the common interests of the people than a large number of independent votes. Cf. Zev M. Trachtenberg, *Making Citizens: Rousseau's Political Theory of Culture* (London: Routledge, 1993), who regards the general will as "an aggregation of the members of society's wants," which is "the result of [a] hypothetical bargain that, given the wants that make up their welfare, would best satisfy the most members of society," pp. 11 and 15. In Trachtenberg's ingenious, but, I believe, errant reading, the general will requires that citizens eschew "intense wants" that make it difficult to find a broadly agreeable distribution of public benefits. The trouble with "partial societies," in this view, is that they are organized "around sets of goods for which they [citizens] have wants above their intensity threshold," i.e., the threshold of intensity at which "the process of formulating the social choice" has become so distorted "that it cannot express the general will," ibid., p. 46.

20. Rousseau, "Social Contract," p. 27.
21. Ibid.
22. In this regard, Rousseau approvingly mentions Machiavelli, who held that " 'there are some divisions that are harmful to a Republic and some that are advantageous.' " Although it is difficult to keep " 'enmities' " from arising, it is essential to " 'prevent them from growing into sects,' " "Social Contract," p. 27.
23. For a more detailed account of collective goods, see Russell Hardin, *Collective Action* (Baltimore: Johns Hopkins University Press, 1982), chaps. 3 and 4.
24. Of course reputation is not always an accurate reflection of a person's true character.
25. The "all else being the same" clause is intended to isolate the consequences of different cooperative dispositions from such factors as economies of scale and complementarities of production. See Jack Hirshleifer, *Price Theory and Applications*, 3rd edition (Englewood Cliffs, NJ: Prentice-Hall, 1984), chap. 11. In saying that, other things being the same, an association with a higher ratio of C_1 to C_2 citizens will always enjoy greater average benefits per member than an association with a lower ratio of C_1 to C_2 citizens, I am stipulating that the increase in total association benefits resulting from the addition of one C_1 citizen to any association, regardless of its size or composition, will always exceed the increase in total benefits resulting from the addition of a C_2 citizen to the same association. Given this stipulation, C_1 citizens will be able to maximize their association benefits by combining exclusively with other C_1 citizens, provided that, either the "supply" of C_1 citizens is unlimited, or all associations face constant or diminishing returns to scale. In the former case, homogenous associations of C_1 citizens can exploit all economies of scale without adding C_2 citizens to their organizations. In the latter case, there are no economies of scale, and, hence, no advantage to be gained by C_1 citizens in expanding the membership of their organizations to include C_2 citizens. Under these conditions, the marginal benefit generated by the addition of a C_2 citizen to an association of C_1 citizens will always be less than the average benefit enjoyed by the current C_1 membership.
26. Circumstances similar to these have been formally modeled with the result that "high-ability agents always have an incentive to match themselves with other high-ability agents," so that "stratification emerges as an equilibrium phenomenon," Steven N. Durlauf, "Associational Redistribution: A Defense," in *Recasting Egalitarianism*, ed. Erik Olin Wright (London: Verso, 1998), p. 269.
27. Talbot Page, Louis Putterman, and Bulent Unel, "Voluntary Association in Public Goods Experiments: Reciprocity, Mimicry, and Efficiency," Brown University Department of Economics Working Paper, May 22, 2002.
28. Rousseau, "Social Contract," p. 29.

29. Rousseau, "Discourse on Political Economy," p. 291.
30. This rule of conduct is troubling both as a moral principle and as a plausible moral psychology. There are moral theories that urge us to act on general principles (Kant) and to take account of everyone's interests (Bentham). But the considerations encompassed by these theories do not stop at the borders of the nation-state; they extend to all of humanity. On the other hand, there are moral theories that acknowledge "agent-relative" rights and obligations, which arise out of our particular projects and relationships. See Samuel Sheffler, *Human Morality* (New York: Oxford, 1996). Yet, a rule which stipulates that when interests conflict, we should act to advance the more general interest, but never against the good of the republic, is unsatisfying insofar as it is "universalist" up to the perimeter of the nation-state at which point it admits one, and only one, overriding agent-relative obligation, i.e., one's obligation as a member of a particular political community.
31. Michael Walzer makes a similar point, arguing that "the stronger the particular identities of men and women are, the stronger their citizenship must be" in *What It Means to Be an American* (New York: Marsilio, 1992), p. 10.
32. One possibility is that C_1 citizens are more inclined to meet their responsibilities within the associations they have *voluntarily joined out of mutual interest*, whereas C_2 citizens are more inclined to fulfill their duties as compatriots of the national community, which forms *an integral part of their identity* and to which they have *belonged since birth*. On this interpretation, C_1 citizens resemble the "unencumbered" agents of liberal political theory, whereas C_2 citizens resemble the "encumbered" selves of communitarian political theory. See Michael J. Sandel, *Liberalism and the Limits of Justice* (Cambridge: Cambridge University Press, 1983).
33. Rousseau, "Discourse on Political Economy," p. 291.
34. Nancy L. Rosenblum, *Membership and Morals* (Princeton: Princeton University Press, 1998), p. 59.
35. The assumed non-overlapping of valuable talents forms an essential premise of Michael Walzer's theory of "complex equality," which becomes less appealing, to egalitarians at least, when there is an overlapping of valued talents. See Michael Walzer, *Spheres of Justice: A Defense of Pluralism and Equality* (New York: Basic Books, 1983).
36. The "tit-for-tat" strategy in an iterated prisoner's dilemma game is only attractive if the player has a relatively low discount rate. See Robert Axelrod, *The Evolution of Cooperation* (New York: Basic Books, 1984).
37. Daniel A. Bell, "Civil Society versus Civic Virtue," in *Freedom of Association*, ed. Amy Gutmann (Princeton: Princeton University Press, 1998), p. 243.
38. The role of association in reinforcing inequality is analyzed in Rene Benabou, "Workings of a City: Location, Education, and Production," *Quarterly Journal of Economics* 108 (1993): 619–652; and Steven N. Durlauf, "A Theory of Persistent Income Inequality," *Journal of Economic Growth* 1 (1996): 75–93.
39. Durlauf, "Associational Redistribution," p. 266.
40. Ibid., p. 269.
41. Samuel Scheffler, *Boundaries and Allegiances* (New York: Oxford University Press, 2001), p. 85.
42. Thomas Nagel, *Equality and Partiality* (Oxford: Oxford University Press, 1991).
43. Nagel, *Equality and Partiality*, p. 11.
44. Rousseau, *Emile*, trans. Allan Bloom (New York: Basic Books, 1979), p. 40.
45. See the references in Durlauf, "Associational Redistribution."
46. See the essays in Gutmann, ed., *Freedom of Association*.
47. Michael Walzer, "Equality and Civil Society," in *Alternative Conceptions of Civic Society*, ed. Simone Chambers and Will Kymlicka (Princeton: Princeton University Press, 2002), p. 39 and p. 49, note 9.
48. See Putnam, *Making Democracy Work*.
49. Edward C. Banfield quoted in ibid., p. 88.
50. Putnam, *Making Democracy Work*, p. 112.
51. Ibid., p. 181.

52. Edward C. Banfield, *The Moral Basis of a Backward Society* (New York: Free Press, 1958), p. 139.

53. Of course the same process could work in reverse; C_2 citizens could offer C_1 citizens membership in C_2 associations.

54. C_2 citizens must also be indifferent to their relative position within associations, for while their absolute benefits will be greater, their membership benefits will be less than the benefits received by C_1 citizens. See Richard Cornes and Todd Sandler, *The Theory of Externalities, Public Goods, and Club Goods*, 2nd edition (Cambridge: Cambridge University Press, 1996), pp. 386–387.

55. To harness the energy of the most talented and ambitious leaders to the interests of the republic, Rousseau proposed a scheme of "purely honorific rewards," which would be distributed solely on the basis of public service, "Considerations on the Government of Poland," in *Jean-Jacques Rousseau: Political Writings*, ed. and trans. Frederick Watkins (Madison: University of Wisconsin Press, 1986), p. 228.

56. Rousseau describes in some detail the many strategies employed by the leaders of Rome to prevent any group from gathering all the reins of power by creating many checks and balances, both within the institutions of government and among the many different tribes and classes. See "Social Contract," pp. 110–121.

57. Although I am mainly interested in the *composition* of associations in opaque societies, it is worthwhile digressing for a moment to consider a different aspect of the matter, viz. the optimal size of an association. Insofar as associations supply non-rival collective goods, i.e., goods whose enjoyment by one member does not reduce their value to other members, they can lower the average cost of supplying these goods by spreading their cost across a larger number of members. Mancur Olson extends this reasoning to virtually every good provided by every association, arguing that the "achievement of any common goal or the satisfaction of any common interest means that a public or collective good has been provided for that group." In other words, "the very fact that a goal or purpose is common to a group means that no one in the group is excluded from the benefit or satisfaction brought about by its achievement." In Olson's account, therefore, nearly all associations always have an interest in expanding their membership. Olson, *Logic of Collective Action*, pp. 15 ff. This argument overlooks an important difference between associations in transparent and opaque societies. Specifically, Olson implicitly assumes that the objectives of an association are permanently fixed, or that the preferences of new members are fully transparent, or both. If, however, the aims of new members are not transparent, then the group's objectives may shift as its membership expands. Adding members to an association does not simply reduce the average cost of supplying a fixed set of goods, it also harbors the possibility that the association will supply a different set of goods. If the interests or beliefs of prospective members are not well known, if they are opaque to some degree, then the admission of new members poses a risk to current members. Thus, while a larger association may be able to achieve some of its goals more effectively, these goals will not necessarily be the goals of the current membership.

58. The probability of getting ten "heads" in a row is approximately 0.1 percent.

59. "Discourse on Political Economy," pp. 290–291.

60. John Rawls, *A Theory of Justice* (Cambridge: Harvard University Press, 1971).

61. On the interrelation between communication and homogeneity, see Mark Granovetter, "The Impact of Social Structure on Economic Outcomes," *The Journal of Economic Perspectives* 19:1 (Winter 2005): 33–50; and Dennis Chong, *Rational Lives: Norms and Values in Politics and Societies* (Chicago: University of Chicago Press, 2000).

62. See Ferdinand Tonnies, *Community and Civil Society*, ed. Jose Harris, trans. Jose Harris and Margaret Hollis (Cambridge: Cambridge University Press, 2001).

63. Quoted in Cass Sunstein, *Republic.com* (Princeton: Princeton University Press, 2001), p. 54.

64. See Sunstein, *Republic.com*.

65. Ibid., p. 59.

66. See Paul F. Lazarsfeld and Robert K. Merton, "Friendship as Social Process: A Substantive and Methodological Analysis," in *Freedom and Control in Modern Society*, ed. Theodore Abel, Monroe Berger, and Charles H. Page (New York: Octagon Books, 1964), pp. 18–66.

67. See Alberto Alesina and Eliana La Ferrara, "Participation in Heterogeneous Communities," *Quarterly Journal of Economics* 115:3 (2000): 847–904.
68. See Mancur Olson, Jr., *The Rise and Decline of Nations* (New Haven, Yale University Press, 1984). This pattern of countervailing power is reminiscent of James Madison's argument in *Federalist Papers #10 and #51*, which contends that an expansive republic will contain many countervailing interests, which will allow elected representatives greater discretion to consider the public interest.
69. See Alberto Alesina and Eliana La Ferrara, "Participation," *Quarterly Journal of Economics* 115 (2000): 847–904.
70. See Ian Molho, *The Economics of Information: Lying and Cheating in Organizations* (Oxford: Blackwell, 1997), part 2, and the references cited therein.
71. See Glenn Loury, "Conceptual Problems in the Enforcement of Anti-Discrimination Laws," in *Meritocracy and Economic Inequality*, ed. Kenneth Arrow, Samuel Bowles, and Steven Durlauf (Princeton, NJ: Princeton University Press, 2000), pp. 296–316.
72. See Olson, *Rise and Decline of Nations*.
73. Tocqueville, *Democracy in America*, p. 506.
74. Ibid., p. 513.
75. Ibid., pp. 513 and 511.
76. Ibid., p. 522.
77. Rawls advances a similar argument in *A Theory of Justice*, pp. 467–72.
78. These and other variables are discussed in Putnam, *Making Democracy Work*; Francis Fukuyama, *Trust: The Social Virtues and the Creation of Prosperity* (New York: Free Press, 1995); Diego Gambetta, *Trust: Making and Breaking Cooperative Relations* (Oxford: Blackwell, 1988); Gabriel Almond and Sidney Verba, *The Civic Culture* (Princeton: Princeton University Press, 1963); Hirschman, *Exit, Voice, and Loyalty*; Albert O. Hirschman, *Shifting Involvements: Private Interest and Public Action* (Princeton: Princeton University Press, 1982); and Burton A. Weisbrod, *The Nonprofit Economy* (Cambridge: Harvard University Press, 1988).
79. See, e.g., J. R. Hicks, *Value and Capital* (Oxford: Clarendon Press, 1946).
80. I continue to assume that at least one significant aspect of being a C_1 citizen, and therefore being eligible for membership in an A_1 association, is beyond a person's control, i.e., not a matter of choice.
81. For a good discussion of the trade-offs between freedom of association and equality of opportunity, see George Kateb, "The Value of Association," in *Freedom of Association*, ed. Amy Gutmann (Princeton: Princeton University Press, 1998); and Nancy L. Rosenblum, "Compelled Association: Public Standing, Self-Respect, and the Dynamic of Exclusion," in *Freedom of Association*, ed. Amy Gutmann (Princeton: Princeton University Press, 1998).
82. I use "joining" loosely here, for this is a purely static analysis, which will become clear shortly.
83. See David Brin, *The Transparent Society* (New York: Perseus, 1999), p. 29. See also Howard Rheingold, *The Virtual Community* (Reading, MA: Addison-Wesley, 1993).
84. This is one effect of offering honors classes and scholarships to bright students from poor families.
85. See Michael Young, *The Rise of the Meritocracy* (New York: Penguin, 1971).
86. Hirschman, *Exit, Voice, and Loyalty*.
87. Insofar as a larger segment of the public will be interested in joining an association under transparent, as opposed to, opaque conditions, the requirement that there be many associations to choose from is likely to be satisfied. Larger associations also favor exit because voice, an individual member's dissent, will have less effect in a large organization than in a small one. Transparency is, of course, only one of several factors that bear on the relative costs of "exit" and "voice." See the discussion in Warren, *Democracy and Association*, pp. 104–109.
88. There are, of course, risks involved in the exercise of "voice."
89. See Charles M. Tiebout, "A Pure Theory of Local Expenditure," *Journal of Political Economy* 64 (October 1956): 416–424.
90. See Warren, *Democracy and Association*, p. 96 ff. and 104.

91. Hirschman, *Exit, Voice, and Loyalty*, p. 53.
92. Ibid.
93. Ibid. Before we leave Hirschman's fruitful typology, let us take note of the fact that while the possibility of "exit" constrains the power of associations over their members, as well as the power of merchants over individual customers, the accelerating trend toward globalization has created a viable "exit" option for both corporations and the wealthy citizens of democratic states. Although this development is relatively new, the "exit" option has nearly always constrained the reach of the subnational governments within nation-states. Cities that impose heavy taxes on business firms and the owners of valuable property in order to finance generous social services for less fortunate citizens often end up with a shrinking tax base and an influx of poverty-stricken citizens from near-by jurisdictions that offer less generous public benefits. See Paul E. Peterson, *City Limits* (Chicago: University of Chicago Press, 1981). The presence of an effective "exit" option thus limits the range of policy alternatives that may be effectively pursued by egalitarian-minded republican regimes.
94. The reader should bear in mind the lower density of associations at the high end of the quality scale.
95. This point is stressed by Judith N. Shklar, *Men and Citizens* (Cambridge: Cambridge University Press, 1969).
96. In order to simply our analysis, we have had to rule out two kinds of relation between the size and composition of an association, on the one hand, and its generation of benefits, on the other hand. These relationships should be addressed, if only briefly. First, if there are significant economies of scale and too few C_1 citizens to exploit these scale economies, then associations of C_1 citizens may be able to increase their average benefits by adding some C_2 citizens to their organizations. Although these circumstances are by no means implausible, the advanced communication and transportation systems necessary to achieve scale economies are much more likely to be used to organize strangers whose cooperative dispositions are opaque to one another, city dwellers in particular, than to organize citizens with transparent dispositions who, if they are transparent to one another, must already interact on a regular basis.

A second relationship not considered earlier is one in which the cooperative contributions of C_1 and C_2 citizens complement one another within an association. In this case, adding a C_2 citizen to an association of C_1 citizens or vice versa would increase the productive contribution of both kinds of citizen. Even if there were such synergy between the two kinds of citizen, it may still not be advantageous for C_1 citizens to invite C_2 citizens to join their associations. Since, in the scenario we have been considering, association benefits are distributed equally, the added productivity resulting from the combination of C_1 and C_2 citizens must be great enough to offset the difference in cooperative productivity between the two types of citizens. To take a simple example, if a C_1 citizen is to find it advantageous to cooperate with a C_2 citizen, then the total benefits generated by the partnership must exceed the total benefits generated by two C_1 citizens working together. Although this is not impossible, especially for organizations that depend on a very fine division of labor, it is unlikely that the combination of the disciplined with the less disciplined will result in greater benefits than a combination of the disciplined among themselves.

If we add these two special cases to the case of associations that offer unequal benefits, there are at least three conditions under which transparent citizens may organize themselves into heterogeneous associations. None, however, is ideal with respect to Rousseau's republican objectives. Heterogeneous associations that capitalize upon economies of scale will not satisfy Rousseau's *desiderata* that "partial societies" be "many in number," for such associations, by definition, will be large in size. Moreover, if one or two associations get a head start in exploiting scale and other economies, these associations will be more powerful than those that get a slower start. Heterogeneous associations that capitalize upon complementarities of production between C_1 and C_2, citizens, apart from being implausible, presuppose an extensive division of labor, which Rousseau regarded as anathema to republican democracy.

Heterogeneous associations in which C_2 citizens enjoy fewer benefits than C_1 citizens are apt to be roughly equal in power, as neither C_1 nor C_2 citizens are isolated in their own homogenous associations, but this external equality is bought at the price of inequality within the associations, themselves, which is not a good training ground for civic virtue.

97. Tocqueville, *Democracy in America*, p. 515.
98. Putnam, *Making Democracy Work*, pp. 89–90. Similar claims are advanced by Michael J. Sandel, *Democracy's Discontent* (Cambridge: Belknap Press of Harvard University Press, 1996); Joshua Cohen and Joel Rogers, "Secondary Associations and Democratic Governance," in *Associations and Democracy*, ed. Erik Olin Wright (New York: Verso, 1995); and Robert N. Bellah, Richard Madsen, William M. Sullivan, Ann Swidler, and Steven M. Tipton, *The Good Society* (New York: Alfred A. Knopf, 1991).
99. Putnam, *Making Democracy Work*, p. 115. This view, it may be noted, is shared by some "republican liberals" who contend that "involvement in organizations of this sort [e.g., neighborhood associations] can improve communications between individuals inside and outside of government while fostering a better understanding of public affairs and a sense of civic responsibility." Richard Dagger, *Civic Virtues: Rights, Citizenship, and Republican Liberalism* (Oxford: Oxford University Press, 1997), p. 199. See also Daniel A. Bell, "Civil Society versus Civic Virtue," pp. 239–272, who characterizes intermediate associations as " 'springboards' for civic virtue"; and John Rawls, *Theory of Justice*, pp. 467–472.
100. See James Coleman, *Foundations of Social Theory* (Cambridge: Harvard University Press, 1990); Samuel Bowles and Herbert Gintis, "How Communities Govern: The Structural Basis of Prosocial Norms," in *Economics, Values, and Organization*, ed. Avner Ben-Ner and Louis Putterman (Cambridge: Cambridge University Press, 1998); and Mark E. Warren, ed., *Democracy and Trust* (Cambridge: Cambridge University Press, 1999).
101. Quoted in Jason Andrew Neidleman, *General Will Is Citizenship*, p. 157. According to one version of the civil society argument, those who engage in association develop trust in one another as they cooperate for mutual advantage. Moreover, the trust that emerges within associations "tends to be generalized to the society as a whole" in Dietland Stolle, "Bowling Together, Bowling Alone: The Development of Generalized Trust in Voluntary Associations," *Political Psychology* 19 (1998), p. 500.
102. Ernest Gellner, *Conditions of Liberty*, p. 100.
103. Robert D. Putnam, "Bowling Alone: Democracy in America at the End of the Twentieth Century," *Journal of Democracy* 6:1 (January 1995), p. 67.
104. See Chong, *Rational Lives*, pp. 53 ff.
105. Ibid., p. 67.
106. The members of an association come to identify with it because "it is in their interest to do so," because "those who identify strongly may gain access to positions under the control of the group and because the group provides a relatively secure and comfortable environment," ibid., p. 67. Under these conditions, one cannot be so confident that associations will enlarge the hearts and minds of their members, not when each member has such strong incentives to conform to the norms of the group and when the group's power, itself, derives in part from this conformity.
107. Rosenblum, *Membership and Morals*, p. 186.
108. Michael A. Mosher, "Conclusion: Are Civil Societies the Transmission Belts of Ethical Tradition?" in *Alternative Conceptions of Civil Society*, ed. Simone Chambers and Will Kymlicka (Princeton: Princeton University Press, 2002), p. 207.
109. Bell, "Civil Society versus Civic Culture," p. 241.
110. Simone Weil, "A Note on the Complete Abolition of Political Parties," in *Rousseau's Political Writings*, ed. Alan Ritter and Julia Conaway Bondanella (New York: Norton, 1988), p. 287.
111. Young, *Democracy and Inclusion*, pp. 6 and 81.
112. Ibid., p. 81.
113. Ibid., p. 7.

114. Young, *Democracy and Inclusion*, p.7.
115. Rousseau, "Discourse on the Origin of Inequality," pp. 250–251.
116. Rousseau, "Social Contract," p. 31.
117. Young, *Democracy and Inclusion*, pp. 30–31.
118. Ibid., pp. 99–102.
119. Rousseau, "Social Contract," p. 27.
120. Let us recall the many cogent critiques of "interest-group liberalism."
121. Of course this is more easily said than done. For example, if labor unions are constrained in the amount of influence they can exercise over their members, the unions are likely to be weakened in bargaining with management, which, in turn, is not likely to be advantageous to the individual members.
122. This policy direction will be more difficult for liberals who attach greater value to the right of individuals to form "partial societies" without restriction. See the essays in Gutmann, ed., *Freedom of Association*.
123. Rousseau, "Social Contract," p. 27, my stress.

Chapter Four   Opaque Traders and the Invisible Hand

1. Adam Smith, *The Wealth of Nations* (Oxford: Clarendon Press, 1976).
2. Smith, *Wealth of Nations*, p. 117.
3. Ibid., p. 118.
4. Ibid., p. 126.
5. See Oliver E. Williamson, *Markets and Hierarchy* (New York: Free Press, 1975), p. 9, who calls this "self-interest seeking with guile."
6. Smith, *Wealth of Nations*, book I, chap. 7.
7. Jean-Jacques Rousseau, "The Social Contract," in *The Social Contract and Discourses*, ed. and trans. G. D. H. Cole (New York: E. P. Dutton, 1950), p. 14.
8. Smith, *Wealth of Nations*, p. 513. See also Michael Ignatieff, *The Needs of Strangers* (New York: Penguin, 1986), chap. 4.
9. See, e.g., Michael Sandel's republican criticisms of globalization in *Democracy's Discontent* (Cambridge: Belknap Press of Harvard University Press, 1996), pp. 338–351.
10. Smith, *Wealth of Nations*, book I, chaps. 5–7.
11. Ibid., chaps. 8–10.
12. See John Bates Clark, *The Distribution of Wealth* [1899] (New York: Macmillan Company, 1920).
13. The *locus classicus* is Leon Walras, *Elements of Pure Political Economy* [1874] (London: George Allen and Unwin, 1965).
14. See Friedrich von Hayek, "Economics and Knowledge," in Hayek, *Individualism and Economic Order* (Chicago: University of Chicago Press, 1980).
15. Smith, *Wealth of Nations*, p. 118.
16. Rousseau quoted in Bertil Friden, *Rousseau's Economic Philosophy* (Dordrecht: Kluwer, 1998), p. 41.
17. Jean Starobinski, *Jean-Jacques Rousseau: Transparency and Obstruction*, trans. Arthur Goldhammer (Chicago: University of Chicago Press, 1988), pp. 104–111.
18. See Friden, *Rousseau's Economic Philosophy*, chap. 3.
19. Jean-Jacques Rousseau, *Confessions*, trans. J. M. Cohen (Harmondsworth, UK: Penguin, 1954), p. 44.

20. Rousseau offers at least one example of *transparent* exchange, citing an account of "Indian traders," who "take one another by the hand and, by varying their grip in ways no one can see, transact all their business . . . without having to exchange a single word." See Jean-Jacques Rousseau, "Essay on the Origin of Languages," in *Discourses and Essay on the Origin of Languages*, ed. and trans. Victor Gourevitch (New York: Harper & Row, 1990), p. 244.

21. Quoted in Friden, *Rousseau's Economic Philosophy*, p. 43.

22. Starobinski, *Jean-Jacques Rousseau*, p. 108. It may be added that Rousseau found it equally important for a country to avoid relying upon imports to meet the community's requirements.

23. See, e.g., Johannes Horner, "Reputation and Competition," *American Economic Review* 92:3 (June 2002): 644–663; and John Muller, *Capitalism, Democracy, and Ralph's Pretty Good Grocery* (Princeton: Princeton University Press, 1999), chap. 2.

24. See David Schmidtz, *The Limits of Government: An Essay on the Public Goods Argument* (Boulder: Westview Press, 1991), chap. 7.

25. Adam Smith, *Lectures on Jurisprudence*, ed. R. L. Meek, D. D. Raphael, and J. C. Bryce (Oxford: Oxford University Press, 1978), p. 538.

26. Smith, *Lectures on Jurisprudence*, p. 539.

27. Jean-Jacques Rousseau, "Discourse on the Origin of Inequality," in *The Social Contract and Discourses*, ed. and trans. G. D. H. Cole (New York: E. P. Dutton, 1950), p. 149.

28. In fact, there are at least three conditions, *in addition to honest dealing*, which must be satisfied before a business can reap economic benefits from its trustworthiness: (1) the business must engage in repeated transactions with the same customers so that the latter are in a position to judge its performance at low cost; (2) customers must be able to differentiate between honest and dishonest businesses; and (3) the business must have an ongoing presence in the market in order to benefit from its investment in a good name. Unless all of these requirements are met, reputation cannot bring transparency to markets. See William J. Baumol, *Perfect Markets and Easy Virtue* (Cambridge, MA: Blackwell, 1991), chap. 1.

29. More precisely, the cost of determining the quality of goods and the integrity of those who sell them must be relatively small.

30. Similarly, buyers who look to a business's "customer base" in hopes of learning something about the quality of its goods are also likely to be disappointed, for the choices made by other consumers are motivated, in varying degrees, by status concerns as opposed to the buyer's real needs. If this extension of Rousseau's complaint about "living in the opinion of others" seems far-fetched, I ask the skeptical reader to consider the volume and variety of advertisements that call attention to the attributes of the people who buy a particular good as opposed to the quality of the good itself. See Horner, "Reputation and Competition"; and Robert H. Frank, *Luxury Fever* (New York: Free Press, 1999).

31. Jean-Jacques Rousseau, "A Discourse on the Arts and Sciences," in *The Social Contract and Discourses*, ed. and trans. G. D. H. Cole (New York: E. P. Dutton, 1950), p. 148.

32. See Baumol, *Perfect Markets and Easy Virtue*, pp. 10–18.

33. Smith's characterization of the market as an institution that liberates individuals from dependence on powerful interests requires the existence of many sellers. When there are a large number of suppliers competing for a contract, no one supplier can dictate the terms of cooperation. But when the contract comes up for renewal, the supplier who won the initial contract will typically have a significant information and cost advantage over other bidders. Thus, what begins as a competition among many bidders wherein the winning bid (or price) is determined by impersonal market forces is often transformed over time into a bargaining situation in which strategic considerations displace the impartial rule of the price system. See Williamson, *Markets and Hierarchies*, pp. 26–30.

34. Joseph E. Stiglitz, *Whither Socialism?* (Cambridge, MA: MIT Press, 1994), p. 95.

35. This example is adapted from George A. Akerlof, "The Market for Lemons," in Akerlof, *An Economic Theorist's Book of Tales* (Cambridge: Cambridge University Press, 1984), pp. 7–22.

36. In some cases, however, a little transparency is worse than pure opacity. See the discussion of health insurance later.
37. Smith, *Wealth of Nations*, p. 119.
38. Ibid., p. 118.
39. The market, itself, has been characterized by Smith's followers as a process through which mutual interests can be discovered and acted upon. See, e.g., Armen A. Alchain, *Economic Forces at Work* (Indianapolis: Liberty Fund, 1977).
40. Rousseau, "Discourse on the Origin of Inequality," p. 248, emphasis added.
41. Cf. Stiglitz, *Whither Socialism?* chap. 1.
42. The 2001 Nobel Prize in economics was awarded to three innovators in information economics, George A. Akerlof, Michael Spence, and Joseph E. Stiglitz. Each prize winner summarizes his work in the *American Economic Review* 92:3 (June 2002).
43. Avner Ben-Ner and Louis Putterman, "Values and Institutions in Economic Analysis," in *Economics, Values, and Organizations*, ed. Ben-Ner and Putterman (Cambridge: Cambridge University Press, 1998), p. 4.
44. Whether a trader's signaling strategy will prove effective depends, in part, on whether those with less to offer can mimic the credentials of those with more to offer, and if so, at what cost. It is hard to predict which kind of market participant will prevail in a contest between those who wish to *reveal* their greater market value and those who wish to *conceal* their lesser value. This much, however, can be said: even if the most productive agents *are* successful in communicating their qualities to others, they must still incur signaling costs that would be unnecessary in a transparent economy where the value of everything was plain to see or, at least, not subject to deliberate distortion. See Joseph E. Stiglitz, "Information and the Change in the Paradigm in Economics," *American Economic Review* 92:3 (June 2002): 471.
45. For a contemporary account of the contest for relative position and its social and economic consequences, see Fred Hirsch, *Social Limits to Growth* (London: Routledge and Kegan Paul, 1977); Frank, *Luxury Fever;* Robert H. Frank, *Choosing the Right Pond* (New York: Oxford, 1985); and Robert H. Frank and Philip J. Cook, *The Winner-Take-All Society* (New York: Free Press, 1995).
46. Armen A. Alchain and Harold Demsetz, "Production, Information Costs and Economic Ownership," *American Economic Review* 62 (1972): 777–795.
47. See Alchain and Demsetz, "Production, Information Costs and Economic Ownership."
48. See Kenneth J. Arrow, *The Limits of Organization* (New York: W. W. Norton, 1974).
49. Smith, *Wealth of Nations*, pp. 113–114.
50. Where monitoring is impractical, firms may instead pay above-market wages in order to elicit a more productive effort from their employees. These so-called efficiency wages exceed the pay that would prevail in a perfectly competitive market, but some firms pay them nevertheless because workers earning efficiency wages are less likely to risk losing their well-paid jobs by shirking. For the firm, the higher wage is more than offset by the increase in worker productivity and the reduction in hiring and training costs. From a wider point of view, however, the trouble with efficiency wages is that some workers, who would be employed in a transparent economy where everyone's level of effort was easily discerned, will be involuntarily unemployed in an opaque economy where firms cannot observe the exertion of their employees. If the productive effort of individual workers were manifest, all of them could find employment at wages commensurate with their productive contribution. But when effort is difficult to monitor, and some firms pay more than the market-clearing wage in order to reduce shirking, fewer workers will be hired in the aggregate than would be the case in a transparent labor market.
51. Ugo Pagano, "Redistribution of Assets and Distributions of Asymmetric Information," in *Recasting Egalitarianism*, ed. Erik Olin Wright (London: Verso, 1998), p. 292.
52. See Joseph H. Carens, *Equality, Moral Incentives & the Market* (Chicago: University of Chicago Press, 1981).

53. See Stiglitz, *Whither Socialism?* p. 49.
54. On the nature of a "separating equilibrium," see Michael Spence, "Signaling in Retrospect and the Informational Structure of Markets," *American Economic Review* 92:3 (June 2002): 434–459.
55. John Rawls, *A Theory of Justice* (Cambridge: Harvard University Press, 1971).
56. See Peter L. Bernstein, *Against the Gods: The Remarkable Story of Risk* (New York, John Wiley and Sons, 1996).
57. See Kenneth J. Arrow, "Uncertainty and the Welfare Economics of Medical Care," *American Economic Review* 53:5 (December 1963): 941–973.
58. Adverse selection provides one of the main arguments in favor of national health insurance. See George A. Ackerlof, "The Market for Lemons," in Akerlof, *An Economic Book of Tales*, (Cambridge: Cambridge University Press, 1984), pp. 13–14.
59. See Nicholas Barr, *The Economics of the Welfare State* (Stanford: Stanford University Press, 1993), chap. 5; and Robert J. Shiller, *Macro Markets: Creating Institutions for Managing Society's Largest Economic Risks* (Oxford: Oxford University Press, 1993).
60. See Brian Barry's conception of the "Public Interest" as those interests we share behind a real-world veil of uncertainty, before we know the specifics of our individual risk exposure, *Political Concepts*, ed. Anthony Quinton (New York: Oxford University Press, 1967), pp. 112–126.
61. Jean-Jacques Rousseau, "Constitutional Project for Corsica," in *Jean Jacques Rousseau: Political Writings*, ed. and trans. Frederick Watkins (Madison: University of Wisconsin Press, 1986), pp. 306–307.
62. If the conduct of insured individuals is publicly observable, then it does not matter whether they behave in a risky manner because insurance coverage can be tailored so that the unwanted consequences of such behavior are excluded from coverage.
63. Robert J. Shiller, *The New Financial Order: Risk in the 21st Century* (Princeton: Princeton University Press, 2003), p. 93.
64. Jean-Jacques Rousseau, "Discourse on Political Economy," in *The Social Contract and Discourses*, ed. and trans. G. D. H. Cole (New York: E. P. Dutton, 1950), p. 323.
65. Adam Smith, *Wealth of Nations*, p. 373.
66. See Anup Shah, *Credit Markets and the Distribution of Income* (London: Academic Press, 1992).
67. See J. E. Stiglitz and A. Weiss, "Credit Rationing in Markets with Imperfect Information," *American Economic Review* 71 (1981): 393–410.
68. Rousseau, "Constitutional Project for Corsica," p. 298. Rousseau's view is shared by a number of contemporary economists one of whom concludes that "poverty of wealth, credit and lifetime earnings can go together." See Shah, *Credit Markets and the Distribution of Income*, p. 84.
69. Adam Smith, *Wealth of Nations*, p. 429.
70. See Shelly J. Lundberg and Richard Startz, "Inequality and Race: Models and Policy," *Meritocracy and Economic Inequality*, eds. Kenneth J. Arrow, Samuel Bowles, and Steven Durlauf (Princeton: Princeton University Press, 2000), pp. 269–295.
71. Such inequalities will, however, be exacerbated by prejudice, especially in segmented societies where discrimination is supported by social norms, and deviance from these norms is costly. See Ackerlof, *An Economist's Book of Tales*, pp. 43–44.
72. See Gary Becker, *The Economics of Discrimination* (Chicago: University of Chicago Press, 1957); and Milton Friedman, *Capitalism and Freedom* (Chicago: University of Chicago Press, 1963).
73. Employer expectations regarding productivity differences are also self-fulfilling. In the first place, the advantaged workers who are hired to fill the best jobs will also get the best training opportunities, hence they will remain more productive. See Lester Thurow, *Generating Inequality* (New York: Basic Books, 1975). And second, insofar as employers make hiring and promotion decisions on the basis of group stereotypes, workers who belong to less productive groups will not receive the full return on their education and training investments. Hence, they will not find it advantageous to invest in the development of their human capital, which reinforces the group's low productivity.
74. Rousseau, "Constitutional Project for Corsica," p. 283.

75. Unlike many of his contemporary followers, Smith actually shared Rousseau's view that the wage bargain favors the employer because, while "many workmen could not subsist a week . . . without employment," employers "could generally live a year or two upon the stocks they have already acquired." Smith, *Wealth of Nations*, p. 169.

76. Rousseau, "Constitutional Project for Corsica," pp. 303–304.

77. Ibid., p. 306. Alternatively, farmers might borrow in order to pay their taxes and other bills. But if they are desperate, there may be no alternative to high-interest loans, which enrich creditors while leaving farmers more vulnerable to bad weather or adverse market conditions in years to come. Consider the problem facing a farmer whose average income net of expenses is five hundred dollars per year, but who may suffer a net loss of one thousand dollars in any given year because of bad weather or low commodity prices. In a transparent economy with competitive markets, farmers would be able to purchase insurance against bad weather or adverse market conditions for a reasonable premium. However, if there is no such insurance (or futures) market, if there are but a few lenders, and if poor harvests or falling prices afflict many farmers at once, then high-interest loans might be the *only* alternative available to farmers who must pay taxes or other bills. Furthermore, if many farmers cannot "wait" for prices to rise, but must sell their crops to pay debts or other obligations, then the increased supply of farm products released upon the market will drive agricultural prices still lower.

78. For a model of self-reinforcing inequalities along these lines, see Karla Hoff, "Market Failures and the Distribution of Wealth: A Perspective from the Economics of Information," in *Recasting Egalitarianism*, ed. Erik Olin Wright (London: Verso, 1998), pp. 332–360.

79. Rousseau, "Constitutional Project for Corsica," p. 303. See also "Discourse on Political Economy." To forestall this outcome, Rousseau proposed changes in the prevailing system of public finance. The problem requiring attention was not just that agriculture labored under a heavy tax burden, but that farmers were sometimes forced to sell their harvest at low prices in order to pay taxes that were coming due. To alleviate this pressure, Rousseau outlined a sophisticated scheme of taxation that provided farmers a modicum of insurance against adverse market conditions. In brief, Rousseau's plan would give farmers the option of paying their taxes in corn or in cash. If corn prices were low, farmers could pay their taxes in corn, and if prices were high, they could pay in cash. Such a mechanism would not only smooth the farmer's income over good and bad harvests, it would, more importantly, reduce the citizen-farmer's dependence on creditors who were unwilling to share the burdens of their fellow citizens. See "Constitutional Project for Corsica," pp. 320–323.

80. See Ronald Dworkin, "What is Equality? Part II: Equality of Resources," *Philosophy and Public Affairs* 10 (Fall 1981): 283–345.

81. See Stiglitz, *Whither Socialism?*

82. Rousseau, "Discourse on the Origin of Inequality," p. 275.

83. Once strategic thinking enters the picture, two things happen. First, the information required for rational decision making by market participants increases sharply. In particular, a knowledge of prices is no longer sufficient because individuals must now predict how others will act, and react, in response to various strategic possibilities. Second, the market's price system now assumes a further burden, in addition to balancing supply and demand. When traders are opaque, prices not only regulate supply and demand, they also influence the quality of the goods brought to market. The quality of used cars offered for sale depends on the prevailing prices, the productivity of workers depends on the level of wages, and the creditworthiness of borrowers depends on the rate of interest. Because of these secondary effects, prices cannot clear markets in the way Smith imagined. See Stiglitz, *Whither Socialism?*

84. See Rawls, *Theory of Justice*; Thomas Nagel, *Equality and Partiality* (Oxford: Oxford University Press, 1991); and Peter Singer, *Practical Ethics* (Cambridge: Cambridge University Press, 1979).

85. John Stuart Mill, *Principles of Political Economy* [1848]. Oxford: Oxford University Press, 1999.

86. Rousseau, "Social Contract," p. 93; and Jean-Jacques Rousseau, *The Government of Poland*, trans. Willmoore Kendall (Bobbs-Merrill: New York, 1972), p. 7. In states, Rousseau

complains, the public's money "is easily diverted and concealed; what is intended for one purpose is utilized for another; those who handle money soon learn how to divert it—and what are all the officials assigned to keep watch on them, except so many more rascals whom one sends along to go shares with them?" *Government of Poland*, p. 70.

87. See Nagel, *Equality and Partiality*, on liberalism's "moral division of labor."

88. It is worth emphasizing that while Rousseau sympathized with the poor, he did not refrain from attributing to them many of the same vices he attributed to the rich. See, e.g., "Discourse on the Origin of Inequality," p. 249.

89. See Rawls, *Theory of Justice*; and Dworkin, "What is Equality? Part II: Equality of Resources."

90. These problems will be compounded in small countries, and in local jurisdictions within larger states, because when these governments raise taxes to provide more generous benefits, they will attract immigrants in need of assistance, while some productive citizens will leave their jurisdictions in search of lower taxes. See Paul E. Peterson, *City Limits* (Chicago: University of Chicago Press, 1981).

91. Nagel, *Equality and Partiality*, p. 86; see also Thomas Nagel and Liam Murphy, *The Myth of Ownership* (New York: Oxford University Press, 2002), p. 72. For a critical view of liberal citizenship and its split personality, as well as an account of Rousseau's influence on Marx, see Lucio Colletti, *From Rousseau to Marx* (New York: Monthly Review Press, 1972), pp. 143–194.

92. Rousseau, "Social Contract," p. 3.

93. Rousseau, "Discourse on Political Economy," p. 306.

94. Rousseau, "Constitutional Project for Corsica," p. 308.

95. Ibid., p. 297.

96. Such an interpretation is consistent with Rousseau's enigmatic remark that while "the will of all" is no more than "a sum of particular wills," if we "but take away from these same wills the pluses and minuses that cancel one another," "the general will remains as the sum of the differences." See "Social Contract," p. 26.

97. Rousseau, "Essay on Political Economy," pp. 307–308.

98. See Bowles and Gintis, "Efficient Redistribution: New Rules for Markets, State and Communities," *Recasting Egalitarianism*, p. 6.

99. According to Bowles and Gintis, "Efficient Redistribution," p. 6, egalitarian communities "may be capable of supporting levels of cooperation and trust unavailable in more economically divided societies."

100. See my earlier discussion of Rousseau's proposed public grain stocks.

101. We noted, however, that health insurance is a special case.

102. Cf. John E. Roemer, *A Future for Socialism* (Cambridge: Harvard University Press, 1994).

103. Bowles and Gintis, "Efficient Redistribution," cite several studies showing that, within the advanced economies, inequalities of wealth and income are negatively correlated with the rate of growth of productivity.

104. See the discussion in Karla Hoff, "Market Failures and the Distribution of Wealth," pp. 332–360.

105. Equality of wealth would also preclude one party from dictating terms to another.

106. According to one proponent of this view, "money liberalism," which aims to preserve some measure of equality by suppressing the increasing disparities of income generated within contemporary global markets, is fighting a losing battle. Attempts to significantly narrow the gap between rich and poor through tax-and-transfer policies, expansion of education and job training programs, increased unionization, trade protection, profit-sharing, and such like will not succeed for both economic and political reasons. See Mickey Kaus, *The End of Equality* (New York: Basic Books, 1992).

107. Kaus, *End of Equality*, pp. 13–14.

108. See Michael Walzer, *Spheres of Justice* (New York: Basic Books, 1983).

109. Rousseau, *Government of Poland*, pp. 14–15. Rousseau seems to be much less concerned about inequality if people do not strive to improve their position, for it is "the continual shifting of rank

and fortune among citizens [that] is fatal to morality and to the Republic," because "neither those who rise nor those who fall are able to assume the rules of conduct" required by "this new condition, still less to discharge the duties it entails," "Discourse on the Origin of Inequality," p. 313.

110. Rousseau, "Discourse on the Origin of Inequality," p. 274.
111. Rousseau, "Constitutional Project for Corsica," p. 318.
112. Ibid., p. 319.
113. Ibid., p. 317.
114. Ibid., p. 320.
115. Ibid.
116. Rousseau, "Considerations on the Government of Poland," p. 74.
117. Rousseau, "Discourse on Political Economy," p. 285, emphasis in the original.
118. Ibid., p. 287.
119. Ibid.
120. Rousseau, "Social Contract," pp. 99–100.
121. Ibid., p. 101.
122. Rousseau, "Discourse on Political Economy," p. 313.
123. See Williamson, *Markets and Hierarchies.*
124. The recent wave of corporate scandals in the United States suggests that principal-agent problems continue to be a pervasive feature of the corporate landscape.
125. In liberal states the task of monitoring is also delegated, in part, to the courts.
126. Indeed, the principal-agent problem is much more severe in this arena than in the corporation. To begin with, there is no single indicator, like a company's stock price or return on investment, against which the management of government can be measured. In addition, significant information costs must be incurred in order to develop a detailed assessment of the government's administrative activities, particularly in the case of a large nation-state.
127. Rousseau, *Government of Poland*, p. 70.
128. Rousseau, "Discourse on the Origin of Inequality," p. 177.
129. See Rousseau, "Social Contract," p. 56.
130. Rousseau, *Government of Poland*, p. 25. In some cases, this may require a federalist government which divides the country up into more manageable units. See ibid., p. 26.
131. Rousseau, *Government of Poland*, p. 70.
132. Ibid., pp. 70–71.
133. Ibid., p. 70.
134. Ibid., p. 72.
135. This requirement, once it is made explicit, may help to explain part of our reticence in accepting Hobbes's version of the social contract. On its face, an arrangement under which an agent, the sovereign authority, promises to act on behalf of its principal, the individual subjects of the commonwealth, who, in turn, promise to obey the sovereign's edicts, seems altogether rational. But one troubling feature of such a contract is that it would be very hard to monitor compliance with its terms. Neither the actions of the central authority and its administrative officials, nor the activities of its subjects would be, at all times publicly observable. Quite apart from its other drawbacks, Hobbes's contract is problematic simply because, in the absence of extensive surveillance, it would be impossible to ascertain whether the parties to the agreement were complying with its terms or not.

Chapter Five   The Ring of Gyges, the Perfect Shield, and the Veil of Ignorance

1. Plato, *Republic*, trans. Francis MacDonald Conford (Oxford: Oxford University Press, 1945), 357a—367e.

2. Ibid., 336b—347e.

3. Ibid., p. 45 (360b).

4. Ibid., p. 46 (361a).

5. Thomas Hobbes, *Leviathan*, ed. C. B. Macpherson (Harmondsworth, Middlesex: Penguin, 1968), pp. 72–75.

6. It could be argued that weak-willed subjects who promise with good intentions, but do not (or cannot) follow through on their promises require a coercive authority. But people subject to frequent lapses of this kind would be excluded from cooperative endeavors just as conniving double-dealers would.

7. David Gauthier, *Morals by Agreement* (Oxford: Oxford University Press, 1986).

8. Gauthier, *Morals by Agreement*, chap. 6.

9. For Gauthier's conception of social contract theory as a response to post-modernism, see David Gauthier, "Why Contractarianism?" in *Contractarianism and Rational* Choice, ed. Peter Vallentyne (Cambridge: Cambridge University Press, 1991).

10. See Peter A. Danielson, *Artificial Morality* (London: Routledge, 1992).

11. See Greg Hill, "The Rational Justification of Moral Constraint," *The Southern Journal of Philosophy* 21:2 (1993): 179–191.

12. Cf. Sissela Bok, *Secrets* (New York: Pantheon, 1982).

13. I borrow the term, "moral distance," from Michael Mosher.

14. See David Gauthier's discussion of the market as a "morally free zone," in his book, *Morals by Agreement* (Oxford: Oxford University Press, 1986), chap. 4.

15. Bruce A. Ackerman, *Social Justice in the Liberal State* (New Haven: Yale University Press, 1980).

16. Ackerman, *Social Justice in the Liberal State*, pp. 170–171.

17. Ibid., p. 173, original emphasis.

18. It is one thing to specify that offers of cooperation must be truthful *in theory*, but quite another to explain how this condition is to be fulfilled in practice. If Rousseau is right, then some kind of mutual surveillance is necessary to ensure truthful offers. But it may be hard to square this requirement with individualistic conceptions of the good.

19. I am here thinking of neutrality in terms of effects rather than justification.

20. See Cass Sunstein, *Republic.com* (Princeton, NJ: Princeton University Press, 2001).

21. Sunstein, *Republic.com*, pp. 48–49.

22. Ibid., p. 49. Solidarity goods will be underproduced if citizens, in programming their Ackermanian technologies, do not take account of the external benefits that are generated simply by virtue of the fact that one more person is sharing in the use of a collective good.

23. Ibid., p. 96.

24. Ackerman, *Social Justice in the Liberal State*, p. 175.

25. Ibid., p. 176.

26. Thomas Nagel, *Concealment and Exposure* (Oxford: Oxford University Press, 2002).

27. Nagel, *Concealment and Exposure*, p. 7.

28. Alexis de Tocqueville, *Democracy in America*, ed. J. P. Mayer, trans. George Lawrence (Garden City, NY: Anchor Books, 1969), p. 567.

29. Nagel, *Concealment and Exposure*, p. 5.

30. See Michael Mosher, "Illiberal Prospects: Observations on Bruce Ackerman's Social Justice in the Liberal State," *Humanities in Society* 4:1 (Winter 1981).

31. See R. G. Lipsey and K. Landcaster, "The General Theory of Second Best," *The Review of Economic Studies* 24 (1956): 11–32.

32. Jean-Jacques Rousseau, "Social Contract," in *Social Contract and Discourses*, ed. and trans. G. D. H. Cole (New York: E. P. Dutton, 1950), p. 18.

33. John Rawls, *A Theory of Justice* (Cambridge, MA: Harvard University Press, 1971), p. 11.

34. Rawls, *Theory of Justice*, p. 11.

35. Rousseau, "Social Contract," p. 14 and p. 3.

36. Rawls, *Theory of Justice*, p. 140.

37. Rawls, *Theory of Justice*, p. 252.
38. Ibid.
39. Ibid.
40. See also John Rawls, *Political Liberalism* (New York: Columbia University Press, 1993).
41. Rousseau, "Social Contract," p. 29.
42. Ibid., p. 30. Since social differentiation and the multitude of interests and outlooks associated with it are precisely the characteristics that define the modern world, one could well criticize Rousseau's general will, or at least its relevance to the more opaque circumstances of modernity, on the Rousseauean grounds that it fails "to take men as they are" and relies too heavily on the kind of self-abnegation that leads Rawls to reject utilitarianism.
43. Ibid.
44. Rawls, *Theory of Justice*, p. 152.
45. See J. C. Harsanyi, "Cardinal Utility in Welfare Economics and the Theory of Risk-Taking," *Journal of Political Economy* (1953); and J. C. Harsanyi, "Cardinal Welfare, Individualistic Ethics, and Interpersonal Comparisons of Utility," *Journal of Political Economy* (1955).
46. See Gauthier, *Morals by Agreement*.
47. Rawls, *Theory of Justice*, p. 101.
48. Ibid., p. 102.
49. Ibid.
50. Ibid., p. 101.
51. Ibid., p. 102.
52. Let us acknowledge that this is not exactly the way Rawls, himself, frames the problem.
53. See Michael Sandel, *Liberalism and the Limits of Justice* (Cambridge: Cambridge University Press, 1982).
54. See Charles Taylor, "Cross-Purposes: The Liberal-Communitarian Debate," in *Liberalism and the Moral Life*, ed. Nancy L. Rosenblum (Cambridge, MA: Harvard University Press, 1989).
55. John Rawls, "The Sense of Justice," *Philosophical Review* 72:3 (1963): pp. 281–305.
56. Rawls, *Theory of Justice*, p. 463, note 9.
57. Ibid., pp. 462–478.
58. Ibid., p. 471.
59. Ibid., pp. 177–182.
60. I assume that "the system of natural liberty" is a "plausible" scheme of justice because it is one of the theories considered in the original position. See ibid., pp. 65–74.
61. Robert Shiller, *Macro Markets: Creating Institutions for Managing Society's Largest Economic Risks* (Oxford: Oxford University Press, 1993), p. v.
62. See Shiller, *Macro Markets*.
63. Robert Shiller, *The New Financial Order: Risk in the 21st Century* (Princeton, NJ: Princeton University Press, 2003), pp. 58–59.
64. See Shiller, *New Financial Order*, chap. 4.
65. See Shiller, *Macro Markets* and *New Financial Order*.
66. Ibid.
67. I ignore incentive effects here.
68. Jean Jacques Rousseau, "A Discourse on Political Economy," in *The Social Contract and Discourses*, ed. and trans. G. D. H. Cole (New York: E. P. Dutton, 1950), p. 313.

Chapter Six   Conclusion

1. David Gauthier, *Morals by Agreement* (Oxford: Oxford University Press, 1986).
2. See Michael Sandel, *Liberalism and the Limits of Justice* (Cambridge: Cambridge University Press, 1983).

3. Thomas Nagel, *The View from Nowhere* (Oxford: Oxford University Press, 1989).
4. Rousseau's contribution, in this regard, was noted by W. G. Runciman and A. K. Sen, "Games, Justice and the General Will," *Mind* (October 1965): 554–562.
5. See Adam B. Seligman, *The Problem of Trust* (Princeton, NJ: Princeton University Press, 1997).
6. Jeremy Bentham, "Panopticon" [1791] in *The Works of Jeremy Bentham* (Edinburgh: William Tait, 1843), vol. IV, p. 45.
7. Michel Foucault, *Discipline and Punish* (New York: Vintage, 1979), pp. 216–217.
8. Foucault, *Discipline and Punish*, p. 146.
9. Ibid., p. 214.
10. Ibid., pp. 216–217.
11. Ibid., p. 216.
12. Ibid., pp. 170 and 184.

BIBLIOGRAPHY

Ackerman, Bruce A. *Social Justice in the Liberal State*. New Haven: Yale University Press, 1980.

Akerlof, George A. "The Market for Lemons." In Akerlof, *An Economic Theorist's Book of Tales*. Cambridge: Cambridge University Press, 1984.

Alchain, Armen A. *Economic Forces at Work*. Indianapolis: Liberty Fund, 1977.

Alchain, Armen A., and Harold Demsetz. "Production, Information Costs and Economic Ownership." *American Economic Review* 62 (1972): 777–795.

Alesina, Alberto, and Eliana La Ferrara. "Participation in Heterogeneous Communities." *Quarterly Journal of Economics* 115 (2000): 847–904.

Alesina, Alberto, and Dani Rodrik. "Distributive Politics and Economic Growth." *The Quarterly Journal of Economics* 109 (1994): 465–489.

Alford, C. Fred. *The Self in Social Theory*. New Haven: Yale University Press, 1991.

Almond, Gabriel, and Sidney Verba. *The Civic Culture*. Princeton: Princeton University Press, 1963.

Arendt, Hannah. *On Revolution*. New York: Viking, 1963.

Aron, Raymond. *Main Currents in Sociological Thought*, vol. I. London: Transaction, 1998.

Arrow, Kenneth J. "Uncertainty and the Welfare Economics of Medical Care." *American Economic Review* 53:3 (December 1963): 941–973.

———. *The Limits of Organization*. New York: W. W. Norton, 1974.

Arrow, Kenneth J., Samuel Bowles, and Steven Durlauf, eds. *Meritocracy and Economic Inequality*. Princeton, NJ: Princeton University Press, 2000.

Axelrod, Robert. *The Evolution of Cooperation*. New York: Basic Books, 1984.

Banfield, Edward C. *The Moral Basis of a Backward Society*. New York: Free Press, 1958.

Barr, Nicholas. *The Economics of the Welfare State*. Stanford: Stanford University Press, 1993.

Barry, Brian. "The Public Interest." In *Political Concepts*, edited by Anthony Quinton. New York: Oxford University Press, 1967.

Baumol, William J. *Perfect Markets and Easy Virtue*. Cambridge, MA: Blackwell, 1991.

Becker, Gary. *The Economics of Discrimination*. Chicago: University of Chicago Press, 1957.

Ben-Ner, Avner, and Louis Putterman. "Values and Institutions in Economic Analysis." In *Economics, Values, and Organizations*, edited by Avner Ben-Ner and Louis Putterman. Cambridge: Cambridge University Press, 1998.

———., eds. *Economics, Values, and Organizations*. Cambridge: Cambridge University Press, 1998.

Beer, Samuel. *To Make a Nation*. Cambridge: Harvard University Press, 1993.

Bell, Daniel A. "Civil Society versus Civic Virtue." In *Freedom of Association*, edited by Amy Gutmann. Princeton: Princeton University Press, 1998.

Bellah, Robert N., Richard Madsen, William M. Sullivan, Ann Swidler, and Steven M. Tipton. *The Good Society*. New York: Alfred A. Knopf, 1991.

Benabou, Roland J. "Workings of a City: Location, Education, and Production." *Quarterly Journal of Economics* 108 (1993): 619–652.

———. "Inequality and Growth." In *NBER Macroeconomic Annual 1996*, edited by B. Bernake and J. Rotemberg. Cambridge: MIT Press, 1996.

Bendor, Jonathan, and Dilip Moskherjee. "Institutional Structure and the Logic of Ongoing Collective Action." *American Political Science Review* 81 (1987): 129–154.

Benichou, Paul. *Man and Ethics*. New York: Anchor, 1971.

Bentham, Jeremy. "Panopticon." In *The Works of Jeremy Bentham*, vol. IV. Edinburgh: William Tait, 1843.

Berman, Marshall. *The Politics of Authenticity*. New York: Atheneum, 1980.

Bernstein, Peter L. *Against the Gods: The Remarkable Story of Risk*. New York: John Wiley and Sons, 1996.

Birdsall, N., and J. L. Londono. "Asset Inequality Matters: An Assessment of the World Bank's Approach to Poverty Reduction." *American Economic Review* (AEA Papers and Proceedings) 82 (1997): 32–37.

Blandshard, William H. *Rousseau and the Spirit of Revolt*. Ann Arbor: University of Michigan Press, 1967.

Blau, Peter M. *Exchange and Power in Social Life*. London: Transaction, 1986.

Bok, Sissela. *Secrets*. New York: Pantheon, 1982.

Bowles, Samuel, and Herbert Gintis. "Efficient Redistribution: New Rules for Markets, State and Communities." In *Recasting Egalitarianism*, edited by Erik Olin Wright. London: Verso, 1998.

———. "How Communities Govern: The Structural Basis of Prosocial Norms." In *Economics, Values, and Organization*, edited by Avner Ben-Ner and Louis Putterman. Cambridge: Cambridge University Press, 1998.

Brin, David. *The Transparent Society*. New York: Perseus, 1999.

Burkholder, Leslie. "Theorem 1." In *Modeling Rationality, Morality, and Evolution*, edited by Peter A. Danielson. New York: Oxford University Press, 1998.

Carens, Joseph H. *Equality, Moral Incentives & the Market*. Chicago: University of Chicago Press, 1981.

Chambers, Simone, and Will Kymlicka, eds. *Alternative Conceptions of Civil Society*. Princeton: Princeton University Press, 2002.

Charvet, John. "Individual Identity and Social Consciousness." In *Hobbes and Rousseau*, edited by Maurice Cranston and Richard S. Peters. Garden City, NY: Anchor Books, 1972.

———. *The Social Problem in the Philosophy of Rousseau*. Cambridge: Cambridge University Press, 1974.

Chong, Dennis. *Rational Lives: Norms and Values in Politics and Societies*. Chicago: University of Chicago Press, 2000.

Clark, John Bates. *The Distribution of Wealth* [1899]. New York: Macmillan Company, 1920.

Chwe, Suk-Young Michael. *Rational Ritual: Culture, Coordination, and Common Knowledge*. Princeton, NJ: Princeton University Press, 2001.

Cohen, Joshua, and Joel Rogers. "Secondary Associations and Democratic Governance." In *Associations and Democracy*, edited by Erik Olin Wright. New York: Verso, 1995.

Coleman, James. *Foundations of Social Theory*. Cambridge: Harvard University Press, 1990.

Colletti, Lucio. *From Rousseau to Marx*. New York: Monthly Review Press, 1972.

Cooper, Laurence W. *Rousseau & Nature: The Problem of the Good Life*. University Park: Pennsylvania University Press, 1999.

Cornes, Richard, and Todd Sandler. *The Theory of Externalities, Public Goods, and Club Goods*, 2nd edition. Cambridge: Cambridge University Press, 1996.

Cranston, Maurice, and Richard S. Peters, eds. *Hobbes and Rousseau*. Garden City, NY: Anchor Books, 1972.

Dagger, Richard. *Civic Virtues: Rights, Citizenship, and Republican Liberalism.* Oxford: Oxford University Press, 1997.

Danielson, Peter A. *Artificial Morality.* London: Routledge, 1992.

Dent, N. J. H. *Rousseau.* Oxford: Basil Blackwell, 1988.

Durkheim, Emile. *Montesquieu and Rousseau: Forerunners of Sociology.* Ann Arbor: University of Michigan Press, 1965.

Durlauf, Steven N. "A Theory of Persistent Income Inequality." *Journal of Economic Growth* 1 (1996): 75–93.

———. "Associational Redistribution: A Defense." In *Recasting Egalitarianism*, edited by Erik Olin Wright. London: Verso, 1998.

Dworkin, Ronald. "What is Equality? Part II: Equality of Resources." *Philosophy and Public Affairs* 10 (Fall 1981): 283–345.

Eberly, Don E. "The Meaning, Origin, and Applications of Civil Society." In *The Essential Civil Society Reader*, edited by Don E. Eberly. Oxford: Rowman & Littlefield, 2000.

———., ed. *The Essential Civil Society Reader.* Oxford: Rowman & Littlefield, 2000.

Etzioni, Amatai. *The Limits of Privacy.* New York: Basic Books, 1999.

Etzioni, Amitai., ed. *The Essential Communitarian Reader.* Oxford: Rowman & Littlefield, 1998.

Forbes, H. D. "Rousseau, Ethnicity, and Difference." In *The Legacy of Rousseau*, edited by Clifford Orwin and Nathan Tarcov. Chicago: University of Chicago Press, 1997.

Foucault, Michel. *Discipline and Punish.* New York: Vintage, 1977.

Frank, Robert H. *Choosing the Right Pond.* New York: Oxford University Press, 1985.

———. *Passions within Reason.* New York: W. W. Norton, 1988.

———. *Luxury Fever.* New York: Free Press, 1999.

Frank, Robert H., and Philip J. Cook *The Winner-Take-All Society.* New York: Free Press, 1995.

Fraser, Nancy. *Unruly Practices: Power, Discourse, and Gender in Contemporary Social Theory.* Minneapolis: University of Minnesota, 1989.

Friden, Bertil. *Rousseau's Economic Philosophy.* Dordrecht: Kluwer, 1998.

Friedman, Milton. *Capitalism and Freedom.* Chicago: University of Chicago Press, 1963.

Fukuyama, Francis. *Trust: The Social Virtues and the Creation of Prosperity.* New York: Free Press, 1995.

Gambetta, Diego. *Trust: Making and Breaking Cooperative Relations.* Oxford: Blackwell, 1988.

Gauthier, David. *The Logic of Leviathan.* Oxford: Oxford University Press, 1969.

———. *Morals by Agreement.* Oxford: Oxford University Press, 1986.

———. *Moral Dealing.* Ithaca, NY: Cornell University Press, 1990.

———. "Why Contractarianism?" In *Contractarianism and Rational Choice*, edited by Peter Vallentyne. Cambridge: Cambridge University Press, 1991.

———. "Hobbes's Social Contract." In *The Social Contract Theorists*, edited by Christopher W. Morris. New York: Rowman & Littlefield, 1999.

Gellner, Ernest. *Conditions of Liberty: Civil Society and Its Rivals.* New York: Penguin Press, 1994.

Gilden, Hilail. *Rousseau's Social Contract: The Design of the Argument.* Chicago: University of Chicago Press, 1983.

Girard, Rene. *Deceit, Desire, & the Novel.* Translated by Yvonne Fressero. Baltimore: Johns Hopkins, 1965.

Goffman, Erving. *The Presentation of Self in Everyday Life.* Woodstock, NY: Overlook Press, 1973.

Granovetter, Mark. "The Impact of Social Structure on Economic Outcomes." *The Journal of Economic Perspectives* 19:1 (Winter 2005): 33–50.

Grimsley, Ronald. *Jean-Jacques Rousseau: A Study in Self-Awareness.* Cardiff, Wales: University of Wales Press, 1961.

Grofman, Bernard, and Scott Feld. "Rousseau's General Will: A Condorcetian Perspective." *American Political Science Review* 82 (1988): 567–576.

Gutmann, Amy., ed. *Freedom of Association*. Princeton: Princeton University Press, 1998.

Hampton, Jean. *Hobbes and the Social Contract Tradition*. New York: Cambridge University Press, 1986.

———. "Two Faces of Contractarian Thought." In *Contractarianism and Rational Choice*, edited by Peter Vallentyne. New York: Cambridge University Press, 1991.

———. "The Failure of Hobbes's Social Contract Argument." In *The Social Contract Theorists*, edited by Christopher W. Morris. New York: Rowman & Littlefield, 1999.

Harsanyi, John C. "Cardinal Utility in Welfare Economics and the Theory of Risk-Taking." *Journal of Political Economy* (1953).

———. "Cardinal Welfare, Individualistic Ethics, and Interpersonal Comparisons of Utility," *Journal of Political Economy* (1955).

Hardin, Russell. *Collective Action*. Baltimore: Johns Hopkins University Press, 1982.

Hargreaves Heap, Shaun P. and Yanis Varoufakis. *Game Theory*. London: Routledge, 1995.

Hauser, Marc D. "Costs of Deception." *Proceedings of the National Academy of Sciences* 89 (1992): 12137–12139.

Hayek, Friedrich von. "Economics and Knowledge." In Hayek, *Individualism and Economic Order*. Chicago: University of Chicago Press, 1980.

Hechter, Michael. *Principles of Group Solidarity*. Berkeley: University of California Press, 1987.

Hicks, J. R. *Value and Capital*. Oxford: Clarendon Press, 1946.

Hill, Greg. "Justice and Natural Inequality." *The Journal of Social Philosophy* (Winter 1997): 16–30.

———. "Solidarity, Objectivity, and the Human Form of Life." *Critical Review* (Fall 1997): 550–580.

———. "The Rational Justification of Moral Constraint." *The Southern Journal of Philosophy* 21:2 (1993): 179–191.

Hirsch, Fred. *Social Limits to Growth*. London: Routledge and Kegan Paul, 1977.

Hirschman, Albert O. *Exit, Voice, and Loyalty*. Cambridge: Harvard University Press, 1970.

———. *Shifting Involvements: Private Interest and Public Action*. Princeton: Princeton University Press, 1982.

Hirshleifer, David, and Eric Rasmusen. "Cooperation in a Repeated Prisoners' Dilemma with Ostracism." *Journal of Economic Behavior and Organization* 12 (1989): 87–106.

Hirshleifer, Jack. *Price Theory and Applications*, 3rd edition. Englewood Cliffs, NJ: Prentice-Hall, 1984.

Hobbes, Thomas. *Leviathan*. Edited by C. B. Macpherson. Middlesex: Penguin, 1968.

Hoff, Karla. "Market Failures and the Distribution of Wealth: A Perspective from the Economics of Information." In *Recasting Egalitarianism*, edited by Erik Olin Wright. London: Verso, 1998.

Holt, John A., ed. *Civil Society*. Cambridge: Polity Press, 1995.

Horner, Johannes. "Reputation and Competition." *American Economic Review* 92:3 (June 2002): 644–663.

Howard, Nigel. *Paradoxes of Rationality*. Cambridge, MA: MIT Press, 1971.

Hulling, Mark. "Rousseau, Voltaire, and the Revenge of Pascal." In *The Cambridge Companion to Rousseau*, edited by Patrick Riley. Cambridge: Cambridge University Press, 2001.

Ignatieff, Michael. *The Needs of Strangers*. New York: Penguin, 1986.

Kateb, George. "The Value of Association." In *Freedom of Association*, edited by Amy Gutmann. Princeton: Princeton University Press, 1998.

Kaus, Mickey. *The End of Equality*. New York: Basic Books, 1992.

Kavka, Gregory S. *Hobbesian Moral and Political Theory*. Princeton: Princeton University Press, 1986.

———. "Hobbes's War of All Against All." In *The Social Contract Theorists*, edited by Christopher W. Morris. New York: Rowman & Littlefield, 1999.

Kelly, Christopher. *Rousseau as Author: Consecrating One's Life to Truth*. Chicago: University of Chicago Press, 2003.

Kelly, George Armstrong. "A General Overview." In *The Cambridge Companion to Rousseau*, edited by Patrick Riley. Cambridge: Cambridge University Press, 2001.

Lazarsfeld, Paul F. and Robert K. Merton. "Friendship as Social Process: A Substantive and Methodological Analysis." In *Freedom and Control in Modern Society*, edited by Theodore Abel, Monroe Berger, and Charles H. Page. New York: Octagon Books, 1964.

Lipsey, R. G., and K. Landcaster. "The General Theory of Second Best." *The Review of Economic Studies* 24 (1956): 11–32.

Loury, Glenn. "Conceptual Problems in the Enforcement of Anti-Discrimination Laws." In *Meritocracy and Economic Inequality*, edited by Kenneth Arrow, Samuel Bowles, and Steven Durlauf. Princeton, NJ: Princeton University Press, 2000.

Lowi, Theodore J. *The End of Liberalism*. New York: W. W. Norton, 1969.

Lundberg, Shelly J., and Richard Startz. "Inequality and Race: Models and Policy." In *Meritocracy and Economic Inequality*, edited by Kenneth Arrow, Samuel Bowles, and Steven Durlauf. Princeton: Princeton University Press, 2000.

Madison, James. *Federalist Papers #10 and #51*.

Margolis, Howard. *Selfishness, Altruism, and Rationality*. Chicago: University of Chicago Press, 1982.

Masters, Roger D. "Rousseau and the Rediscovery of Human Nature." In *The Legacy of Rousseau*, edited by Clifford Orwin and Nathan Tarcov. Chicago: University of Chicago Press, 1997.

McConnell, Grant. *Private Power and American Democracy*. New York: Vintage, 1966.

Mead, George Herbert. *Mind, Self, and Society*. Chicago: University of Chicago Press, 1934.

Melzer, Arthur M. "Rousseau and the Modern Cult of Sincerity." In *The Legacy of Rousseau*, edited by Clifford Orwin and Nathan Tarcov. Chicago: University of Chicago Press, 1997.

Mill, J. S. *Principles of Political Economy* [1848]. Oxford: Oxford University Press, 1999.

Miller, Gary J. *Managerial Dilemmas*. Cambridge: Cambridge University Press, 1992.

Miller, James. *Rousseau: Dreamer of Democracy*. New Haven: Yale University Press, 1984.

Molho, Ian. *The Economics of Information: Lying and Cheating in Organizations*. Oxford: Blackwell, 1997.

Montesquieu, Charles de Secondat. *Spirit of the Laws*. Edited by Ann M. Cohler. Cambridge: Cambridge University Press, 1989.

Morgenstern, Mira. *Rousseau and the Politics of Ambiguity*. University Park, PA: Penn State Press, 1996.

Morris, Christopher W., ed. *The Social Contract Theorists*. New York: Rowman & Littlefield, 1999.

Mosher, Michael A. "Conclusion: Are Civil Societies the Transmission Belts of Ethical Tradition?" In *Alternative Conceptions of Civil Society*, edited by Simone Chambers and Will Kymlicka. Princeton: Princeton University Press, 2002.

———. "Illiberal Prospects: Observations on Bruce Ackerman's Social Justice in the Liberal State." *Humanities in Society* 4:1 (Winter 1981).

Muller, John. *Capitalism, Democracy, and Ralph's Pretty Good Grocery*. Princeton: Princeton University Press, 1999.

Nagel, Thomas. *The View from Nowhere*. Oxford: Oxford University Press, 1989.

———. *Equality and Partiality*. Oxford: Oxford University Press, 1991.

———. *Concealment and Exposure*. Oxford: Oxford University Press, 2002.

Nagel, Thomas, and Liam Murphy. *The Myth of Ownership*. New York: Oxford University Press, 2002.

Neidleman, Jason Andrew. *The General Will Is Citizenship*. New York: Rowman & Littlefield, 2001.

Noble, Richard. *Language, Subjectivity, and Freedom in Rousseau's Moral Philosophy*. New York: Garland Press, 1991.

Nozick, Robert. *The Nature of Rationality*. Princeton: Princeton University Press, 1993.

Nussbaum, Martha C. *Upheavals of Thought*. Cambridge: Cambridge University Press, 2001.

Oakeshott, Michael. *Rationalism in Politics*. Indianapolis: Liberty Press, 1991.

Ockenfels, Peter. "Cooperation in the Prisoner's Dilemma." *European Journal of Political Economy* 9 (1993): 567–579.

Olson, Jr., Mancur. *The Logic of Collective Action*. New York: Schocken, 1968.

———. *The Rise and Decline of Nations*. New Haven: Yale University Press, 1984.

Orwin, Clifford, and Nathan Tarcov, eds. *The Legacy of Rousseau*. Chicago: University of Chicago Press, 1997.

Ostrom, Eleanor. "Collective Action and the Evolution of Norms." *Journal of Economic Perspectives* 14:3 (Summer 2000): 137–158.

Pagano, Ugo. "Redistribution of Assets and Distributions of Asymmetric Information." In *Recasting Egalitarianism*, edited by Erik Olin Wright. London: Verso, 1998.

Page, Talbot, Louis Putterman, and Bulent Unel. "Voluntary Association in Public Goods Experiments: Reciprocity, Mimicry, and Efficiency." Brown University Department of Economics Working Paper, May 22, 2002.

Parry, Geriant. "Emile: Learning to be Men, Women, and Citizens." In *The Cambridge Companion to Rousseau*, edited by Patrick Riley. Cambridge: Cambridge University Press, 2001.

Persson, Torsten, and Guido Tabellini. "Is Inequality Harmful to Growth? Theory and Evidence." *American Economic Review* 84:3 (1994): 600–621.

Peterson, Paul E. *City Limits*. Chicago: University of Chicago Press, 1981.

Plato. *Republic*. Translated by Francis MacDonaldCornford. Oxford: Oxford University Press, 1945.

Posner, Richard A. *The Economics of Justice*. Cambridge, MA: Harvard University Press, 1981.

Putnam, Robert D. *Making Democracy Work: Civic Traditions in Modern Italy*. Princeton: Princeton University Press, 1993.

———. "Bowling Alone: Democracy in America at the End of the Twentieth Century." *Journal of Democracy* 6:1 (January 1995): 65–78.

———. *Bowling Alone: The Collapse and Revival of American Community*. New York: Simon & Schuster, 2000.

Qvortrup, Mads. *The Political Philosophy of Jean-Jacques Rousseau: The Impossibility of Reason*. Manchester: Manchester University Press, 2003.

Rawls, John. "The Sense of Justice." *Philosophical Review* 72:3 (July 1963): 281–305.

———. *A Theory of Justice*. Cambridge, MA: Harvard University Press, 1971.

———. *Political Liberalism*. New York: Columbia University Press, 1993.

Reisman, W. Michael. *Law in Brief Encounters*. New Haven: Yale University Press, 1999.

Rhees, Rush. *Wittgenstein and the Possibility of Discourse*. Edited by D. Z. Phillips. Cambridge: Cambridge University Press, 1998.

Rheingold, Howard. *The Virtual Community*. Reading, MA: Addison-Wesley, 1993.

Riley, Patrick. "Rousseau's General Will." In *The Cambridge Companion to Rousseau*, edited by Patrick Riley. Cambridge: Cambridge University Press, 2001.

———., ed. *The Cambridge Companion to Rousseau*. Cambridge: Cambridge University Press, 2001.

Roemer, John E. *A Future for Socialism*. Cambridge: Harvard University Press, 1994.

Rosen, Jeffery. *The Unwanted Gaze*. New York: Random House, 2000.

Rosenblum, Nancy L. "Compelled Association: Public Standing, Self-Respect, and The Dynamic of Exclusion." In *Freedom of Association*, edited by Amy Gutmann. Princeton: Princeton University Press, 1998.

———, ed. *Liberalism and the Moral Life*. Cambridge: Harvard University Press, 1989.

———. *Membership and Morals*. Princeton: Princeton University Press, 1998.

Rousseau, Jean-Jacques. "A Discourse on the Arts and Sciences." In *The Social Contract and Discourses*, edited and translated by G. D. H. Cole. New York: E. P. Dutton, 1950.

———. "A Discourse on the Origin of Inequality." In *The Social Contract and Discourses*, edited and translated by G. D. H. Cole. New York: E. P. Dutton, 1950.

———. "A Discourse on Political Economy." In *The Social Contract and Discourses*, edited and translated by G. D. H. Cole. New York: E. P. Dutton, 1950.

———. "The Social Contract." In *The Social Contract and Discourses*, edited and translated by G. D. H. Cole. New York: E. P. Dutton, 1950.

———. "Letter to M. D'Alembert on the Theatre." In *Politics and the Arts*, edited and translated by Allan Bloom. Ithaca: Cornell University Press, 1960.

———. *The Reveries of a Solitary Walker*. Translated and edited by C. Butterworth. Hammondsworth, UK: Penguin, 1964.

———. *The Government of Poland*. Translated by Willmoore Kendall. Bobbs-Merrill: New York, 1972.

———. "Geneva Manuscript." In *Jean-Jacques Rousseau, On The Social Contract*, edited by Roger D. Masters, translated by Judith R. Masters. New York: St. Martins, 1978.

———. *Emile*. Translated by Allan Bloom. New York: Basic Books, 1979.

———. *Confessions*. Translated by J. M. Cohen. Hammondsworth: Penguin, 1984.

———. "Considerations on the Government of Poland." In *Jean Jacques Rousseau: Political Writings*, edited and translated by Frederick Watkins. Madison: University of Wisconsin Press, 1986.

———. "Constitutional Project for Corsica." In *Jean-Jacques Rousseau, Political Writings*, edited and translated by Fredrick Watkins. Madison: University of Wisconsin Press, 1986.

———. "Essay on the Origin of Languages." In *Discourses and Essay on the Origin of Languages*, edited and translated by Victor Gourevitch. New York: Harper & Row, 1990.

Rue, Loyal. *By the Grace of Guile*. New York: Oxford University Press, 1994.

Runciman, W. G. and A. K. Sen. "Games, Justice and the General Will." *Mind* (October 1965): 554–562.

Sahlins, Marshall. *Stone Age Economics*. Hawthorne, NY: Aldine de Gruyter, 1972.

Sandel, Michael J. *Liberalism and the Limits of Justice*. Cambridge: Cambridge University Press, 1982.

———. *Democracy's Discontent*. Cambridge: Belknap Press of Harvard University Press, 1996.

Scheffler, Samuel. *Human Morality*. New York: Oxford University Press, 1996.

———. *Boundaries and Allegiances*. New York: Oxford University Press, 2001.

Schmidtz, David. *The Limits of Government: An Essay on the Public Goods Argument*. Boulder: Westview Press, 1991.

Schuessler, Rudolf. "Threshold Effects and the Decline of Cooperation." *Journal of Conflict Resolution* 34 (1990): 476–494.

Seligman, Adam B. *The Problem of Trust*. Princeton, NJ: Princeton University Press, 1997.

Shah, Anup. *Credit Markets and the Distribution of Income*. London: Academic Press, 1992.

Shama, Simon. *Citizens*. New York: A. Knopf, 1989.

Shiller, Robert J. *Macro Markets: Creating Institutions for Managing Society's Largest Economic Risks*. Oxford: Oxford University Press, 1993.

———. *The New Financial Order: Risk in the 21st Century*. Princeton: Princeton University Press, 2003.

Shklar, Judith N. *Men and Citizens*. Cambridge: Cambridge University Press, 1969.

———. *Montesquieu*. Oxford: Oxford University Press, 1987.

Skyrms, Brian. *Evolution of the Social Contract*. Cambridge: Cambridge University Press, 1996.

Singer, Peter. *Practical Ethics*. Cambridge: Cambridge University Press, 1979.

Smith, Adam. *The Wealth of Nations*. Oxford: Clarendon Press, 1976.

———. *Lectures on Jurisprudence*. Edited by R. L. Meek, D. D. Raphael, and J. C. Bryce. Oxford: Oxford University Press, 1978.

———. *Theory of Moral Sentiments*. Edited by D. D. Raphael and A. L. Mackie. Indianapolis: Liberty Fund, 1990.

Smith, John Maynard. *Evolution and the Theory of Games*. Cambridge: Cambridge University Press, 1982.

Sober, Elliot. "Stable Cooperation in Iterated Prisoners' Dilemmas." *Economics and Philosophy* 8 (1992): 127–139.

Spence, Michael. "Signaling in Retrospect and the Informational Structure of Markets." *American Economic Review* 92:3 (June 2002): 434–459.

Starobinski, Jean. *Jean-Jacques Rousseau: Transparency and Obstruction*. Translated by Arthur Goldhammer. Chicago: Chicago University Press, 1988.

———. "The Political Thought of Jean Jacques Rousseau." In *Rousseau's Political Writings*, edited by Alan Ritter and Julia Conaway Bondanella. New York: Norton, 1988.

Stiglitz, J. E., and A. Weiss. "Credit Rationing in Markets with Imperfect Information." *American Economic Review* 71 (1981): 393–410.

———. *Whither Socialism?* Cambridge: MIT Press, 1994.

———. "Information and the Change in the Paradigm in Economics." *American Economic Review* 92:3 (June 2002): 460–501.

Stolle, Dietlind. "Bowling Together, Bowling Alone: The Development of Generalized Trust in Voluntary Associations." *Political Psychology* 19 (1998): 497–525.

Sunstein, Cass. *Republic.com*. Princeton, NJ: Princeton University Press, 2001.

Talmon, J. L. *The Origins of Totalitarian Democracy*. New York: Praeger, 1960.

Taylor, Charles. "Cross-Purposes: The Liberal—Communitarian Debate." In *Liberalism and the Moral Life*, edited by Nancy L. Rosenblum. Cambridge: Harvard University Press, 1989.

Taylor, Michael. *Anarchy and Cooperation*. London: John Wiley, 1976.

———. *The Possibility of Cooperation*. Cambridge: Cambridge University Press, 1987.

Thurow, Lester. *Generating Inequality*. New York: Basic Books, 1975.

Tiebout, Charles M. "A Pure Theory of Local Expenditure." *Journal of Political Economy* 64 (October 1956): 416–424.

Tocqueville, Alexis de. *Democracy in America*. Edited by J. P. Mayer, translated by George Lawrence. New York: Anchor Books, 1969.

Tonnies, Ferdinand. *Community and Civil Society*. Edited by Jose Harris, translated by Jose Harris and Margaret Hollis. Cambridge: Cambridge University Press, 2001.

Trachtenberg, Zev M. *Making Citizens: Rousseau's Political Theory of Culture*. London: Routledge, 1993.

Trivers, R. L. "The Evolution of Reciprocal Altruism." *Quarterly Review of Biology* 46 (1971): 35–57.

Tullock, Gordon. *Rent Seeking*. Brookfield, VT: Edward Elgar, 1993.

Ullmann-Margalit, Edna. *The Emergence of Norms*. Oxford: Oxford University Press, 1977.

Vallentyne, Peter., ed. *Contractarianism and Rational Choice*. Cambridge: Cambridge University Press, 1991.

Viroli, Maurizio. *Jean-Jacques Rousseau and the "Well-Ordered Society."* Translated by Derek Hanson. Cambridge: Cambridge University Press, 1988.

Waldron, Jeremy. *Liberal Rights*. Cambridge: Cambridge University Press, 1993.

Walras, Leon. *Elements of Pure Political Economy* [1874]. London: George Allen and Unwin, 1965.

Walzer, Michael. *Spheres of Justice: A Defense of Pluralism and Equality*. New York: Basic Books, 1983.

———. *What It Means to Be an American*. New York: Marsilio, 1992.

———. "Equality and Civil Society." In *Alternative Conceptions of Civic Society*, edited by Simone Chambers and Will Kymlicka. Princeton: Princeton University Press, 2002.

Warren, Mark E. *Democracy and Association.* Princeton: Princeton University Press, 2001.

————., ed. *Democracy and Trust.* Cambridge: Cambridge University Press, 1999.

Weil, Simone. "A Note on the Complete Abolition of Political Parties." In *Rousseau's Political Writings,* edited by Alan Ritter and Julia Conaway Bondanella. New York: Norton, 1988.

Weisbrod, Burton A. *The Nonprofit Economy.* Cambridge: Harvard University Press, 1988.

Williams, Bernard. *Shame and Necessity.* Berkeley: University of California Press, 1993.

Williamson, Oliver E. *Markets and Hierarchy.* New York: Free Press, 1975.

Wingrove, Elizabeth. *Rousseau's Republican Romance.* Princeton: Princeton University Press, 2000.

Wittgenstein, Ludwig. *Philosophical Investigations.* Translated by G. E. M. Anscombe. Oxford: Blackwell, 1958.

————. *On Certainty.* Edited by G. E. M. Anscombe and G. H. von Wright, translated by G. E. M. Anscombe. Oxford: Blackwell, 1969.

Wollheim, Richard. *The Thread of Life.* Cambridge: Harvard University Press, 1984.

Wright, Erik Olin., ed. *Associations and Democracy.* New York: Verso, 1995.

————. *Recasting Egalitarianism.* London: Verso, 1998.

Young, Iris Marion. *Inclusion and Democracy.* Oxford: Oxford University Press, 2000.

Young, Michael. *The Rise of the Meritocracy.* New York: Penguin, 1971.

INDEX

Abel, Theodore, 174*n*
accurate recognition, 16–17, 25, 27–28,
    31–33, 36, 43–44, 164*n*, 167*n*
Ackerman, Bruce A., 10, 127, 135–142,
    155, 159, 160, 162*n*, 185*n*
Akerlof, George A., 179*n*, 180*n*, 181*n*
Alchain, Armen A., 180*n*
Alesina, Alberto, 174*n*
Alford, C. Fred, 169*n*
Almond, Gabriel, 175*n*
ambitions, 1, 8, 26, 49, 109, 134,
    157, 160
amour de soi, 2, 8, 13–14, 16, 26–28,
    30–33, 40–41, 43, 47, 79, 167*n*
amour-propre, 2, 8, 25–28, 30–31, 33,
    40–44, 48, 55–56, 123, 157,
    163*n*, 167*n*, 170*n*
Anscombe, G. E. M., 162*n*, 165*n*
anticipatory violence, 14, 164*n*
Arendt, Hannah, 32, 168*n*
Aron, Raymond, 11, 162*n*
Arrow, Kenneth J., 175*n*, 180*n*, 181*n*
association, modes of, 40–44, 146
asymmetric information, 93, 95, 103,
    105, 110–111, 124, 133, 158
Axelrod, Robert, 165*n*, 173*n*

Banfield, Edward C., 69, 173*n*, 174*n*
bargaining, 63, 87, 91, 94, 105–106,
    112–114, 124, 127, 147, 155,
    178*n*, 179*n*

Barr, Nicholas, 181*n*
Barry, Brian, 181*n*
Baumol, William J., 179*n*
Becker, Gary, 181*n*
Beer, Samuel, 171*n*
Bell, Daniel A., 84, 173*n*, 177*n*
Bellah, Robert N., 177*n*
Benabou, Rene, 173*n*
Bendor, Jonathan, 166*n*
Benichou, Paul, 167*n*
Ben-Ner, Avner, 177*n*, 180*n*
Bentham, Jeremy, 39, 159, 162*n*,
    173*n*, 187*n*
Berger, Monroe, 174*n*
Berman, Marshall, 161*n*
Bernstein, Peter, 181*n*
Blandshard, William H., 166*n*
Blau, Peter M., 166*n*
Bloom, Allan, 166*n*, 173*n*
Bok, Sissela, 185*n*
Bondanella, Conaway, 168*n*, 171*n*, 177*n*
Bowles, Samuel, 175*n*, 177*n*, 181*n*, 183*n*
Brin, David, 162*n*, 175*n*
Burkholder, Leslie, 163*n*
Butterworth, C., 162*n*

capitalist authority, 103–107
Carens, Joseph H., 180*n*
Chambers, Simone, 171*n*, 173*n*, 177*n*
Charvet, John, 165*n*
Chong, Dennis, 83, 174*n*, 177*n*

Chwe, Michael Suk-Young, 170*n*

civil society, 1, 3, 6, 9, 37, 45, 47, 55, 58, 63, 65, 70, 84–89, 101, 102, 124, 127, 137, 155, 177*n*

Clark, John Bates, 178*n*

Cohen, J. M., 162*n*, 167*n*, 178*n*

Cohen, Joshua, 177*n*

Cohler, Ann M., 162*n*

Cole, G. D. H., 161*n*, 162*n*, 168*n*, 171*n*, 178*n*, 179*n*, 181*n*, 185*n*, 186*n*

Coleman, James, 177*n*

Colletti, Lucio, 183*n*

compassion, 2, 9, 12, 29–34, 40–44, 132–133, 167–168*n*, 170*n*

compassion games, 9, 30–32

competitive markets, 9, 89–91, 98, 99, 114–116, 180*n*, 182*n*

compliance, 89, 105, 120, 146–147, 184*n*

conditional cooperation, 14–18, 21, 24–27, 31–33, 96–97, 132, 156, 163*n*, 164*n*, 165*n*

Condorcet, Marquis de, 49, 108

Conford, Francis MacDonald, 162*n*, 184*n*

constrained maximizers, 10, 131–132

Cook, Philip J., 180*n*

cooperation partner, 55, 58, 66, 69, 79, 130, 155

cooperative disposition, 9, 46, 50, 58–60, 78, 79, 81, 172*n*, 176*n*

Cornes, Richard, 174*n*

corvée (compulsory community service), 86, 123

Dagger, Richard, 177*n*

Danielson, Peter A., 163*n*, 166*n*, 185*n*

deception, 3–4, 7, 8, 14–16, 18–26, 29, 36, 39, 42, 102, 115, 116, 128–129, 156, 163*n*, 166*n*

deer (stag) hunt, 165–166*n*

Demsetz, Harold, 180*n*

Dent, N. J. H., 165*n*

difference principle, 146–151

distribution of wealth, 10, 34, 103, 107, 110–112, 119–121, 135, 149, 162, 183*n*

division of labor, 5, 22, 56, 64, 90, 103–106, 107, 112, 124, 176*n*

moral, 118, 183*n*

duplicity, 1, 15, 21–22, 26, 35, 49, 91, 95, 102, 107, 114, 128, 129, 133, 134, 157

Durlauf, Steven N., 172*n*, 173*n*, 175*n*, 181*n*

Dworkin, Ronald, 182*n*, 183*n*

Eberly, Don E., 170*n*, 171*n*

egalitarianism, 6, 10, 20, 32–34, 55, 59, 70, 88, 90, 106, 107, 109, 121–123, 145, 149, 173*n*, 176*n*, 183*n*

egalitarian liberalism, 116–118

enforceable contracts, 116, 120, 163*n*

Etzioni, Amitai, 162*n*, 171*n*

externalities, 101, 116, 120, 141, 155

Feld, Scott, 171*n*

"foole," 10, 130–131

Foucault, Michel, 6, 39–40, 159–160, 162*n*, 170*n*, 187*n*

Frank, Robert H., 163*n*, 166*n*, 167*n*, 168*n*, 179*n*, 180*n*

free exchange, 10, 90, 141

Fressero, Yvonne, 170*n*

Friden, Bertil, 93, 168*n*, 178*n*, 179*n*

Friedman, Milton, 181*n*

Fukuyama, Francis, 175*n*

Gambetta, Diego, 175*n*

Gauthier, David, 10, 127, 131–133, 135, 145, 154, 162*n*, 163*n*, 168*n*, 185*n*, 186*n*

Gellner, Ernest, 82, 171*n*, 177*n*

general will, 3, 38–39, 45–50, 53, 57, 60, 64, 76, 78, 80, 84, 86, 91, 106, 109, 119, 123–124, 143–146, 149, 169*n*, 172*n*, 183*n*, 186*n*

Gilden, Hilail, 171*n*

Gintis, Herbert, 177*n*, 183*n*

globalization, 6–7, 117, 176*n*, 178*n*

Goffman, Erving, 167*n*

Goldhammer, Arthur, 161*n*, 166*n*, 178*n*

goodness, 12, 154
Gourevitch, Victor, 165*n*, 179*n*
Granovetter, Mark, 174*n*
Grimsley, Ronald, 161*n*
Grofman, Bernard, 171*n*
Gutmann, Amy, 170*n*, 173*n*,
    175*n*, 178*n*

Hampton, Jean, 163*n*, 168*n*
happiness, 1, 124, 144
Hardin, Russell, 172*n*
Hargreaves Heap, Shaun P., 163*n*
Harris, Jose, 174*n*
Harsanyi, J. C., 186*n*
Hayek, Friederich Von, 178*n*
Hechter, Michael, 167*n*, 168*n*
Hicks, J. R., 175*n*
Hill, Greg, 162*n*, 185*n*
Hirsch, Fred, 167*n*, 180*n*
Hirschman, Albert O., 47, 75–77, 171*n*,
    175*n*, 176*n*
Hirshleifer, David, 166*n*
Hirshleifer, Jack, 172*n*
Hobbes, Thomas, xiv, 2–3, 5–6, 10,
    12–18, 22, 27–29, 39, 41, 43–44,
    59, 89, 92–93, 104–105, 107,
    130–134, 154, 156, 162*n*, 163*n*,
    164*n*, 167*n*, 170*n*, 184*n*, 185*n*
Hoff, Karla, 182*n*
Hollis, Margaret, 174*n*
Horner, Johannes, 179*n*
Howard, Nigel, 163*n*
Hulling, Mark, 168*n*

ignorance, veil of, 10, 63, 108, 137,
    142–147, 149–151, 154–155
individualism, 9, 46–47, 68–70, 75,
    79, 157
inequalities of wealth. *See* distribution of
    wealth
information, asymmetric. *See* asymmetric
    information
information externalities, 101, 116
insurance, 7, 86, 107–110, 116–117, 120,
    150–153, 180, 181*n*, 182*n*, 183*n*

intentions, 4, 5, 28–29, 32, 35, 43, 78,
    133–134, 140, 163*n*, 185*n*
    cooperative, 82
    opaque, 2, 7, 40–41, 89, 157–158,
        164*n*, 166*n*, 167*n*
    real, 1, 8, 15, 16, 24, 40, 116, 131
    transparent, 9, 14–18, 38–41,
        116, 131, 133, 156, 164*n*,
        165*n*, 167*n*
Internet, 7, 64–65, 73, 138–139
invisible hand, 6, 89–92, 101, 114–116,
    157–158

justice, 10, 84, 108, 127–130,
    135, 137, 138, 142–149,
    152, 186*n*

Kant, Immanuel, 119, 142, 144, 173*n*
Kateb, George, 175*n*
Kaus, Mickey, 183*n*
Kavka, Gregory F., 162*n*, 163*n*, 164*n*
Kelly, Christopher, 161*n*
Kelly, George Armstrong, 161*n*, 168*n*
Kendall, Willmoore, 182*n*
Kymlicka, Will, 171*n*, 173*n*, 177*n*

La Ferrara, Eliana, 175*n*
Landcaster, K., 185*n*
law of large numbers (law of averages),
    62, 171–172*n*
Lawrence, George, 162*n*, 165*n*,
    171*n*, 185*n*
Lazarsfeld, Paul F., 174*n*
liberalism, 3, 155, 178*n*, 183*n*
    egalitarian, 117, 118
Lipsey, R. G., 185*n*
Loury, Glenn, 175*n*
lucidity, 2, 12, 15, 20, 127
Lundberg, Shelly J., 181*n*

Machiavelli, 172*n*
Macpherson, C. B., 163*n*, 185*n*
Madison, James, 175*n*
Madsen, Richard, 177*n*
Margolis, Howard, 167*n*

market economy, 4, 6, 7, 75, 89–91, 98, 102, 110, 114, 115, 123–124, 155, 157. *See also* competitive markets

Masters, Judith R., 169*n*

Masters, Roger D., 165*n*, 169*n*

maximizers. *See* constrained maximizers; straightforward maximizers

Mayer, J. P., 162*n*, 165*n*, 171*n*, 185*n*

Melzer, Arthur M., 167*n*

Merton, Robert K., 174*n*

Mill, John Stuart, 182*n*

Miller, Gary J., 167*n*

Miller, James, 170*n*

modernity, 158–159, 186*n*

modus vivendi, 128, 130

Molho, Ian, 175*n*

Moliere (Jean-Baptiste Poquelin), 166*n*

Montesquieu, Charles de Secondat, 11, 27, 28, 41, 43, 44, 68, 87, 134, 157, 162*n*, 167*n*

morals by agreement, 131, 133, 135

Morgenstern, Mira, 162*n*

Morris, Christopher W., 162*n*, 163*n*

Mosher, Michael A., 177*n*, 185*n*

Moskherjee, Dilip, 166*n*

Muller, John, 179*n*

Murphy, Liam, 183

mutual defection, 12, 13, 15, 21, 132, 164*n*

mutual respect, 23, 27, 157

Nagel, Thomas, 57, 118, 139–140, 162*n*, 170*n*, 173*n*, 182*n*, 183*n*, 185*n*, 187*n*

Neidleman, Jason Andrew, 163*n*, 170*n*, 171*n*, 177*n*

Noble, Richard, 165*n*

Nozick, Robert, 163*n*

Nussbaum, Martha, 168*n*

Oakeshott, Michael, 27, 167*n*

Ockenfels, Peter, 164*n*

Olson, Mancur, Jr., 171*n*, 174*n*, 175*n*

opaque cities, 4–5, 20–34, 36, 133

opaque economies, 90, 101, 109, 113, 115, 121, 180*n*

opaque markets, 3, 6–7, 97, 100, 103, 114–116, 127

Orwin, Clifford, 161*n*, 165*n*, 167*n*, 169*n*

Ostrom, Eleanor, 163*n*

Pagano, Ugo, 180*n*

Page, Charles H., 174*n*

Page, Talbot, 172*n*

Parry, Geraint, 170*n*

partial societies, 7, 9, 45–54, 57, 60–61, 63–68, 76–81, 84, 86–88, 137, 149, 157, 172*n*, 176*n*, 178*n*

passions. See *amour de soi; amour-propre*; compassion

perfect transactional flexibility, 10, 136–142, 155

persona, 2, 18, 156

Peterson, Paul E., 175*n*, 183*n*

Phillips, D. Z., 165*n*

Plato, 127, 140, 154, 162*n*, 184*n*

Posner, Richard A., 166*n*

preeminence, 1, 3, 12, 25, 27, 28, 48, 132, 157

principal-agent problem, 110, 121–122, 124–126, 184*n*

prisoner's dilemma, 8, 12–13, 15, 21, 26, 30, 33–34, 43, 44, 52, 96, 131, 157, 163*n*, 164*n*, 169*n*, 173*n*

productivity, 90–91, 103, 104, 107, 110, 112, 120, 122, 176*n*, 180*n*, 181*n*, 182*n*, 183*n*

public surface, smoothly fitting, 139–140

Putnam, Robert D., 58–59, 81–84, 171*n*, 173*n*, 175*n*, 177*n*

Putterman, Louis, 172*n*, 177*n*, 180*n*

Quinton, Anthony, 181*n*

Rasmusen, Eric, 166*n*

rational choice, 3–4, 25

rational egoists, 3, 21, 25, 39, 59, 131, 134, 167*n*

Rawls, John, 10, 63, 107–108, 110, 127, 137, 142–152, 154–155, 159, 162*n*, 170*n*, 174*n*, 175*n*, 181*n*, 182*n*, 183*n*, 185*n*, 186*n*
receivers, 10, 136–138, 140–142
recognition, 15–17, 25, 27, 28, 31–33, 36, 38, 43–44, 58, 124, 128, 163*n*, 164*n*, 167*n*. *See also* accurate recognition
Reisman, W. Michael, 170*n*
republican state, 46, 47–50, 59, 78, 81, 106, 119–120, 122, 149
reputation, 1, 4, 22, 29, 35, 36, 51, 64, 67, 102, 114, 115, 129, 130, 154, 157, 172*n*, 179*n*
   limits of, 96–99
Rhees, Rush, 165*n*
Rheingold, Howard, 175*n*
Riley, Patrick, 161*n*, 168*n*, 170*n*
Ring of Gyges, 4, 10, 129–130, 133–135, 140, 154–156, 162*n*
risk-pooling, 108–109, 147
risk-sharing, 109–110, 150, 151, 152
Ritter, Alan, 168*n*, 171*n*, 177*n*
Robespierre, Maximilien, 170*n*
Roemer, John E., 183*n*
Rogers, Joel, 177*n*
Rosen, Jeffrey, 162*n*, 170*n*
Rosenblum, Nancy L, 54, 169*n*, 173*n*, 175*n*, 177*n*, 186*n*
Rousseauean typology, 11, 40–44, 127
Rue, Loyal, 165*n*
Runciman, W. G., 169*n*, 187*n*

Sahlins, Marshall, 166*n*
Sandel, Michael J., 162*n*, 169*n*, 173*n*, 177*n*, 178*n*, 186*n*
Sandler, Todd, 174*n*
Scheffler, Samuel, 56, 173*n*
Schmidtz, David, 169*n*, 179*n*
Schuessler, Rudolf, 166*n*
second best, theory of, 65, 80, 135, 141
self-aggrandizement, 4, 19, 29, 128–130, 154

self-interest, 27, 34–35, 57, 80, 89–90, 101–102, 104, 107, 109, 117, 120, 125, 143, 156, 158, 178*n*
self-restraint, 12–15, 17–18, 23, 28, 89, 119, 128–129, 133, 154
Seligman, Adam B., 166*n*, 187*n*
Sen, A. K., 169*n*, 187*n*
separating equilibrium, 107
Shah, Anup, 181*n*
Shama, Simon, 170*n*
shield, perfect, 139–142, 160
Shiller, Robert J., 150, 181*n*, 186*n*
Shklar, Judith N., 167*n*, 176*n*
signaling, 101–103, 180*n*
simple souls, 8, 11–12, 15, 17, 164*n*
Singer, Peter, 182*n*
Skyrms, Brian, 164*n*
Smith, Adam, 1, 6–7, 9–10, 89–93, 96, 98, 101–107, 110–116, 127, 157–158, 162*n*, 164*n*, 178*n*, 179*n*, 180*n*, 181*n*, 182*n*
Smith, John Maynard, 164*n*
Sober, Elliot, 165*n*
social contract, 97, 127–131, 142–143, 145, 158, 184*n*, 185*n*
   in Plato's *Republic*, 127–128
   Rousseau's characterization of, 143
   transparent economy and, 118–124
Spence, Michael, 180*n*, 181*n*
Starobinski, Jean, xiii, 38, 93, 96, 161*n*, 166*n*, 168*n*, 169*n*, 171*n*, 178*n*, 179*n*
Startz, Richard, 181*n*
statistical discrimination, 66, 67, 112
Stiglitz, Joseph E., 162*n*, 179*n*, 180*n*, 181*n*, 182*n*
Stolle, Dietlind, 177*n*
straightforward maximizers, 131–132
Sullivan, Willam M., 177*n*
Sunstein, Cass, 64, 138, 139, 174*n*, 185*n*
super-transparency, 136–138
surveillance, mutual, 9, 12, 34–40, 47, 50, 106–107, 119, 135, 140, 149, 158, 160, 168*n*, 170*n*, 185*n*
Swidler, Ann, 177*n*

Talmon, J. L., 170*n*

Tarcov, Nathan, 161*n*, 165*n*, 167*n*, 169*n*

taxes and taxation, 6, 34, 83, 113, 116–118, 123, 141, 152, 176*n*, 182*n*, 183*n*

Taylor, Charles, 169*n*, 186*n*

Taylor, Michael, 165*n*, 167*n*

Thurow, Lester, 181*n*

Tiebout, Charles M., 175*n*

Tipton, Steven M., 177*n*

tit-for-tat, 21, 25, 156, 167*n*, 173*n*

Tocqueville, Alexis de, 9, 20, 32, 40, 42, 43, 46–47, 68, 75–77, 81–82, 87, 140, 157, 162*n*, 165*n*, 167*n*, 168*n*, 170*n*, 171*n*, 175*n*, 177*n*, 185*n*

Tonnies, Ferdinand, 174*n*

Trachtenberg, Zev M., 166*n*, 172*n*

transactional flexibility, 10, 135–142, 155

transmitters, 10, 136–138, 140, 141

transparent economy, 94, 108, 118–124, 180*n*, 182*n*

transparent exchange, 101, 179*n*

transparent republic, 5–6, 8, 29–34, 41, 135

Trivers, R. L., 164*n*

Ulmann-Margalit, Edna, 161*n*, 162*n*, 168*n*

unconditional cooperators, 24, 132–133, 166*n*

unconditional defection, 14–17, 25, 29, 31, 35, 36, 163–164*n*

Unel, Bulent, 172*n*

unequal associations, 9, 60

unhappiness, 32, 38, 40

unilateral cooperation, 12

unilateral defection, 12

Vallentyne, Peter, 168*n*, 185*n*

Varoufakis, Yanis, 163*n*

Verba, Sidney, 175*n*

violence, anticipatory. *See* anticipatory violence

violent death, 17–18, 165*n*

virtue, 2, 4–6, 9, 11, 23, 44, 55, 57, 96, 115, 119, 124, 129, 130, 133, 159, 170*n*
  civic, 9, 34–40, 46, 50, 54, 68, 78, 84, 137, 141, 143, 153, 169*n*, 177*n*
  cooperative, 58, 62, 66

von Wright, G. H., 165*n*

Waldron, Jeremy, 171*n*

Walras, Leon, 178*n*

Walzer, Michael, 58, 173*n*, 183*n*

Warren, Mark E., 171*n*, 175*n*, 177*n*

Watkins, Frederick, 161*n*, 168*n*, 174*n*, 181*n*

wealth. *See* distribution of wealth

Weil, Simone, 84, 177*n*

Weisbrod, Burton A., 175*n*

Weiss, A., 181*n*

welfare state, 90, 116–117

will of all, 169*n*, 183*n*. *See also* general will

Williams, Bernard, 169*n*

Williamson, Oliver, E., 178*n*, 179*n*, 184*n*

Wingrove, Elizabeth, 161*n*

Wittgenstein, Ludwig, 20, 162*n*, 165*n*

Wolker, Robert, 161*n*

Wollheim, Richard, 169*n*

Wright, Erik Olin, 172*n*, 177*n*, 180*n*, 182*n*

wrongdoer/wrongdoing, 128–129

Young, Iris Marion, 85–86, 171*n*, 177*n*, 178*n*

Young, Michael, 175*n*